A New Beginning for Humankind

A RECIPE FOR LASTING PEACE ON EARTH

R. B. Herath

iUniverse, Inc.
Bloomington

A New Beginning for Humankind
A Recipe for Lasting Peace on Earth

iUniverse books may be ordered through booksellers or by contacting:

iUniverse
1663 Liberty Drive
Bloomington, IN 47403
www.iuniverse.com
1-800-Authors (1-800-288-4677)

ISBN: 978-1-4759-3952-1 (sc)
ISBN: 978-1-4759-3953-8 (hc)
ISBN: 978-1-4759-3954-5 (e)

Library of Congress Control Number: 2012913910

Printed in the United States of America

iUniverse rev. date: 8/31/2012

Also By R. B. Herath

Desappremayen Odavadiwa Darudariyanta
Kavivalinma Liyu Lipiyak (1979)
(translation reads as A Letter to Our Children in
Poems Written through Patriotism)

Sri Lanka Desapalanaya, Ayanna, Aayanna, Eyanna, Eeyanna (1979)
(translation reads as A, B, C, D of Sri Lankan Politics)

Sri Lankan Ethnic Crisis: Towards a Resolution (2002)

Real Power to the People: A Novel Approach to Electoral Reform in
British Columbia (2007)

To
my daughters Lucky, Anoja and Tikiri,
my granddaughter Chantal
and
the youth of the world,
for their future

"I know not with what weapons World War III
will be fought, but World War IV would be
fought with sticks and stones"

-ALBERT EINSTEIN (1879 – 1955)

Contents

FOREWORD xiii

PREFACE xvii

ACKNOWLEDGEMENTS. xix

ACRONYMS xxi

CHAPTER 1: INTRODUCTION. 1

CHAPTER 2: VIOLENT CONFLICTS IN AND ABOUT STATES. 9
   Inter-state Violent Conflicts 9
   Intrastate Violent Conflicts. 33
   A Sober Reflection 61

CHAPTER 3: A VIOLENT CONFLICT WITH NO BORDERS 65
   Primary Target 67
   Primary Suspect. 70
   Mother of all Terrorist Attacks. 71
   US War on Terror 72
   A Sober Reflection 93

CHAPTER 4: GLOBAL ATTEMPTS TO BRING ORDER 97
   Peace Efforts Prior to WWI 97
   Peace Efforts through the League of Nations 99
   Peace Efforts through the United Nations. 107
   A Sober Reflection 118

CHAPTER 5: CHANGING WORLD DYNAMICS 121
    Before WWII 121
    A Major Shift after WWII 123
    Another Major Shift in the Early Nineties 132
    Future Possibilities 141

CHAPTER 6: AVOID THE LOOMING DANGER 151
    End Unilateral Global Policing. 152
    End the War on Terror 154
    Destroy All Weapons of Mass Destruction 161
    Adopt non-violent means of conflict resolution 167
    Reform or Replace the United Nations Organization 171

CHAPTER 7: LASTING PEACE ON EARTH 175
    Challenges 175
    A New Beginning for Humankind. 190

CHAPTER 8: SUMMARY AND CONCLUSION 199

ABOUT THE AUTHOR 207

REFERENCES 209

INDEX. 223

Foreword

To HAVE KNOWN AND interacted intimately with Dr R. B. Herath, known warmly among his circle as RB, is indeed a privilege. It is a greater privilege now to have been asked to write a foreword to his latest book of this voluminous writer, the present volume, appropriately titled *A New Beginning for Humankind: A Recipe for Lasting Peace on Earth.*

Dr Herath, a professional engineer, is a poet in his heart. And he has enthusiastically flirted, in a very good sense, with politics from a very early time of his life. He has always been an active peace-maker, deeply involved in local community, national and international affairs, agitating always for non-violence and promoting an authentic democracy.

The planet we live in and share with others has immense capacity for healing and recovery. The inner peace of humans expands to embrace the fullness of life of this planet. In places where conflict has caused enormous damage, or even raged for years or centuries, peace is still possible. And peace needs to be pursued at all cost, particularly for the sake of our progenies. This optimism is the passion of Dr Herath, an ambassador for peace who, in this book, offers us a recipe for lasting peace to our globe. How do we generate this perpetual peace? Dr Herath patiently and precisely addresses this concern in the following pages.

This book on global peace has been, in a sense, evolving from the very body, mind and soul of Dr Herath for a very long time. He has always stood up for the democratic rights of individuals. He demonstrated these traits early on during his high school time developing them through his university and into the present. It was no surprise to those who knew RB, when he founded the Peoples' Party in Sri Lanka. This centrist party was rooted in non-violence and was concerned about democracy and consensus among all ethnic groups in the country.

The relevance of Herath's new recipe is also related to its boldness to question the older strategies of conflict resolution. These strategies have not helped resolve past wars or continuing skirmishes that can easily loom into global nuclear catastrophe. Herath recognizes and announces courageously the impotency of the existing peacemaking agencies, and shows us radical structural and essential changes that will reassure peace activists of varied levels. He implies that it is the present generation's responsibility to promptly deal with the current "dismal human destiny" rather than passing it to the future generation. In that sense, there is urgency in RB's call for peace.

But that call is delivered to the humankind born with certain inherent human virtues, that RB has rightly identified: caring "for the needs of others" and sharing "what is available in an equitable manner"; forgiving and forgetting "any harm done by others"; acting "responsibly in a trustworthy and reliable manner"; and treating "the wellbeing and happiness of all humans just as one's own, irrespective of race, ethnicity, tribe, religion, language, culture, ideology, and the like". The potential to enact these four virtues are deeply embedded in human nature. Every human should consciously and consistently revisit this potential if peace is to last. This is Dr Herath's argument. This book is an invitation to that "revisiting." Here I am reminded of that famous quote from Ralph Waldo Emerson: "What lies behind us and what lies before us are tiny matters compared to what lies within us." Dr R.B. Herath unfalteringly believes that the fundamental human virtues that could result in global peace lie deep within every human soul.

I congratulate RB for this book and wish him every success in his future peace efforts in this world inclined to cherish short term wars based on failed and unworkable strategies for conflict resolution. We welcome his novel peace-making approach, which emerges from thinking outside the box.

REV. HENRY VICTOR, PhD (B'HAM)
Former Senior Lecturer in Comparative Religion, Eastern University, Sri Lanka
Adjunct Professor of Religious Studies, University of Alberta, Canada
16205-55 Street
Edmonton, Alberta
Canada
T5Y 0G1
Tel (780) 473-5161
hvictor@telus.net

Preface

WILL THERE BE A new world war in the near future? If so, will it be fought with nuclear weapons?

Perhaps not everyone would answer either of these questions affirmatively. Nevertheless, there are many reasons that suggest the likelihood of both the dire predicaments. Some of the reasons are obvious. The ominous possibility of further nuclear proliferation and the cavalier approach of the major global powers to current volatile issues in the world offer two such reasons. The continuing mistrust and rivalry among humans on varied fronts is another. The continued dependence on the outdated conflict resolution strategy of eliminating the enemy, instead of the *enmity*, is yet another. The list goes on. Based on these and other reasons, some experts have already warned of a looming global nuclear catastrophe. This catastrophe, if triggered, could have a destructive power many thousand times greater than the combined effect of the atomic bombs dropped over the Japanese cities of Hiroshima and Nagasaki during World War II (WWII). In the face of this potential devastation and other new challenges to world peace, the United Nations (UN) - created after WWII to prevent further wars – now stands impotent. In any event, we, the present occupants of the planet, have no choice but to find a way to prevent the outbreak of the impending global nuclear disaster, before it becomes too late.

However, the mere avoidance of this or any other future global war, by whatever means, would not necessarily guarantee lasting peace on

Earth. With or without a new global war, existing conflicts among humans will continue until the parties involved resolve them amicably. At the same time, new conflicts will crop up from time to time, and it is unrealistic to think otherwise. In time, some of these existing or even new conflicts could re-create the same state of affairs that we have now, with a renewed threat of a global calamity. This only points to a dismal human destiny – one of humans living under intermittent clouds of a potential global catastrophe. We should not simply pass this bleak human destiny on to future generations. Instead, we should step up to the plate and do what we can to change it to one of lasting peace on Earth.

This demonstrates that the challenges to world peace are primarily two-fold: a possible outbreak of a worldwide nuclear disaster and the potential human fate of living under intermittent clouds of a global war. The good news is that we can overcome both the challenges. However, this is not possible if we continue to depend on conventional peace-building measures. It will become possible only if we think creatively, outside the box, for new and different solutions. We have a special and urgent need to do this now. Unfortunately, thus far, no one at any level has engaged in a serious attempt to meet this need in a meaningful way. Although bookstore shelves abound with books on world peace and related subjects, none has addressed this special need in a wholesome manner. *A New Beginning for Humankind: A Recipe for Lasting Peace on Earth* fills this niche.

R. B. Herath
July 2012

Acknowledgements

I WAS PLANNING TO write this book for more than a decade now. All previous attempts to do so ended up in procrastination. All this changed after my daughter Anoja gave birth to Chantal, her first child and my first grandchild. I was overwhelmed with joy to see the new addition to the family. At the same time, I was also struck with certain pain and agony, thinking of the potential dangers of a global nuclear disaster she may have to endure if a third world war broke out in her lifetime. This gave me the extra motivation I needed to write the book.

Once started, there were many to help complete it. They came from a wide spectrum of religious, cultural, and ideological backgrounds. There were clergymen, academics, social workers, humanists, computer experts, colleagues, friends, and family among them. Some of them helped formulate ideas through one-on-one and group discussions and provided vital information that was not freely available. The computer experts helped clear glitches I encountered in preparing the manuscript. A selected few reviewed its earlier drafts and made comments and suggestions for their further improvement. Then, some came up with ideas for the book cover, and even talked about post-publication strategies and processes for propagating the peace mission promoted in the book. The support I got from all of them became an additional source of motivation and inspiration. It is impossible to mention here the names of all those who helped so much, as the list is quite long. However, I must mention the names of several persons from whom I received special help.

The initial discussions I had with Venerable Bhikkhu Pavaro of the Sītavana (Birken Forest) Monastery, Kamloops, Canada, and my friends Mohammed Alam, Bill Howden, Neil Turner, Dr. Mohan Thiagarajah, Amin Kabani, and Kirthi Senarathne helped define the scope of the book. Then, the earlier drafts of the manuscript were reviewed by Venerable Ajahn Sona (Abbot of the Sītavana Monastery), Venerable (Dr.) Henry Victor (Anglican minister and Adjunct Professor of Religious Studies of the University of Alberta), and friends Mohammed, Mohan, and Kirthi. Their penetrating critiques on those earlier drafts became valuable beyond measure in further improving the manuscript. Mary Guilfoyle edited its final draft, making it a better read. Palitha Ranasighe, a friend, and two students, Devin Ariyarathne (Simon Fraser University) and Sanjog Sidhu (Tamanawis Secondary), offered numerous suggestions for the book cover. Mary Montica Poole finally designed the cover, putting a visual face to the book's message that we as a society need to awake from our complacency and act with urgency or we could be doomed with annihilation.

My immediate family were always there to help complete the book just as in all my previous book projects. In particular, I am indebted to my wife Hemamala for helping me refine my ideas through frequent discussions and relentless reviews of my daily writings. My youngest daughter Lucky, a political science graduate, reviewed an interim draft of the manuscript and offered invaluable suggestions for its improvement.

I sincerely thank all those who helped me write this book. At the same time, I must say that although all these considerate people contributed to the book in numerous ways, I alone am responsible for the views expressed in it. All its shortcomings are also my own.

R. B. Herath
Surrey, British Columbia
Canada
July 2012

Acronyms

ETA	Euskadi t Euskadi ta Askatasuna
FAO	Food and Agriculture Organization
FIS	Islamic Salvation Front
IAEA	International Atomic Energy Agency
ICBMs	intercontinental ballistic missiles
ICU	Islamic Courts Union
IMF	International Monetary Fund
INFT	Intermediate Nuclear Forces Treaty
JEM	Justice and Equality Movement
LON	League of Nations
LTBT	Limited Test Ban Treaty
LTTE	Liberation Tigers of Tamil Eelam
NAM	Non-Aligned Movement
NATO	North Atlantic Treaty Organization
NLD	National League for Democracy
NPT	Nuclear Non-Proliferation Treaty
PKK	Kurdish Workers Party
PLO	Palestine Liberation Movement
PNA	Palestinian National Authority
SALT	Strategic Arms Limitation Talks

SLA	Sudan Liberation Army
SORT	Strategic Offensive Reduction Treaty
START	Strategic Arms Reduction Treaty
TFG	Transitional Federal Government
UN	United Nations
UNDP	United Nations Development Programme
UNESCO	United Nations Educational, Scientific and Cultural Org.
UNICEF	United Nations International Children's Emergency Fund
UNSCOM	United Nations Special Commission
US	United States of America
WHO	World Health Organization
WMD	Weapons of Mass Destruction
WOT	War on Terror
WWI	World War I
WWII	World War II

Chapter 1:
Introduction

THE ODDS ARE THAT humans will fight the next world war with nuclear weapons. The types of nuclear weapons used in that war could be much more sophisticated and dangerous than anything known so far, thanks to the continuing 'successes' of science and technology. The extent of the potential destruction to life and property in that war would be far beyond anyone's comprehension. In comparison, the level of destruction witnessed during the First and Second World Wars would appear simply scanty. World War I (WWI) fought with conventional weapons killed over 15 million people; it occurred long before the invention of the atomic bomb. World War II (WWII), also fought with conventional weapons, except for two atomic bomb attacks, killed 65 million people. These atomic bomb attacks were the first nuclear assaults in the history of humanity. In these attacks, the United States (US) dropped two atomic bombs over the Japanese cities of Hiroshima and Nagasaki, one on each. These bombings flattened the two cities and instantly killed more than 100,000 people. There were many more deaths afterwards resulting from the fallout of the bombs. These ferocious nuclear attacks managed to end WWII, as only the United States had nuclear weapons capability at the time.

Today's situation is very different for two main reasons. First, not one but nine countries possess nuclear weapons, and nuclear proliferation is continuing in an uncontrollable manner. Second, it is unlikely that all the nuclear weapons countries would team up to fight a common enemy at the time of a new world war. All indications are that in the next world war, if it became inevitable, the concerned countries would separate themselves into two or more competing camps and engage in nuclear warfare. In such an eventuality, there would be nuclear bombs of the latest models falling over most, if not all, of the major cities in the world. What would then happen to the millions of people living in those cities is too dreadful to imagine. The eyewitness accounts of what actually occurred in Hiroshima on the day of the first US nuclear attack may help us understand and feel, at least in a symbolic way, the extent of the horror associated with such a new world war predicament. The following are excerpts from two such accounts.

The first account is a 2005 recollection of Tomiko Morimoto, a 13-year-old schoolgirl at the time of the Hiroshima atomic bomb attack. The following is an abstract from Adam Phillips' (2005) written version of this recollection.

> Everything started falling down; all the buildings started flying around all over the place. Then something wet started coming down, like rain. I guess that's what they call black rain. In my child's mind, I thought it was oil. I thought the Americans were going to burn us to death. And we kept running. And fire was coming out right behind us, you know. (para. 4)

> Dead people all over! Particularly, I saw a Japanese soldier that was still mounted right on his horse... just dead! Also that a streetcar had stopped just at the moment [of the bomb] and the people still standing, dead. (para. 6)

> I saw [while looking down from a railway river bridge] a sea of dead people. There was not one space for the water, just people lying there and dead. (para. 7)

The second eyewitness account is a memo of Dr. Michihiko Hachiya. He was one of the doctors of the Hiroshima Communications Hospital who survived the attack. What follows below are excerpts from this account (World War II, n.d.).

My breath became short, my heart pounded, and my legs gave way under me. An overpowering thirst seized me and I begged Yaeko-san [wife] to find me some water. But there was no water to be found. (para. 3)

I paused to rest. Gradually things around me came into focus. There were the shadowy forms of people, some of whom looked like walking ghosts. Others moved as though in pain, like scarecrows, their arms held out from their bodies with forearms and hands dangling. These people puzzled me until I suddenly realized that they had been burned and were holding their arms out to prevent the painful friction of raw surfaces rubbing together. A naked woman carrying a naked baby came into view. I averted my gaze. Perhaps they had been in the bath. But then I saw a naked man, and it occurred to me that, like myself, some strange thing had deprived them of their clothes. An old woman lay near me with an expression of suffering on her face; but she made no sound. Indeed one thing was common to everyone I saw--complete silence. (para. 5)

The streets were deserted except for the dead. Some looked as if they had been frozen by death while in the full action of flight; others lay sprawled as though some giant had flung them to their death from a great height. (para. 6)

Between the Red Cross Hospital and the center of the city, I saw nothing that was not burned to a crisp. Streetcars were standing and inside were dozens of bodies, blackened beyond recognition. I saw fire reservoirs filled to the brim with dead people who looked as though they had been boiled alive. In one reservoir I saw one man, horribly burned, crouching beside another man who was dead. He was drinking bloodstained water out of the reservoir. In one reservoir, there were so many dead people there was not enough room for them to fall over. They must have died sitting in the water. (para. 8)

Are these abstracts of the two eyewitness accounts of the first nuclear bombing not terrifying enough? No person with a right mind wants to go through a similar experience any time, ever. Yet, there may be ground conditions boiling under our own feet waiting to trigger a new world war of much worse consequences. One of these consequences could very well be the extinction or near-extinction of humans and, perhaps, many other species now living on this green planet.

In any event, going by what triggered WWI and WWII, the world is certainly not in a better place now than at any time before. WWI started with the assassination of Archduke Franz Ferdinand of Austria, heir to the Austro-Hungarian throne, by a Bosnian-Serb nationalist. This happened on June 28, 1914. In time, the military conflict that erupted between Austria-Hungary and the Kingdom of Serbia because of the assassination gained momentum with all the major European powers taking part in it. The colonies of the European powers at the time also joined the war in support of their respective imperial masters. All this helped spread the war worldwide. Later, WWII resulted from a merger of two separate inter-state wars that broke out on the continents of Asia and Europe. The war in Asia started in September 1931 with the Japanese invasion of Manchuria, a vast geographic region in northeast Asia. The war in Europe began with the German invasion of Poland in September 1939. These two wars later grew in intensity and merged into one gigantic, worldwide war. The ways in which WWI and WWII broke out show the vulnerability of the present world with all its ongoing violent conflicts. We live with the possibility that one or more of the current conflicts, given the right conditions, could develop into a world war that would likely be fought with nuclear weapons.

Some may simply argue that there would not be any nuclear confrontations just because such weapons do exist. The main thinking behind such arguments appears to rest on the assured mutual destruction inevitable in such confrontations. It is true that any first nuclear attack by a party would inanely invite its enemy powers to respond with similar attacks. The end result would be colossal destruction to life and property at both the ends. This blatant realism, no doubt, does install a sense of restraint in the use of nuclear weapons by those who possess them. However, this cannot be construed as a total constraint in the use of nuclear weapons by any power in future confrontations. There are three main reasons for this. First, history has shown that some leaders at the helm of power have acted irrationally at their times of desperation. How Adolf Hitler, who was brought to power through democratic elections, brought Germany to its ruination in the WWII is a case in point. Second, a first nuclear attack could result from a human error. It could simply be an error in handling an active nuclear warhead for maintenance or improvement purposes. At the same time, an intelligence failure, falsely accusing one party of an imminent nuclear attack against another, could also lead to the same end. The world now knows how the United States, for example, waged war against Iraq in 2003 because of an intelligence failure. Third, more and more nations are attempting to develop nuclear weapons not because there is assurance that such weapons will never be used in future confrontations. Instead, they are doing so in order to prepare themselves for any possible nuclear attack they may face in the future. In any event, however, experts hold the common view that all those who possess nuclear weapons would use them in the next world war. At stake in all this today is the very survival of humans as a species on Planet Earth. The only way to avoid such a nuclear holocaust is not to have another world war, ever. Such sentiments have echoed throughout the globe from the time of the Hiroshima bombing. For example, in their joint manifesto of July 9, 1955, two well-known and respected intellects, Bertrand Russell (1872–1970) and Albert Einstein (1879–1955), stated, "In view of the fact that in any future world war nuclear weapons will certainly be employed, and that such weapons threaten the continued existence of mankind, we urge the Governments of the world to realize, and to acknowledge publicly, that their purpose cannot be furthered by a world war, and we urge them, consequently, to find peaceful means for the settlement of all matters of dispute between them." ("Russell-Einstein Manifesto" 1955, para. 17)

These sentiments came from Einstein and Russell with a stern warning about the perils of nuclear weapons and the escalating arms race at the time. Later, these and many other intellectuals around the world have repeatedly expressed the same concerns and called for full, global disarmament. Despite such concerns and sage warnings, certain parties have chosen to build the nuclear arsenals now stockpiled around the globe. If we fail to get rid of them, we know that a nuclear holocaust will occur, sooner or later. It is only a matter of time. This shows, as Jonathan Schell says in his *The Fate of the Earth*, that "We have come to live on borrowed time: every year of continued human life on Earth is a borrowed year, every day a borrowed day" (1982, 184).

In the event that the contemplated nuclear holocaust becomes a reality, we humans would either face the same fate as that of the dinosaurs some 65 million years ago, or revert to our own Stone Age. In his time, Einstein appeared to have thought that the latter was still a possibility. That may be why when someone asked him after WWII with what kind of weapons the next world war would be fought, he responded, "I know not with what weapons World War III will be fought, but World War IV will be fought with sticks and stones" ("Quotation details", n.d. para.1). The British statesman and naval officer Lord Louis Mountbatten (1900 – 1979) also expressed similar sentiments, when he said, "If the Third World War is fought with nuclear weapons, the fourth will be fought with bows and arrows" (*Who said: the fourth world war*, n.d., para.5).

Despite such warnings, some seem to think that although the nuclear threat is real, no one has yet seen a sign of an imminent nuclear confrontation. According to experts, however, this is not the case. For example, according to a related report (Schultz, Perry, Kissinger, and Nunn 2008), a group of influential former Cold War warriors, based at Stanford University's Hoover Institution, has categorically stated, "The accelerating spread of nuclear weapons, nuclear know-how and nuclear material has [already] brought us to a nuclear tipping point" (para. 1). It is a warning no one should ignore. Those who have issued the warning have extensive knowledge and experience in world matters. They include former US Secretaries of State George Shultz and Henry Kissinger, former US Defence Secretary William Perry, and former US Senator Sam Nunn. This and other expert opinions clearly indicate that a looming global nuclear catastrophe is awaiting an opportune time to explode. The world will face dire consequences if it fails to prevent the outbreak of this catastrophe with prompt and timely action.

In this situation, as the present occupants of the planet, we have an unwritten but conscionable duty to prevent the outbreak of the looming catastrophe before it becomes too late. At the same time, however, the mere avoidance of this fiasco would not necessarily guarantee lasting peace on Earth. This is so because the world's history of wars could repeat itself yet again. Thus, we also have a paramount duty to change the present dismal human destiny of living under war threats to one of lasting peace. Any serious attempt to accomplish these two noble duties must begin with a thorough examination of the existing major conflicts in the world, the likelihood of any of them turning into a worldwide fiasco, the specific measures to prevent such an eventuality if such a likelihood does exist, and what more is needed to be done to establish lasting peace on Earth. The rest of the book conducts this examination by answering four critical questions:

(1) What are the major violent conflicts in the world today?

(2) Is there any guarantee that none of the ongoing violent conflicts will deteriorate into a worldwide fiasco?

(3) If there is no such guarantee, what needs to be done to prevent such an eventuality? and

(4) Is there anything more to be done to ensure lasting peace on the planet?

Chapters 2 and 3 answer the first question by identifying the current major violent conflicts in the world. Chapter 2, in particular, gives an updated account of ongoing violent conflicts of major concern within and among states. Chapter 3 describes the series of violent attacks of similar concern that have been staged across the globe by some Islamic militant groups against those whom they perceive as enemies of the Muslim world. In discussing these conflicts, these chapters explore their historic context to the extent deemed essential for the reader to understand reasonably well their present and future predicaments. Those readers who are already familiar with the present status of these conflicts to some degree also will find these chapters somewhat informative and helpful.

Chapter 4, together with Chapter 5, attempts to answer the second question. Chapter 4, in particular, examines the successes and failures of the global attempts made since WWI to bring order to our conflicted world. Chapter 5 examines the changing world dynamics and their potential impact on ongoing major conflicts.

Chapter 6 attempts to answer the third question. It outlines five specific measures as a means to prevent the outbreak of the looming global catastrophe. Chapter 7 tries to answer the last question. This chapter first explains that avoiding wars at the worst of times is a strategy for only short-term peace on the planet. It then suggests a unique and revolutionary approach to lasting peace on Earth with a New Beginning for Humankind. Chapter 8, the last chapter, summarises and concludes the book.

Chapter 2:
Violent Conflicts In and About States

THIS CHAPTER DISCUSSES VIOLENT conflicts of major concern in and about states, under two main categories: inter-state and intrastate. The *inter-state* category consists of violent conflicts between and across independent states, while the *intrastate* category consists of violent conflicts confined to a single state. The focus of this chapter is to discuss only the currently active conflicts of greatest concern in both categories. However, it also provides some basic information about similar conflicts in the past that have recently concluded. This will help the reader see the nature and extent of major conflicts in the big picture. The specific discussions of the currently active major conflicts include their historic context, present status, and future possibilities. The historic contexts of the conflicts vary in length, depending on their individual merit. For convenience, the discussions of the concerned conflicts begin with those of the inter-state category.

INTER-STATE VIOLENT CONFLICTS

Currently, there are four major inter-state violent conflicts of greatest concern: two in the Middle East and two in Asia. The concerned conflicts in the Middle East are the ones between Israel and Palestine and between Iran and Israel. The discussions of these conflicts below will show how they are closely interrelated. Of these two inter-state conflicts, the former appears to be the older. Many, in fact, consider the Israel-Palestine conflict to be the oldest in the world. It is also the scariest of all the current inter-state conflicts. In this particular dispute, the existing ceasefire arrangement between the parties has failed to halt the bloodshed. Israel has gathered momentous support from its allies in the West to help prevent the Palestinian Hamas group taking control over the Gaza Strip, but to no avail. The Israeli government has since added fuel to the fire by refusing to acknowledge the globally accepted two-state solution to the continuing conflict and by allowing illegal occupation of the West Bank, despite worldwide objection. This has kept the two opposing sides in a vicious cycle of attacks and counter-attacks. The latter conflict, between Iran and Israel, has not yet flared up in flames. So far, these two countries have only been exchanging threats of violence from time to time. Both sides seem to be awaiting an opportune time to 'fight the unknown.' On its part, Iran, which allegedly develops nuclear weapons, has tested missiles that could blow its foes 'to hell.' However, Israel has boasted that it has ballistic missiles to counter any Iranian nuclear threat.

The two ongoing conflicts of greatest concern in Asia are between India and Pakistan and between North Korea and its adversaries in its neighbourhood. In the former, the ongoing troubles in Kashmir keep the two parties in a state of constant agitation. India also blames 'Pakistan state actors' for the infamous 2008 Mumbai attacks. At the same time, Pakistan points its finger at India over the 2008 violent assault on the visiting Sri Lankan cricket team on Pakistani soil. India was also plagued with anti-Muslim signs during some of its past general elections. Both countries have tested nuclear weapons, and their silent nuclear arms race has become a main threat to peace in the region, and the world. At the same time, in the Korean peninsula, North Korea has vowed to 'punish South Korea' and 'attack Japan'. No one should completely ignore such vows and threats of North Korea. This is specially so, considering how it went ahead and developed nuclear weapons - disregarding related international laws and mounting worldwide objection. Let us now examine these four inter-state conflicts of greatest concern in more detail.

The oldest and the scariest. The conflict between Israel and Palestine is the oldest and the scariest conflict in the world. It is also the most dominant cause of instability in the entire Middle East, and the world. Many believe that it has the greatest potential to trigger a global catastrophe. This conflict is primarily about the ownership of land, now known as Israel, the West Bank, and the Gaza Strip. Currently, Jews predominately occupy Israel, while Palestinian Arabs predominately occupy the West Bank and the Gaza Strip. Cultural intolerance and poor governance are among the other issues affecting the dispute. Both sides stick to their uncompromising positions, primarily based on their previous occupation of the land, at different times in history. This shows the need to understand first the historic context of this conflict to a fair degree, before attempting to assess its present state and future possibilities.

Both sides agree that the first known inhabitants of the land were the Canaanites. They were, notably, a collection of Semitic people ancestrally connected to both the Jews and the Arabs. The dominant religion among the Semitic Jews was Judaism, while that of the Arab Semites was Islam – just as at the present time. According to biblical and historical records, historians say that Jews took possession of the land from the Canaanites sometime around the 13th century BC. The new Kingdom of Israel that the Jews established, with Jerusalem as its capital, flourished and expanded for the next 500 years or so, until the Assyrians took control in 720 BC. During their period of rule, Jews had built their first temple in Jerusalem in 965 BC. Ever since, they have treated Jerusalem as their holiest city and spiritual homeland. Later, the Assyrians, Babylonians, Greeks, and Hasmoneans took possession of the land, until it became a part of the Roman Empire in 70 AD. Romans ruled the land until 615 AD. For the next 900 years or so, the rule of the land went back and forth among various invading forces, including the Byzantines, the Arabs, the Christian Crusaders, and the Mamluks until it became a part of the Ottoman Empire in 1517 AD. The Ottoman rule of the land lasted for four hundred years and ended with a British conquest in 1917 AD.

The early periods of non-Jewish rule on the land had a devastating effect in many ways on the Jewish community who lived there. In the process, they even lost their holiest shrine, more than once. In 586 BC, the Babylonians destroyed the first Jewish temple, built in 965 BC. Then, in 70 AD, the Romans destroyed the second Jewish temple, built in 516 BC to replace the first. At the same time, Jews lost ten out of their 12 main tribes in their dispersion, mostly after the Assyrian rule. During the period of Roman rule, Christianity became the official religion of the disputed land in the fourth century AD. Roman Emperor Constantine 1 (306 – 337) constructed Christian sites such as the Church of Holy Sepulchre in Jerusalem. During the Constantine time and thereafter until the seventh century, Jews were banned from Jerusalem. Most of the Jews later chose to go and live all over the world outside Israel, in the Diaspora. Some of these Jews went to live in Arabic countries. Later, many Roman Christians suspected that the Jews were helping the Arabs in the region in their early seventh century attacks against the Roman Empire. This, in fact, led to a new wave of Christian persecutions of Jews, not only in the Roman Empire in the Eastern Mediterranean, but also in the western kingdoms. After Jerusalem fell to Arabs in 637 AD, they built the Al-Aqsa Mosque (Dome of the Rock) on the site of the destroyed Jewish temple in 705 AD.

Because of these and other historic reasons, Jerusalem slowly and surely became a place of close affinity to Christians and Muslims as well. Christians, in fact, have treated Jerusalem as their holiest place, even before the construction of the Church of Holy Sepulchre. There were a number of reasons for this. Jerusalem was the place where Jesus grew up as a child, and had his last supper, trial, crucifixion, and burial. It was also the site of his resurrection and ascension. For Muslims, the Al-Aqsa Mosque is their third holiest site. For them, Jerusalem was also the first qibla (direction of prayer) in Islam, before Kaaba in Mecca. In addition, Muslims believe Jerusalem is the site from which prophet Mohammad ascended to heaven. Meanwhile, Jews - now mostly dispersed in the Diaspora - never gave up their claim to the disputed land.

The issue of ownership of the disputed land took centre stage during the period of its British rule. In 1915, the British government indicated its preparedness to recognize and uphold the independence of Arabs in the region. The area was part of the Ottoman Empire at the time. This British position was made clear in the "Hussein-McMahon Correspondence" (Gerner 1994). Two years later, the same British government issued a special declaration favouring the establishment of a national home for the Jewish people in the disputed land. The British called it the Balfour Declaration of 1917. These two undertakings of the British government were mutually exclusive and contradictory. This led to rising tension between the Arabs and Jews in the region. The

League of Nations discussed this new situation in depth with a view to finding a solution. In the end, what the League did was to mandate Britain to put into effect its 1917 declaration. This, in turn, led to violent confrontations between the Jews and the Arabs in the region. These confrontations include the infamous 1920 and 1921 Palestine riots, the 1929 Hebron massacre, and the 1936-39 Arab revolts in Palestine. After numerous failed attempts by Britain to resolve the worsening crisis, the United Nations (UN), which had by now replaced the League of Nations, intervened in the late forties and partitioned Palestine into two states, one Jewish and one Arab. The Arab leaders of Palestine and the entire Arab League rejected the partition proposal. The Jewish leaders, however, promptly accepted the partition plan as proposed, and declared the independence of their State of Israel on May 14, 1948. This led to a historic Arab-Israel War in the same year. This war started with the invasion of Palestine by five Arab League countries: Egypt, Lebanon, Syria, Transjordan, and Iraq. By the time this war ended, Israel had captured more land than had been partitioned for it by the UN. The invading nations, except Iraq, took over the Palestinian land not captured by Israel, leaving Jerusalem as a divided city. Millions of Palestinian Arabs who had left their homes during and after the war became refugees in neighbouring Arab states. Arab governments, on their part, continued to refuse to recognize Israel. Then in 1964, the Palestinian Arabs formed a new multi-party confederation called the Palestine Liberation Organization (PLO). Fatah, one of the parties that joined, was its largest faction. The central tenant of the PLO was that Palestine was an indivisible homeland of the Arab Palestinian people; it should remain intact as originally recognized by the British under their Palestine Mandate in 1915. This now set the tone for further escalation of the Arab-Israeli conflict in the coming years.

It took two more bloody wars between the conflicting parties to pave the way for a peace negotiation process: the infamous Six-Day-War of 1967 and the Yom Kippur War of 1973. Together, they claimed tens of thousands of lives. The first peace agreement of any sort between of the two sides was the Camp David Accord of 1978. It set a precedent for future peace talks between the warring parties. Despite ongoing peace efforts, violent confrontations continued between the factions. The Lebanon War of 1982 and the First Intifada of 1987 were two such major clashes. One significant event that occurred during the First

Intifada was the emergence of a new Palestinian Arab organization called Hamas. It called for armed resistance against Israel, and later became a dominant force in the region.

The Oslo Peace Process that began in 1993 was significant. During this peace process, the two confronting parties failed to come to a mutually acceptable agreement. However, the same process authorized the PLO to establish an autonomous Palestinian National Authority (PNA). The intended task of the PNA was to run Palestinian affairs in the West Bank and the Gaza Strip. For this purpose, the PNA could have its own governing bodies. All this, of course, was subject to the PLO's recognition of and mutual coexistence with Israel. Israel's obligation was to stop its settlement activities in these areas. The PNA took effect with its first Presidential and Legislative elections of 1996. The second Presidential and Legislative elections took place in 2005 and 2006, respectively. Fatah, the principle component of the PLO, dominated these elections. Yasser Arafat, who was the founder and leader of Fatah, became the first PNA President. After his death in November 2004, Mahmoud Abbas became the next PNA resident in January 2005.

Meanwhile, the Second Intifada began in 2000, primarily due to the failure of the ongoing peace process. Then in 2006, Hamas won the second Legislative elections (Palestinian Legislative Council). This was fourteen and a half months after the death of Yasser Arafat. In this election, Hamas secured a clear majority of seats in the PNA Legislature. The result was a Hamas-led government, while the Presidency remained in the hands of Fatah. Ismail Haniyeh of Hamas became the new Prime Minister.

In government, Hamas offered to extend the truce that was in place. It was, however, not prepared to honour past agreements between the previous Fatah-led Palestinian government and Israel. This brought Hamas in direct conflict with Fatah internally, and resulted in an internal war between them. In this internal war, Israel and its allies, including the United States, solidly stood behind Fatah forces. The two regional powers, Iran and Saudi Arabia, stood divided, supporting the two conflicting Palestinian camps. Critics say that by taking a side in this internal war, Israel and its allies have shown complete disregard for the wishes of a democratically elected Hamas government; they also continued to label Hamas as a terrorist organization. This internal war finally resulted in Hamas taking full control of the Gaza Strip; only the West Bank continued to remain under PNA control. President Mahmoud Abbas responded to this new situation by doing five things. First, he dissolved the existing coalition government (Fatah, Hamas, and others). Second, he removed the incumbent Prime Minister Ismail Haniya (Hamas member) from his position in government. Third, he formed a new governing coalition excluding Hamas. Fourth, he consolidated his power over both the Gaza Strip and the West Bank by a presidential decree on June 14, 2007. And, fifth, he changed the voting system, prohibiting those parties that did not acknowledge the PLO's right to represent the Palestinian people from contesting future elections.

The tension between Israel and Hamas further escalated during 2008 on two main issues. One issue was Israel's reluctance to lift the blockage it imposed on the Gaza Strip following the internal war between the Hamas and Fatah forces. The other issue was the November 4, 2008 Israeli raid on an alleged cross-border tunnel in the Gaza Strip, while a six-month truce was still in effect. The increased tension resulted in a series of rocket attacks by Hamas against southern Israel, also while the truce was still in effect. Israel responded to this with military operations against the attackers. Once the truce was over, both the sides intensified their violent attacks. A report on the attacks, prepared by the international war crimes prosecutor Richard Goldstone, blamed both sides, more so Israel, for war crimes. Based on the report, the Geneva-based UN Human Rights Council voted 26 to 6 in favour of a resolution on October 16, 2009. This resolution condemned Israel for a number of alleged human rights abuses. It also called on the UN Secretary General Ban Ki-moon to follow up the issue with the UN Security Council. The Western countries did not support the Human Rights Council resolution: the United States and five other Western countries, in particular, voted against it.

Meanwhile, the Netanyahu government of Israel elected in 2009, added fuel to the fire by doing two things. First, it announced its objection to a two-state solution to the question of the ownership of the disputed land. With this action, it showed its complete disregard for the solution that had been adopted by the UN, taking the conflict back to square one. Second, the Netanyahu government gave its green light to new

Jewish settlements in the West Bank. Both these actions met with widespread protests and objections. Some of the strongest objections came from its closest allies. Sometime later, the Netanyahu government took a new position on the issue of a two-state proposal. According to its new position, it would agree to a two-state solution only if the proposed Palestinian state did not have its own armed forces. Instead, the Netanyahu government wanted to retain its own military presence inside an eventual Palestinian state.

It is clear that both Jews and Arabs have occupied and ruled the disputed land. Jews had occupied and ruled the land long before Arabs. As well, many others also have occupied and ruled the land at different times in history. At the time of adoption of the UN resolution dividing the land into two states, it was in the hands of the Palestinian Arabs. The Arabs' main concerns about the new Israeli state appear to be three-fold. First, the Israeli government refuses to accept the return of the Palestinian Arabs who fled their homes in 1948 and 1967. BADIL, a Palestinian non-government organization, has estimated that "there were more than 7.2 million Palestinian refugees and displaced persons at the beginning of 2005" (IMEU, n.d., para. 3). Second, Israel continues to promote Jewish settlements on extra land it illegally grabbed from Palestinians during past wars. By doing this, Palestinians say that the Israelis have evicted Arabs from Palestinian lands and farms they have already developed. Palestinians also charge that the intruding Israeli troops humiliate, sexually assault, and even kill their women. Third, despite continuous atrocities committed against the Palestinians by the Israeli government, the West continues to support and protect its interests. Many have criticised the United States and its allies for sheltering Israel under their defence umbrella. These critics say that this has made it possible for Israel to possess the atomic bomb and become a force in the region more powerful than any combination of Arab forces.

The UN, in particular, has shown its strong objection to the Jewish settlements in the occupied territories. UN Secretary-General Ban Ki-moon called on the Israeli authorities to fulfill their obligations under the ongoing peace process. These obligations include a complete freeze on new settlement activities. The Netanyahu government, however, is willing to consider only a partial freeze. The partial freeze it proposed was inadequate both in time (only 10 months) and space (only the

West bank, leaving out Jerusalem). Palestinian leaders do not consider this partial freeze to be adequate to bring them to the peace table. In this uncompromising situation, Israel carries on with its new Jewish settlements, to the sounds of protests and objections - even from within. In one such internal protest, the Israeli government jailed two Israeli soldiers for 30 days in November 2009. These soldiers had refused to evacuate Arabs from a new Jewish settlement area in the occupied West Bank. There was also an Israeli army radio report that twenty-five Israeli reservists had signed a petition asking for exemption from such evacuation duties. There were some officers among the concerned reservists. Arabs in the region view such internal protests to new Jewish settlements as a clear testimony of objection to the Israeli government's strong resistance to the ongoing peace process.

At the same time there has been a change in the US' approach to the issue of these Jewish settlements. The Obama administration that assumed its duties in January 2009 has openly expressed its objection to such new settlements. President Barack Obama said that Israel's plans to build new Jewish settlements on occupied territories could lead to a very dangerous situation. He also said that such plans could seriously obstruct the ongoing Middle East peace process. With further deterioration of the US-led Middle East peace process, President Obama in May 2011 called for both the Israelis and Palestinians to accept Israel-Palestine borders established before the 1967 Arab-Israel War as a starting point for future negotiations. Israel promptly rejected this proposition, saying that those borders would be indefensible. At the same time, Israel insisted on its right to retain a military presence inside an eventual Palestinian state and continued with its refusal to admit the descendents of Palestinians who left the disputed land during and after the 1948 Palestine War. In the heat of all this, in September 2011, Palestinian President Mahmoud Abbas handed UN Secretary-General Ban Ki-moon a letter of application requesting full UN membership for Palestine. While a large number of UN member-states pledged to support the application, Israel and the United States vowed to work against it. The United States pledged to use its veto power at the UN Security Council, if necessary, to reject the application. In response to this situation, the UN, as well as all other outside mediators, including the United States, the European Union, and Russia asked the Israeli and Palestinian leaders to resume peace talks; already there have been two decades of on-again, off-again negotiations with no tangible results. Israeli leaders would like to enter into new peace talks without any pre-conditions. However, the Palestinian leaders would cooperate only if Israel first commits to stop new settlements on occupied lands: the West Bank and East Jerusalem. Even before the talks on these preconditions had ended, Israel went ahead and announced plans to build 1,100 new homes in East Jerusalem, which was annexed to its territory in the 1967 war. On their part, Palestinians want East Jerusalem to be the capital of a future Palestinian state. A report by Jeffrey Heller (*Vancouver Sun*, October 3, 2007, B4) suggests that there are already some 500,000 Israelis living in the West Bank and East Jerusalem, areas that are home to 2.5 million Palestinians.

Meanwhile, the United Nations Educational, Scientific and Cultural Organization (UNESCO) accepted Palestine as a full member on October 31, 2011. UNESCO did this in spite of US threats to eliminate its funding to the organization, amounting to more than 20 percent of its budget. The United States is known for such action in the past as well. In 1984, it pulled itself out of UNESCO, claiming that it had an anti-US slant. The United States rejoined the organization only twenty long years later. On their part, Palestinians believe that their UNESCO membership would be a springboard to joining other international bodies.

At the same time, Palestinians also see that the Israeli government has no genuine support for the Israel-Palestine peace movements. Among the Palestinian Arabs, this has contributed to an ever-growing anger and hatred against Israel and its allies. This hatred and anger permeates through the Arabs living outside Palestine, and the entire Muslim world. This will keep the Arabs and the Israelis in a perpetual war situation. Only a lasting solution to the Israeli-Palestinian conflict could remedy this situation. In the interim, the violent confrontations staged by Muslim militants against the United States and its allies are also likely to continue. Many believe that if the Palestine issue is not resolved soon, it could deteriorate into a global fiasco in the near future.

Fighting the unknown. Iran's opposition to Israel as a state is even louder and stronger than Palestinians.' At least some Palestinian Arab leaders have expressed their willingness to accept Israel's right to exist as a separate state in the Middle East. Despite that, Iran is vowing to "wipe Israel off the map" (MacAskill and McGreal 2005, para. 1). According to Iranian President Mahmoud Ahmadinejad, the Holocaust is simply a lie and he appears to believe that the Zionists propagated it as a pretext for creating the Israeli regime. In a national address he once said, "Confronting the Zionist regime is a national and religious duty" (Hafezi and Sedarat 2009, para. 3). This is a strong opposition to the Israel state from a very powerful regional player.

At the same time, Israel and its Western allies strongly suspect that Iran is pursuing a covert nuclear weapons programme. This suspicion rose to a new level in 2009, after the International Atomic Energy Agency (IAEA) inspectors had access to an undeclared Iranian uranium enrichment plant near the city of Qom. This uranium enrichment plant was still under construction. The IAEA inspectors who examined the site had two important observations. First, Iran had failed to provide credible evidence to show that the plant was being built for civilian (general power generation) purposes only. Second, its construction appeared to have been under way for a longer period than admitted. This, in turn, raised a new cloud of doubt that Iran could have other similar facilities, probably some still under construction. Iran later announced that it, in fact, had planned to build ten more uranium enrichment plants. It also kept insisting that it would use all its uranium plants, both new and old, exclusively for civilian purposes. Further, Iran made an agreement with the IAEA to continue its civilian nuclear programme in an unsuspicious manner. This agreement required Iran to send 75 percent of its low-enriched uranium to Russia and France. Then, these countries would turn it into fuel for the Iranian civilian nuclear facilities. Later, however, Iran put forward a precondition for the implementation of the agreement, requiring that the process of turning low-enriched uranium into fuel remain under Iranian supervision inside Iran. This has raised more doubts about the sincerity of Iran's intention to limit its nuclear programmes to civilian purposes. When the United States and other major powers wanted to respond to this new situation with a strong set of UN sanctions against Iran, it went ahead and entered into a special pact with Turkey and Brazil for storing some of its medium-enriched uranium in May 2010. Israel and its allies consider that this was a move to undermine the US' efforts to secure universal backing for the intended UN sanctions. Then, in November 2011, there was a special IAEA report on Iran, suggesting that it had carried out a number of activities key to the development of nuclear weapons. The suspicious activities include high-powered explosives testing and the development of an atomic bomb trigger. This particular IAIE report renewed the warning of the Iranian nuclear threat in the region, especially against Israel. In responding to this new situation, the major powers - United States, Russia, China, France, Britain, and Germany - issued a joint resolution condemning Iran for its continuing research for developing nuclear weapons. Earlier that year, a UN panel had concluded that Iran was cooperating with North Korea to develop nuclear weapon systems. North Korea, which had already developed its own nuclear weapons, was operating in defiance of the United Nations.

Iran may or may not succeed in producing nuclear weapons. However, one thing appears certain: if ever Iran gains access to the atomic bomb, Israel would be the most vulnerable state in the Middle East. Because of this, Israel is actively engaged in an attempt to stop Iran from producing nuclear weapons by any means possible. In 2008, the Israeli transport minister Shaul Mofaz publicly warned, "If Iran continues with its programme for developing nuclear weapons, we will attack it" ("Israeli minister threatens Iran" 2008, para. 7). If such an attack took place, Iranians would face the wrath of all the defenders and protectors of Israel as well. The United States would be at the top of a long list of them. In 2007, there were reports that Israel was preparing for a nuclear strike on Iranian enrichment facilities. Israel wanted to do this with the help of bunker-buster bombs. In the process, they had sought negotiations with the United States for permission to use Iraqi air space for an air strike on Iran. Iran dismissed any such potential attacks by Israel or the United States as simply impossible or crazy. Iran has also made it clear that in the event of any such attack its first target will be Israel. The head of the UN nuclear watchdog agency, Mohamed El Baradei, says such an airstrike by Israel, if ever occurred, would turn the Middle East "into a ball of fire" (Middle East Online 2009, para. 6). It is, indeed, too dreadful to imagine what would happen to the world around us if Iran and Israel had equal access to nuclear weapons with the hostility between them still unsettled.

On its part, Israel has kept out of the Nuclear Non-Proliferation Treaty of 1968. It is also continuing with its policy of deliberate ambiguity on whether or not it possesses nuclear weapons. Every other country, however, appears to believe that Israel does possess such weapons. Against this background, Israel is opposing possible Iranian nuclear weapons programmes. It also continues to call for more and more international sanctions against Iran. By doing all this, many believe that Israel has put itself on a warpath with Iran.

Meanwhile, the hostility of the West towards Iran had particularly worsened following the 1979 Iranian Revolution. This revolution overthrew the West-supported Shah of Iran. The new Islamic government of Iran proclaimed its desire to overthrow monarchs and dictators in the Middle East who oversaw the interests of the West. With such proclamations, Iran has become the leading opponent of the United States and its Western allies in the Islamic world. In this situation, the US-led West, no doubt clamours for a change of government in Iran. Iran knows the West's capability in such matters. It was not that long ago, in 1953, that the United States and the United Kingdom staged a joint coup and brought displaced Shah Reza back to power, displacing the West-unfriendly government led by Dr. Mohammed Mossadegh.

In the middle of the growing tension between Iran and the West, Israel has become more and more vulnerable in the Middle East. The West has particularly blamed Iran for the continuing support it gives to Hezbollah and Hamas in their military confrontations with Israel. This explains why Israel and its western allies are most concerned about the possibility of Iran becoming a nuclear weapons state. If Iran succeeds in developing nuclear weapons, it would very likely trigger a dangerous nuclear arms race between that country and Israel. Such an arms race could eventually shift the balance of power in the Middle East to the detriment of Israel. This also shows the possibility that Iran could emerge as a dominating Islamic power in the region, and the world. In such a situation, any attempt by Israel to go to war with Iran could turn not only the Middle East, but also many other regions of the world into a "ball of fire".

Two rival nuclear neighbours. India and Pakistan are two nuclear weapons states that share a common border. Their relationship has never been friendly. The people of India are mostly Hindus, while those of Pakistan are mostly Muslims. These two peoples had the common heritage of one country, India, until 1947. It was the departing colonialists, the British, who partitioned it into the two new states of India, as

now known, and Pakistan. Historically, the disputes between Hindus
and Muslims of (former) India reached a new height when its regime
changed hands from Muslims to Hindus in the mid-nineteenth century.
Many measures that the subsequent Hindu-dominated governments
adopted on religious grounds have caused conflicts. These measures
included separate electorates, weighted representation, quotas in the
public service, and preservation of religious liberties and cultural values.
The Hindu-dominated governments continued to fail in addressing the
widespread concerns on these measures to the satisfaction of Muslims
living in the country. The divide-and-rule policy of the colonizing
British later exacerbated the existing mistrust and enmity between the
two religious groups. This eventually led to calls for a separate state for
Muslims as the colonial rule was ending. The chaos and pandemonium
that followed took the lives of nearly a million people. All this has left
a region with seemingly permanent wounds in the minds of those who
survived and their descendents.

The partitioning of India left one of its Muslim-majority areas - the
mountainous Kashmir region - in dispute between new, partitioned
India and Pakistan. Neighbouring China also had interests in this land.
The British left it out of its partition plan. They wanted the residents
of the disputed land to decide on its future. The Muslim majority
(80 percent) living there wanted to join Pakistan. However, the rest
(mainly Hindus, Sikhs, and Buddhists) chose to join India. The Hindu
maharaja of Kashmir at the time had the final say. He opted to join
India, disregarding the majority's decision. Kashmir thus became a land
of contention among three concerned states: India, Pakistan, and China.
Later, however, China got control over about one-fifth of the disputed
land. This became possible after it waged a war with India and entered
into a bilateral agreement with Pakistan. The rest of Kashmir now
remains as a land of contention between India and Pakistan. India treats
the presently disputed land (still a Muslim majority) as an integral part
of its territory. Pakistan wants the people who live there to determine its
status. Some organizations of Kashmir residents want present Kashmir
to be independent of both India and Pakistan. India and Pakistan have
already had three wars over the disputed land: in 1947, 1965, and 1999.
India currently controls 54% of Kashmir, while Pakistan holds 46%
of the area. Kashmiri Muslim separatist militants often fight with

the Indian armed forces, despite heavy casualties on both sides. India blames Pakistan for supporting the Muslim militants.

Some deadly terrorist attacks, seemingly related to the Kashmir dispute, have occurred on Indian soil even outside Kashmir. This has particularly angered the Indian administration in New Delhi. Such attacks have occurred in 2001, 2008, and 2011. In the 2001 incident, five gunmen attacked the Indian Parliament in New Delhi, soon after it had adjourned its sessions on December 13th. Many believed that Kashmir separatist groups were responsible for this attack. The Indian government also blamed Lashkar-e-Tayyiba, an Islamic militant movement operating in neighbouring Pakistan. All five militant gunmen died during the attack. The motive of the attackers was not evident. In the 2008 incident, the India's commercial capital Mumbai came under a wave of terrorist attacks. Ten militants carried out the assaults between November 26th and 29th of that year. They used automatic weapons and grenades in their attacks, which took place at ten different locations within the Mumbai City. The resulting death toll was 164, including 30 foreign nationals from ten countries. During the period of these attacks, the Indian security forces killed nine of the attackers, and captured the tenth alive. The one captured alive informed the Indian authorities that all the ten attackers were members of the Pakistan-based Lashkar-e-Tayyiba organization. In the 2011 incident, some militants set off three remote-controlled bombs, within a few minutes of each other, in busy and crowded venues in Bombay, killing 18 people and injuring 130 others. The famous jewellery market of Jhaveri Bazaar and a popular opera house some seven kilometres away were two of the attack venues. It remains unclear whether a local Islamic group or perhaps some militants linked to the Lashkar-e-Tayyiba group carried out these bomb attacks.

Meanwhile, Indian intelligence agencies have observed a growing link between the Islamic militant groups in Afghanistan and the Kashmir separatists. There were also reports that the al-Qaeda movement provides ideological and financial support to the Kashmir separatists. The al-Qaeda leader Osama bin Laden had repeatedly called for jihad against India. All these have contributed to the rising tension between the two neighbouring nuclear states.

The word 'jihad' appears about 40 times in the holiest book of Islam, the Quran. Jihadists, or mujahedeen, are those who engage in acts of jihad. According to the Quran, jihad is a system of checks and balances. It applies to situations where a person or group of persons violates the rights of Muslims. Jihad specifically calls for striving in God's name to bring the violators back into line. Such striving begins with the intention to help those who have lost their rights. Later, it transcends to speeches, verbalizing the intention. Physical action, violent or not, comes when mere verbalizing the intention is not enough. According to classical Islamic writers, jihad also refers to spiritual struggles against the evil within oneself. These writers refer to this kind of jihad as "the greater jihad."

In any event, the rising tension between India and Pakistan is a major global concern. This is especially so because both countries possess nuclear weapons. It is also an "open secret" that the two countries are presently engaged in an arms race, each trying to be ahead of the other in terms of military capability. In this regard, India is particularly concerned about the growing defence ties Pakistan has with China, a very powerful country hostile to India. For example, there were reports in early 2011 that China was planning to accelerate the supply of 50 new JF-17 Thunder multirole combat jets to Pakistan under a co-production pact. In responding to these reports, Indian Defence Minister A. K. Antony has said, "It is a matter of serious concern for us. The main thing is we have to increase our capability - that is the only answer" (*India says Sino-Pakistan ties* 2011, para. 2). This arms race is likely to continue.

In April 2009, US President Barak Obama had a special meeting with Indian Prime Minister Manmohan Singh in London. At this meeting, Prime Minister Manmohan Singh expressed his interest and willingness to discuss all outstanding issues between India and Pakistan. He, however, has added, "But these discussions cannot proceed if hundreds of people are killed as happened in Mumbai. ....We expect Pakistan to do all that it is required to bring perpetrators of the Mumbai attacks to book" ("India, Pakistan dialogue" 2009, 4). Later, Prime Minister Manmohan Singh insisted at a press conference that a sincere assurance from Pakistan not to allow its soil to promote terrorism "is a minimum precondition" ("India, Pakistan dialogue" 2009) for resumption of discussions between the two countries.

At the same time, there is also a growing possibility that the Islamic militants with al-Qaeda links who are now fighting with the government of Pakistan could gain access to its nuclear weapons. Any use of such weapons against India by the militants or the Pakistani government could easily lead to a nuclear war in the region, and the world. Kashmir, of course, would remain the central issue in any such confrontation. In his book *American Raj: Liberation or Domination*, Eric S. Margolis, an expert on the subject, explains:

> Kashmir represents probably the most dangerous current threat to world security: the ongoing risk of nuclear war between two old enemies, India and Pakistan. Kashmir has poisoned relations between India and Pakistan for over half a century, led them into three full-scale wars, and continues to pose the danger of a nuclear exchange between them that could instantly kill an estimated 2 million people, injure 100 million, and contaminate the entire globe with radioactive dust. (Margolis 2008, 307)

Threats of a defiant state. The war threats of North Korea against South Korea and Japan since 2009 have sent new shockwaves across the geopolitical landscape of the region, and the world. North Korea's rivalry and enmity with these countries date back to the time of the infamous 1950–53 Korean War that killed three million people. The United States and its allies have remained solidly behind South Korea both during and after the war. The differences North Korea had with South Korea and Japan at the time were primarily ideological and have not changed since. However, the military capacity of North Korea has since changed in a significant manner. At the time of the Korean War, it did not have access to nuclear weapons. As a result, it had to depend exclusively on traditional weapons. Today it has nuclear weapons as well. Against this background, its current threats to South Korea and Japan need serious consideration.

North Korea has always remained a threat to the international community with its secretive and provocative behaviour. In developing its nuclear weapons, it surprised the world by taking four stunning steps. First, it expelled the inspectors from the International Atomic Energy Agency. Second, it reaffirmed its withdrawal from the Nuclear Non-Proliferation Treaty. Third, it started enriching plutonium rods into bomb-making material. Fourth, it went ahead and carried out nuclear tests. After all that, and in a confrontational manner, it pledged to keep its nuclear weapons as long as it wanted. In summing up the situation, newspaper columnist Jonathan Manthorpe (*Vancouver Sun*, February 24, 2009, B7) stated, "Pyongyang greeted the inauguration of [President] Obama with a full-throated threat to keep its nuclear weapons so long as it feels the slightest threat from the United States forces, and to adopt an 'all-out confrontational posture' by its 1.19 million-strong military against South Korea on land and at sea"

Today, North Korea is not only in possession of nuclear weapons. It is also allegedly exporting nuclear materials and technology to others. Some suspect that this could potentially lead to further nuclear proliferation to the benefit of terrorist groups of global reach.

There were two major incidents orchestrated by North Korea in 2010 that were particularly provocative. One incident occurred in March 2010. In this incident, North Korea sank a South Korean navy ship, killing 46 people. Jonathan Manthorpe viewed this incident as "one of Pyongyang's worst military provocations since the 1950-53 civil war on the peninsula" (*Vancouver Sun*, May 21, 2010, B6). In the other incident, which occurred in November 2010, North Korea fired dozens of artillery shells across the marine border, targeting the South Korean Yellow Sea Island of Yeonpyeong. These shell attacks killed four and injured twenty others. The dead included two South Korean marines. This reckless military provocation drove the South Koreans to retaliate, bringing the Korean peninsula to the brink of war.

The world rushed to condemn this provocative act of North Korea. Russia, in particular, saw this as a wake-up call that the ongoing negotiations to bring peace to the Korean peninsula were not working. According to a report by John McElroy, Russian Foreign Minister Sergei Lavrov said, "It is necessary to immediately end all strikes. ... There is a colossal danger, which must be avoided. Tensions in the region are growing. This could degenerate into military actions" (*Vancouver Sun*, November 24, 2010, B5). China showed its interest to settle the dispute through dialogue. A report by Barbara Demick, John M. Glionna, and Paul Richter later confirmed this. According to this report, Hong Lei, a Chinese foreign ministry spokesperson had said, "China strongly urges both North and South Korea exercise calm and restraint, and as quickly as possible engage in dialogue and contacts" (*Vancouver Sun*,

November 25, 2010, B1). The United States, however, rebuffed China's call for dialogue, reiterated its defence guarantee for South Korea, and immediately dispatched one of its most powerful aircraft carriers to the region.

The aircraft carrier sent to the region was the nuclear powered USS *George Washington*. It carries 75 warplanes and has a crew of over 6,000. The United States explained that it would include the carrier in a four-day joint naval exercise with South Korea in the Korean waters of the Yellow Sea. The United States also explained that it had planned such a joint naval exercise sometime back, long before the provocative shelling of North Koreans. The subsequent developments, however, show that such action by the United States has further enraged North Korea and made its most powerful ally, China, somewhat uncomfortable. In this situation, North Korea increased its artillery practices near the border. As Barbara Demick reported, it did so with a clear warning that it would unleash "a shower of dreadful fire and blow up the bulwark of the enemies" (*Vancouver Sun*, November 27, 2010, B8). China made clear to South Korean authorities its own 'principled approach' to naval exercises in the Yellow Sea. After that, there was a stern warning by the Chinese Premier Wen Jiabao against any provocative military behaviour on the Korean Peninsula. These and other developments point to one thing: tensions in the region are building. In summing up the situation in the region, as Barbara Demick further reported, Xu Guangyu, an analyst with the China Arms Control and Disarmament Association said, "Sending in an aircraft carrier is only going to make everybody in the neighbourhood nervous and is not going to help the United States to achieve their goals" (*Vancouver Sun*, November 27, 2010, B8).

Meanwhile, there is also the dire possibility that South Korea and Japan will develop their own nuclear arsenals in the face of North Korea's on-and-off provocative war threats and aggression in the region. At the same time, South Korea and Japan, together with the United States, have shown interest to help North Korea to recover from its collapsed economy in exchange for ending its nuclear weapons programmes. However, North Korea has less and less interest in accepting such a deal. Instead, it continues to depend on China for economic assistance when needed. In this situation, if a military clash ever occurs between North Korea and South Korea or Japan, it would likely involve the United

States and China, and, through them, other major world powers as well. There is also no guarantee that any of the parties involved would not use nuclear weapons in such an eventuality. In short, the situation in the Korean Peninsula has already drawn together enough ingredients to trigger a global nuclear catastrophe.

Inter-state conflicts concluded. In addition to the ongoing, violent inter-state conflicts recorded above, the list below shows similar violent inter-state conflicts concluded since WWII. It is possible that some of them, given the right conditions, could revivify at a future time with serious consequences. In this instance, they help show the overall picture of the nature and extent of the animosity and hatred among states.

Inter-state war	Dates	Death toll	Comment
Lebanon (Hezbollah forces) – Israel War	2006 34-day war	1,300	Hezbollah started this war with rocket and ground attacks on two Israeli Humvees patrolling the Israeli side of the border, killing 3 Israeli soldiers and capturing two others. Israel responded with rescue attacks, massive airstrikes, air and naval blockages, and artillery fire on Lebanese infrastructure targets. The war ended with an UN-brokered ceasefire.

Kivu Conflict in Congo	2004-09	500 (Death toll in Africa's World War was 3.9 million)	This conflict was a sequel to the Second Congo War, Africa's World War involving eight African states, (1998-2004), the deadliest since WWII. Laurent Nkunda, a general of the Congo Transitional Government (CTG), rejected its authority and launched a rebellion. He blamed the CTG for widespread corruption and the intended genocide of ethnic Tutsis in Eastern Congo. The neighbouring Rwandan Tutsi government was allegedly behind the rebellion. A few other African states came to support the government. After Nkunda was arrested in 2009, his group entered into a peace treaty.
Eritrean-Ethiopian War	1998-2000	53,000 -300,000 Varying estimates	According to an international commission in The Hague, Eritrea started the war by invading Ethiopia. At the end, Ethiopia held all the disputed territory and some extra land from Eritrea.

Gulf War – Iraqi Invasion of Kuwait	1990-91	21,000-35,000 Varying estimates	Kuwait's excessive oil extraction, lowering oil prices to the detriment of Iraq's already devastated economy (due to its war with Iran), allegedly triggered this war. A huge US-led coalition joined the Kuwaitis and pushed the Iraqis out of Kuwait. The US had targeted Iraq because of its position on a number of issues related to Israel and the rest of the Middle East. Iraq also had claimed Kuwait as an Iraqi territory, and challenged the creation of Kuwait by the departing British colonialists.
Persian Gulf War – Iraqi Invasion of Iran	1980-88	800,000-1,300,000 Varying estimates	Border / land dispute and Iran's alleged support of Shia insurgency within Iraq led to the invasion. Chemical weapons were also used in the war. Iranians gained virtually all lost territory by 1982, but they continued to fight on the offensive. This war has not resulted in any border changes.

Soviet War in Afghanistan	1979-1989	1,000,000	Soviets went to support the Marxist-Leninist government of Afghanistan in its struggle against the Mujahedeen, a resistance movement within the country. A lengthy war developed when countries adversarial to the Soviets (Cold War) joined in support of the Mujahedeen. These countries include the US, the UK, Saudi Arabia, Pakistan, Egypt, and some other Muslim nations.
Sino-Vietnamese War	1979	46,000	China started the war in response to Vietnam's invasion and occupation of Cambodia, ending the infamous reign of the China-backed Khmer Rouge.

Bangladesh Liberation War	1971	500,000 – 3,000,000 Varying estimates	This war started with military operations launched by West Pakistan against the separatist Bengalis (students, intelligentsia, and armed persons). This united the Bengali military, paramilitary, and civilian forces as the Bengali Liberation Army. The Indian army helped it win the war and create the state of Bangladesh. This Indian involvement led to the 1971 Indo-Pakistani War.
Vietnam War	1955-75	4,500,000 – 6,000,000 (Vietnamese, Laotians, Cambodians & Americans)	This war was between North Vietnam, supported by its communist allies, and South Vietnam, backed by the US and other anti-communist countries (Cold War). War operations on or near the border led to heavy bombings in Laos and Cambodia as well. The war ended with the capture of Saigon by North Vietnam and the subsequent reunification of the two Vietnamese states.

France-Algerian War	1954-62	960,000-1,500,000 Varying estimates	Independence war (with France), and some internal fighting among rival groups, all characterized by guerrilla warfare, terrorism against civilians, torture, and counter-terrorism operations. Independence movements were supported by other Arab countries, and, in the end, Algeria gained independence from France.
Korean War: between communist North Korea and non-communist South Korea	1950-53	3,000,000	This war started with the invasion of South Korea by North Korea. It developed into a proxy war between the superpowers, the US and the Soviets. The UN sent troops to repel the invading forces. When the UN (& US) counter attacks repelled the invaders, Chinese troops came to their aid. The soviets gave them material help. A threat of a nuclear war finally led to a ceasefire armistice.

This ends the account of the major violent confrontations in the interstate category. Let us now turn to the intrastate category to examine the key aggressive conflicts confined within a single state.

Intrastate Violent Conflicts

The violent conflicts in the intrastate category appear in two main subcategories. One of these consists of bloody confrontations launched by one or more groups of people in a state against their own government. Such confrontations are civil wars. The other subcategory consists of violent confrontations among two or more groups of people within a state. In intrastate confrontations of the civil war subcategory, those who fight the government typically seek redemption from the laws, policies, and programmes that they perceive to be discriminatory against them. Some may attempt to replace the existing government with one of their choice or create a separate state as a means to end such discrimination. In intrastate confrontations of the latter subcategory, each group appears to fight for the superiority of its identity and influence in the society and the country. There can also be drug wars among different factions of the narcotic drug dealers within a state.

Currently, there are a considerable number of intrastate violent confrontations belonging to both subcategories. The world regions mostly affected by these confrontations include Asia, Africa, Europe, South America, and the Middle East. The biggest and the worst of the intrastate conflicts, in fact, appear even deadlier than some inter-state conflicts. Given the right conditions, some of intrastate conflicts could expand beyond the boundaries of their respective state jurisdictions. In any event, it is prudent to examine ongoing major intrastate conflicts at this stage for two main reasons. First, it will help show the totality of violence created by humans on Earth to the detriment of themselves and all other living species. Second, it will show the dire complexity and the vastness of the hatred and hostility among humans. What follows is a summary of the current intrastate conflicts of most concern.

Columbia. The government of Columbia is fighting a major internal war against Marxist guerrilla groups operating in the country. What fuels the war is the groups' commitment to Marxist ideology. The largest of these groups is the Revolutionary Armed Forces of Columbia. It is also the largest Marxist guerrilla group in Latin America. This particular group has been waging guerrilla warfare against the Columbian government for the last 40 years and has carried out numerous acts of violence. In 2008, in neighbouring Ecuadorean territory, Columbian government forces killed Raul Reyes, the group's leader. This increased the tension among the countries in the region, including Columbia, Ecuador, Venezuela, and Nicaragua. In November 2011, the Columbian government forces also killed Alfonso Cano, the leader of the revolutionary movement after 2008. Although the government thinks that Cano's death is a resounding blow to the revolutionary organization, the group may continue with its operations regardless of the loss.

During the same time period, Columbia has also been marred with a drug war. Drug trafficking in the country started in the mid-1970s with drug dealers smuggling small quantities of cocaine to the United States hidden in suitcases. Columbia has now become home to some of the most violent and sophisticated international drug trafficking organizations in the world, motivated by the 'easy money' made through numerous drug deals. While the government has waged war against these organizations, they have been fighting on and off their own internal battles as well, for reasons best known to them. In time, all these bloody conflicts in the country have created the worst humanitarian crisis in the Western Hemisphere, with more than two million people fleeing their homes. In addition, several Indigenous tribes have reached virtual extinction.

Spain. In Europe, Spain is under sporadic terrorist attacks by a revolutionary Marxist group, the Euskadi ta Askatasuna (ETA). The group aims to win independence for the Basque region in northern Spain and southwestern France. The ETA emerged in 1959 to fight against General Francisco Franco's alleged suppression of the Basque language and culture. According to numerous reports, the ETA has so far carried out over 1,600 terrorist attacks, killing more than 800 people. Those primarily targeted in these attacks include government officials, police and military personnel, politicians, and tourists. Among the victims were a police chief in1968, Franco's apparent successor Admiral Luis Carrero Blanco in 1973, and a former city councillor in northern Spain in 2008. In 1995, the ETA almost killed the conservative Popular Party leader Maria Aznar; she later served as Spain's Prime Minister. They also engaged in a failed attempt to assassinate King Juan Carlos in the same year. In July 2007, the government blamed the ETA for an enormous explosion outside a police barracks in the Basque town of Durango. The ETA bomb attacks have been frequent since that time. Allegedly, al-Qaeda has also engaged in attacks in Spain, including the infamous 2004 commuter train bombings in Madrid. These bombings killed two hundred people and injured hundreds of others on the eve of that year's Spanish national election. As in other Marxist struggles, the ETA members' continued commitment to Marxist revolutionary ideology is keeping the conflict alive.

The Russian Federation. The Russian Federation government fought two wars with the Islamic separatist rebels of Chechnya. In the first Chechen war (1994-96), the Chechen region gained de facto independence as a separate Republic and was named the Chechen Republic of Ichkeria. Although it was an internal war within the Russian Federation, large numbers of foreign fighters took part in it. The second Chechen war (1999-2000) helped the Russian Federation establish its direct rule over Chechnya by May 2000. Since then, the Chechen rebels have engaged in guerrilla resistance to Federation rule, but by 2009, Russia gained significant control over the situation. However, sporadic violence continues with rebel attacks throughout the region. There are already 25,000 – 50,000 people assumed dead or missing, mostly civilians. The goal of the Islamic rebels is a separate state for the Chechnya region, where the traditional religion is Islam.

Turkey. An ethnic Kurdish guerrilla group is fighting a separatist war in Turkey. They first emerged as the Kurdish Workers Party (PKK) and took up arms against the government in 1984. According to a report ("Turkey-Kurdistan Workers' Party conflict," n. d.), the war that followed had claimed more than 44,000 lives, mostly PKK members, by the end of 2008. The PKK uses Kurdistan in northern Iraq as the base for its Turkish separatist war. The UN had established no-fly zones in Kurdish areas of Iraq in the aftermath of the failed 1991 uprising against the Iraqi government. These Kurdish areas then became a safe haven for the PKK cadres. According to one report, more than 70% of the PKK members now operate from northern Iraq. Then, the 2003 US invasion of Iraq also helped the PKK by providing them with access to Iraqi weapons in the region, which had now fallen into the hands of Iraqi Kurdish Peshmerga militias. Since then, the PKK assaults on Turkish targets - bombings, ambushes, and suicide attacks originating in northern Iraq - have grown in number and intensity. The attacks escalated to an alarming number by 2007. In response, Turkish fighter jets and ground troops started to attack the PKK forces on the Iraqi side of the border; the government of Turkey believed that they had the right to carry out military raids against the PKK in Iraqi Kurdistan. When the Turkish Parliament extended this action for an additional year in

2008, it sparked a new wave of PKK attacks. The PKK has openly warned the Turkish government of the catastrophic consequences if it decides to continue to attack its cadres on Iraqi Kurdistan soil. Bozan Takeen, a senior PKK leader, based in Iraqi Kurdistan's Qandil Mountains, declared, "We are ready and our forces are ready. We are not afraid of them [Turkey government forces]. If they want to attack Iraqi Kurdistan, then the Middle East will turn into a ball of fire" (Ahmed 2008, para 1). Only time will tell what will happen in the region in the coming years.

Yemen. For some years now, the government of Yemen, led by President Ali Abdullah Saleh, has faced not one, but three violent confrontations. It has a Shiite insurgency in the north, a separatist struggle in the south, and al Qaeda attacks across the country. The northern insurgency started in 2004. One report ("Sa'dah insurgency", n.d.) suggests that by 2008, this rebellion had claimed about 4,000 lives, mostly civilians, and displaced internally 77,000 people. The Yemeni government alleges that the northern rebels want to overthrow it and implement Sharia law. On the other hand, the rebels claim that they are "defending their community against discrimination and government aggression" (Aljazeera 2010, para. 14). The Yemen government has also accused Iran of directing and financing the insurgency. According to one report (Novak, 2008a), however, Iran's Grand Ayatollah Ali al-Sistani has characterized the Yemeni government's operations as a jihad against the insurgents. A report on the southern separatist forces (Novak, 2008b) says that this group challenges the Yemen government's legitimacy in their part of the country. The disputed southern part only became part of Yemen in 1990. Before that, it was a separate entity called South Yemen. Prior to the April 2009 Parliamentary elections, the same Novak report says that angry citizens in the south repeatedly attacked and then expelled voter registration committees. At these elections, the southerners elected their own representative body, the Southern Arabian Liberation Council, instead of members of the Yemen Parliament.

Meanwhile, in and around 2008, the central powerbase of the al-Qaeda movement shifted from Osama bin Laden's supposed hiding place in the mountains bordering Pakistan and Afghanistan to Yemen. Yemen was also Osama bin Laden's ancestral home, and it was where al-Qaeda's war against the West began in the late nineties. In explaining this, Praveen

Swami (*Vancouver Sun*, October 30, 2010, B1) says, "It was where [in Yemen] a little-known Islamist group responded to his [Laden's] calls for attacks on U. S. and British targets by kidnapping 16 tourists. Three British citizens and one Australian were killed when Yemeni forces stormed the kidnappers' safe house, 280 kilometres south of the Yemeni capital of Sana'a."

Once again, Yemen has become al-Qaeda's operational centre. Swami (*Vancouver Sun*, October 30, 2010, B1) says, according to intelligence estimates, the number of al-Qaeda militants concentrated in Yemen could be as many as several hundred, mostly Yemenis, although there have been at least 50 foreign nationals linked to al-Qaeda among those arrested by the Yemeni security forces. These foreign nationals have come from a number of Muslim and non-Muslim countries, including Malaysia, the United States, the United Kingdom, and France. Al-Qaeda militants continue to carry out sporadic bombings wherever they want within Yemen. The Yemeni security forces have great difficulty in containing their activities. As a result, many Yemeni troops have lost their lives.

The threats of al-Qaeda operatives located in Yemen are not confined to that country. Instead, these threats have begun to spread far beyond the country and the region. For example, in October 2010, two packages of explosives were en route from Yemen to the United States in cargo planes. The West believes that the al-Qaeda operatives in Yemen had dispatched them for terrorist attacks on two Jewish centres in Chicago. Fortunately, authorities in Europe and the Middle East managed to intercept them, preventing a terrible disaster. There seems to be a general upswing in the number of acts and threats of violence attributed to al-Qaeda worldwide. For example, according to a report by Robert Spencer, the Islamic insurgents in Iraq have warned of new attacks on Christians "wherever they can be found" (*Vancouver Sun*, November 4, 2010, B5). In the same warning, they have also claimed, "We will open upon them the doors of destruction and rivers of blood" (*Vancouver Sun*, November 4, 2010, B5). Following this declaration, there was a series of incidents involving suicide bombs and mail bombs. Iraq and Pakistan received the worst of the suicide bomb attacks. Two mail bombs exploded at the Swiss and Russian embassies in Athens. Another was intercepted at the German Chancellor's office. The list continues.

Meanwhile, popular street protests began in the capital city of Sana'a in mid-February 2011, calling for the immediate resignation of President Saleh. These protests are an extension of the wave of public protests launched against the authoritarian rulers holding office in North Africa and the Middle East. The protests began in Tunisia in early January 2011 and, in no time, spread to a number of neighbouring countries, including Egypt, Libya, Yemen, Bahrain, Jordan, Saudi Arabia, Syria, and Morocco. The protesters in Tunisia, Egypt, Libya, and Yemen demanded, from their first day, the immediate resignation of their incumbent rulers and their governments. In the other countries, the protesters first called for democracy and social justice. The protests in Tunisia and Egypt ended within weeks, with the resignation of the incumbent presidents and their governments. Libyan President Moammar Gadhafi, however, chose to fight back using all the ground, naval, and air forces at his disposal. This led to indiscriminate killings of civilians. In response, the UN decided to intervene with air strikes and other necessary measures to protect Libyan civilians threatened by the murderous acts of their own government. President Gadhafi, however, vowed to avenge any foreign attacks. This, in turn, led to more fights in the country. In the end, on October 20, 2011, the Libyan protesters managed to capture and kill President Gadhafi in a field about three kilometres west of his birthplace, Sirte, taking control of the country.

In Yemen, after 30 days of protests, President Saleh came up with a reconciliation package. It pledged, among other things, to devolve power to parliament with a new constitution. It was too little, too late. As the protests grew, some key army generals, cabinet ministers, and government diplomats defected to the opposition. However, there appeared no immediate successor to President Saleh. This uncertain situation, together with the other violent conflicts in the country stated earlier, showed the possible downfall of the Saleh regime. It also pointed to more violent struggles than ever before and to the breakup of the country.

Lebanon. In May 2007, an Islamist militant group called Fatah al-Islam started to fight with the Lebanese Armed Forces in two major Palestinian refugee camps in the country, the Nahr al-Bared Palestinian camp near Tripoli and the Ain al-Hilweh refugee camp in the south. During this fight, the militant group also engaged in terrorist bombings in and around the capital, Beirut. Lebanon had not witnessed internal fighting to this extent since its civil war of 1975-90. The new fighting continued for four months until the Lebanese Armed Forces brought the situation under control. By the time the fighting ended, hundreds of soldiers, militants, and civilians – mostly Palestinians - had perished. Most of the 31,000 Palestinian refugees housed in the camps fled the fighting areas to go to refugee camps elsewhere in the country.

Then, in May 2008, some political protests in the country turned to bloody street battles. A number of groups opposing the Western-backed Lebanese government of Prime Minister Fouad Siniora had staged the protests and were seeking the creation of a national government. Two specific actions taken by the government had triggered the protests. One was the shutting down of the existing telecommunication network belonging to Hezbollah, a political party and Shia Muslim militant group operating in the country. The other was the removal of the incumbent Beirut Airport security chief Wafic Shkeir over his alleged ties to Hezbollah. In turn, Hezbollah treated these government actions as a declaration of war and led the protests and street battles. The fighting led to the fall of Beirut and the eastern Aley area to the Hezbollah forces. After the battles, however, Hezbollah handed over the control of its newly won areas to the army, thinking that it would remain neutral. Many subsequent attempts by the country's parliament to elect a new civilian president also ended without success. As a compromise, the parliament finally elected the Chief General Michel Suleiman as president. Then, after five months of negotiations following the 2009 parliamentary elections, the major political parties and groups in the country formed a national unity government, under the premiership of Saad Hariri. Saad Hariri is a Sunni and the son of the former Prime Minister Rafik Hariri, who was assassinated, along with 22 others, in a bomb attack in Beirut in 2005. Hezbollah secured two cabinet positions in this unity government.

About a year after the inauguration of the unity government, Hezbollah and its allies pulled out in January 2011. This forced the unity government to collapse, while also raising fears of a fresh crisis in the country. Some new information unveiled by a UN-backed special tribunal, suggesting the likelihood of indictment of several members of Hezbollah and its allies for the 2005 assassination of the former Prime Minister, had triggered the crisis. Within months of the assassination, a UN-mandated prosecutor had concluded that Syrian security forces, together with some high-ranking Lebanese military men, were responsible for it. However, the UN special tribunal later found that there was no evidence to prove their guilt. Instead, the special tribunal came up with recommendations for new indictments against Rafik Hariri's killers. Hezbollah, for the most part, sees the UN special tribunal as an Israeli initiative to create trouble in Lebanon, and wants all parties in Lebanon to reject its recommendations. The odds were that Prime Minister Saad Hariri would follow through with the recommendations. In this situation, Hezbollah and its allies in the opposition did not want to see Saad Hariri back as the Prime Minister. They now supported another Sunni candidate for that position. Irrespective of who would be the next premier, Hezbollah prepared to fight back with all its might to prevent the arrest of any of its members based on new indictments against Rafik Hariri's alleged killers. This is now keeping the country on the brink of a new civil war.

In general, Lebanon has become a centre for confrontations among many adversarial groups: Arabs and Israelis, Arabs and Persians, Shiites and Sunnis, and pro-American states and anti-American states. Some of these confrontations could bring devastating results to the entire region, and the world. For example, in the event of a future confrontation between Arab Shia Hezbollah and Israeli forces, their respective international allies would invariably join in. Iran and Syria would be among those that would support Hezbollah. The United States and its allies would support Israel. In early January 2009, one of Hezbollah supporters, who identified himself only with his first name Rabih, pronounced, "We want more fire... We want the order to attack Israel directly. We would like to start a war with Israel today. We've got to crush Israel" (Cambanis 2009, para. 5). With such a statement, he has shown the true spirit and desires of the Hezbollah supporters of the time. He made the statement during a speech by Hezbollah's leader Hassan Nasrallah.

In response to previous attacks on Israel, the G8 summit declaration of February 2009 blamed both Hamas and Hezbollah, and by implication, their allies in Iran and Syria. The statement categorically warned, "These extreme elements and those who support them cannot be allowed to plunge the Middle East into chaos and provoke a wider conflict. The extremists must immediately halt their attacks" (Guardia 2009, para. 4).

Palestinian Territory. Earlier, this chapter discussed how the Palestinian Territory plunged into a violent internal conflict between the Hamas and Fatah groups in 2007. There were two main reasons to believe that this conflict could deteriorate further in the coming years. First, it is unlikely that Hamas would change its position on the issue of Israel's right to exist, at least in the near future. This position of Hamas has differentiated it most from its rival Fatah, and remains unchanged especially due to the moral and material support received from outside Palestine, particularly from Iran and Syria. If Iran becomes a nuclear weapons state, it will only make the conflicted situation in the region much worse. Second, the Palestinian Fatah government (as well as Israel) has received strong support from the United States and its allies. Hamas would continue to make use of this situation to gather momentum with an enhanced anti-American, anti-Israel, and anti-West propaganda programme. For the four years of the conflict, 2007-11, the relationship between Hamas and Fatah remained the same, if not worsened.

Then, in a somewhat surprise move, the two groups signed a reconciliation pact in Cairo on May 4, 2011, ending their bloody four-year split. This pact, they thought, would help them work together to end Israel's occupation and to form an independent Palestinian state. There were mixed reactions to the pact both within and outside the region. For example, Jack Khoury (2011) reported that the Israel government condemned the reconciliation pact, and called on Palestinian President Mahmoud Abbas (Fatah) to choose between peace with Israel and peace with Hamas. According to the same report, some Israelis expressed the view that the pact would be short-lived. Another report (Glick 2011) said that *The New York Times* also emphasized the pack's high chances of failure. The report also stated that the senior political commentator, Raviv Ducker of Israel's Channel 10 was of the opinion that the pact may increase the chance of peace between Israel and Palestine. Then, according to the same report, former US President Jimmy Carter had praised the deal as a step forward and said that it could increase the chances for a ceasefire between Hamas and Israel and peace between Israel and Palestine. In spite of all these comments, the fact remains that the implementation of the pact is extremely challenging, especially considering the deep ideological and strategic differences between Hamas and Fatah on key issues. On his part, Hamas leader Khaled Meshaal said, "Hamas is ready to pay any price for internal Palestinian reconciliation ... [as] the only battle of the Palestinians is against Israel" (Khoury 2011, para. 5). At the same time, the fact that this pack was signed under the auspices of the new Muslim Brotherhood-friendly Egyptian intelligence services indicated the instant support it would receive from the new power brokers in the Arabic world.

If Hamas and Fatah somehow manage to implement the pact, it would increase pressure on Israel to recognize Palestinian demands. In addition, it would enhance Palestine's chances of becoming an independent state in the near future. Israel's blatant refusal to consider Palestinian demands in such a situation would only further increase the tension in the region. If, on the other hand, Hamas and Fatah fail to implement the pact, the status quo will prevail, with on and off violent confrontations between themselves as well as between Hamas and Israel.

India. India has three major internal conflicts. First, there is a separatist Kashmir insurgency in the north-west region of the country. This insurgency was discussed earlier in the chapter, under the heading 'Two Rival Nuclear Neighbours.'

The second conflict is an insurgent movement in Assam in the northeast region of the country triggered by an influx of illegal immigrants to the area from neighbouring Bangladesh. In trying to curb this insurgency, the Indian government adopted a twofold strategy. It called for counter-offensive military operations, while facilitating negotiations with the insurgents. There was a ceasefire in 2006. However, the violence associated with this insurgent movement escalated with a sharp increase in the death toll in 2007. Later, there was a split among the senior cadres of the major insurgency movement, the United Liberation Front of Assam. Six of its disengaged commanders enforced a unilateral declaration of ceasefire. This helped decrease the violence significantly. However, the potential for an escalation to greater violence remains high.

Third, there is a not-so-publicised Maoist-Naxalite communist insurgency, which appears to be a more dangerous threat to India's national security than the Kashmir conflict or the Assam insurgency.

The Maoist-Naxalite rebellion started in West Bengal and has spread to less developed areas in rural central and eastern India. According to a report, it "spread to nearly 40% of the country's geographical area and is a major political force in poor tribal states such as Chhattisgarh, Jharkhand and Orissa" (Thapaliya 2007, para. 1). According to a separate report ("NAXAL/ MAOISTS threats and movements", n.d., para. 1), the Research and Analysis Wing of India's intelligence agency has estimated the total number of armed Naxalites in operation to be around 20,000. According to the same report, the Indian Ministry of Home Affairs estimated the death toll related to the Maoist-Naxalite insurgency for the period from 1996 to 2009 to be over 6,000. These rebels usually step up their attacks during general election times. Such attacks became prominent during the 2009 April/May general election. In one of them, the insurgents took hostage more than 300 train passengers in the eastern state of Jharkhand. According to a report on the incident, "at least 200 armed rebels swooped on the train ... and held the passengers for about four hours" (Geopolitical 2009, para. 2). This, many believe, was aimed at enforcing a general strike they had called in the area. As the situation continued to worsen by the year, the central government of India announced a simultaneous, coordinated counter operation with the intended purpose to plug all possible escape routes of Naxalites in the troubled states: Chhattisgarh, Orissa, Andra Pradesh, Maharashtra, Jharkhand, Bihar, Uttar Pradesh, and West Bengal. The future would tell to what extent the Indian government would be able to control the Naxalite movement by this and other measures.

Pakistan. Pakistan is engaged in a deadly confrontation with al-Qaeda and Taliban forces that moved in from Afghanistan. Their Pakistani supporters have further strengthened their ability to fight. These rebel forces fight the Pakistani government because of its role in the US-led War on Terror (WOT). The al-Qaeda and Taliban forces have a hideout based in the Swat Valley in the northwest part of Pakistan, an area not under the direct control of the Pakistani government. The rebels' violent attacks have spread far beyond their hideouts in the north-west. For example, in April 2009, the rebels attacked a police barracks near the country's capital, Islamabad. A few days later, the Pakistani police in Karachi arrested five suspected militants with links to al-Qaeda. In this arrest, the police also uncovered a large cache of weapons and explosives used in suicide attacks. In Lahore, authorities advised private schools to develop security plans to cope with possible militant attacks. It was also in Lahore that a group of insurgents attacked a visiting Sri Lankan cricket team in 2009. Over the years, Pakistan Army convoys and checkpoints, rural police stations, government offices, schools, hotels, and restaurants, have all become targets of indiscriminate suicide attacks conducted by the rebel forces. Shiite mosques also became targets. In a related article (*National Post*, November 18, 2009, para. 23), Peter Goodspeed noted, "more than 1,500 have been killed in Swat and at least 100,000 made homeless" during 2007 and 2008. The frequency and the intensity of the attacks have since increased. This resulted in deadly US drone attacks aimed at the rebels within Pakistan. US military agencies direct and control these attacks from their offices in America, using missile-armed remote-controlled drone aircraft. Such attacks have killed both the targeted militants and innocent bystanders, including women and children. By the end of December 2009, the death toll had surpassed 7,000 and more than 3.4 million people were displaced from their homes in the Swat area. Meanwhile, Peter Goodspeed reported Hakimullah Mehsud, a deputy to Pakistani Taliban leader Baitullah Mehsud, vowed to carry out "two suicide bombings a week until the US military stops attacking Taliban targets inside Pakistan with predator drone aircraft" (*National Post*, April 10, 2009, para. 12). At the same time, on an al-Qaeda website, Pakistani Taliban commander Mullah Nazeer Ahmed has said, "The day is not far when Islamabad will be in the hands of the mujahedeen" (*National Post*, April 10, 2009, para. 11). Should this happen, the nuclear weapons of the country also would fall into the hands of the rebellious forces operating there.

Overall, the continuing violent confrontations in Pakistan appear to threaten its very survival as a stable democratic state. A report prepared by the Atlantic Council task force and led by former Nebraska senator Chuck Hagel and Massachusetts Senator John Kerry in 2009 suggests, "Pakistan is on a rapid trajectory toward becoming a failing or failed state ....We cannot stress the magnitude of the dangers enough nor the need for greater action now. Pakistan faces dire economic and security threats that threaten both the existence of Pakistan as a democratic and stable state and the region as a whole." (*National Post*, April 10, 2009, para. 2). In the same year, US General David Petraeus in Iraq told The Washington Post, "We're now reaching the point where, within one to six months, we could see the collapse of the Pakistani state. ... Pakistan is 173 million people, 100 nuclear weapons, and an army bigger than the US Army and al-Qaeda headquarters sitting right there in the two thirds of the country that the government doesn't control" ("Key quotes" 2009, para. 11).

Although the Pakistani state has not collapsed as predicted, its condition remains tense and insecure. The Pakistani Army maintains its actions against the Taliban and al-Qaeda militants, especially in the tribal regions of the country. The United States continues to assist the Pakistani army in these offensives with continued drone attacks aimed at the militant groups. Occasionally, there have been popular protests within Pakistan against all types of US and other cross-border aerial attacks on Pakistani soil. These protests clearly show the leverage Pakistan has in its alliance with the United States and its allies in fighting the WOT. At times of such major protests, the occasional threats by the Pakistani government to stop protecting the US and allied supply lines to Afghanistan indicate a clear sign of Pakistan's uneasiness over the cross-border attacks.

The killing of the al-Qaeda leader Osama bin Laden on Pakistani soil by a US Special Forces military unit on May 2, 2011 only worsened the uneasy US-Pakistan relationship. The military unit launched the raid on bin Laden's compound in Pakistan from neighbouring Afghanistan, and was aided by CIA operatives on the ground. The bin Laden compound was located in the city of Abbottabad, a military town about 50 kilometres north-east of the Pakistan's capital, Islamabad. It became evident that Bin Laden had been living there under cover for some years. After the killing of bin Laden, the United States pressed Pakistan to probe into how he managed to live there for years under the military's nose, suggesting that he must have had a Pakistani government support system of some kind. Pakistan strongly dismissed such suggestions. In explaining the situation, according to a report by Rob Crilly, Pakistani Prime Minister Yusuf Raza Gilani said, "It is disingenuous for anyone to blame Pakistan or state institutions of Pakistan, including Pakistan's ISI [Inter-Services Intelligence] and the armed forces, for being in cahoots with al-Qaeda. .. It was al-Qaeda and its affiliates that carried out hundreds of suicide bombings in nearly every town and city of Pakistan and targeted political leaders, state institutions, the ISI and the General Headquarters" (*Vancouver Sun*, May 10, 2011, B3).

The mistrust that developed between the United States and Pakistan only got worse over time. In September 2011, the United States blamed Pakistan's ISI for using some Afghan militant groups as proxies to fight with US forces in Afghanistan. The United States even claimed that one such proxy group had attacked the US embassy in Kabul earlier in the same month. This claim came with a threat to send US ground troops to Pakistan to fight these proxy groups. Pakistan vehemently protested against such a move.

Meanwhile, the killing of Osama bin Laden, in particular, led to a new wave of popular protests in Pakistan, and all around the Muslim world. In these protests, masked militants stormed towns and cities, blazed US flags, burned effigies of US leaders, and vowed to avenge bin Laden's death with bombings. In one of these protests that took place on May 23, 2011, the protesters attacked a naval airbase in Karachi with rockets, grenades, and machine guns. In this particular attack, the protesters destroyed two US maritime-surveillance airplanes, killing 10 Pakistani security personnel. Then, Chris Allbritton and Missy Ryan reported, a poll of June 2011 showed that "almost two-thirds of the population considered the United States as an enemy" (*Vancouver Sun*, October 1, 2011, B3).

Myanmar. The military junta of Myanmar (formerly known as Burma) faces confrontations on two fronts: the ethnic minorities in the country and its democratic movement. On the ethnic front, there are five minority groups: Muslims in the west, the Kachin in the far north, the Chin in the central western region, the Mon in the south, and the people living in the eastern states along the Burmese border with Thailand. The Burmese junta has signed many ceasefire agreements with the conflicting parties. Many of these agreements allow the fighting ethnic groups to keep their arms. The only conflict not covered by any ceasefire agreement is the Karen separatist struggle concentrated in the Karen and Shan states; these states lie on the Thai border. A report on this particular conflict says, "The Karen, the Shan and other minority groups who live along the Myanmar-Thai border have been attacked, raped and killed by government soldiers. Their thatch-roofed, bamboo homes have been torched. Men have been seized into forced labour for the army, while women, children and the elderly either hide out in nearby jungles until the soldiers leave or flee over the mountains to crowded, makeshift refugee camps." (Elmore 2009, para. 2).

The armed struggle for Karen autonomy started in 1947; the dominant party involved is the Christian Karen National Union. Some believe that it is the oldest ongoing war in the world. It has so far killed over 7,000 people and displaced tens of thousands within eastern Myanmar. It has also forced more than 160,000 out of the country to neighbouring Thailand as refugees. More than 60 percent of the refugees are Karen. Many believe that the situation with this and other ethnic struggles in Myanmar worsened after its government made Buddhism the official religion of the country in 1960.

The National League for Democracy (NLD) is the main democracy movement in Myanmar with Aung San Suu Kyi as its leader. She is the daughter of the country's founding father, Aung San. His declared mission was to establish a post-independence Myanmar representing the interests of all the ethnic groups in the country. However, he was assassinated before he could become the post-independence prime minister when the country gained independence from Britain in 1947. Ever since independence, the ethnic minority groups, more than 200 in number, sought a federal system of government. As their cry for such a governing system gathered momentum, the military, dominated by the majority Burmans, staged a coup and took over the government in 1962. At an election held in 1990, the NLD won a landslide victory. The ruling junta, however, ignored the results of the election and put the NLD leader under house arrest. Then, in 2007, the junta drafted a new constitution and later ratified it through a questionable (no foreign observers allowed) referendum. The junta also banned the opposition leader from holding office. These actions resulted in widespread demonstrations against the junta government. The junta, however, cracked down mercilessly, and severely punished all political activists who had played a leading role in organizing them. There were many Buddhist monks and students among the leading activists. In secret trials, the junta sentenced some of them to prison terms up to 65 years. Despite the junta's harsh crackdown on the leaders of the protests, the pro-democracy demonstrations continued. In 2010, the junta held another election, further consolidating its power. After the election, however, the junta released the NLD leader from house arrest. Only time will tell whether the junta will readily allow the country to return to genuine democracy in the coming years.

Thailand. There are three separate insurgency movements in the Muslim-dominated southern provinces of Thailand. The violence caused by the insurgencies occasionally spills over to the other provinces of the country. According to experts, there are a number of historic grounds for these insurgent uprisings. A 200-year Thai occupation and the resettlement of northeastern Thais in the conflicted areas in the 1960s are two of the reasons. Another is the alleged Thai cultural and economic imperialism in the country's southern provinces. Muslims concentrated in these provinces make up approximately 4.5 percent of the total population of the country. They complain of police brutality and disrespect for Islam. From their religious perspective, they have shown strong opposition to the presence of culturally sensitive businesses such as bars and drug trafficking. This area's insurgency started decades ago and, over time, it has become a major offensive against the government. The year 2004 was particularly troublesome; the insurgents in these provinces raided an army ammunition depot, attacked 11 police outposts, and set 20 schools and two police posts on fire. In the same year, they also slaughtered 15 Buddhists. In one of the counter-operations, government forces entered a historic mosque with grenades and slaughtered 32 militants, and allowed 78 others to die of asphyxiation. This particular counter-operation causing so many deaths led to the sharp escalation of the insurgent activities in the area. The total number of casualties resulting from the insurgency in 2004 alone exceeded 700. The rebellious activities that occurred after 2004 included major bomb explosions and attacks, drive-by shootings, ambushes, and arson. June 15, 2006 was the 60th anniversary of the accession of King Bhumibol Adulyadej to the Thai throne. The militants marked the occasion with a series of coordinated bomb-attacks against at least 40 government and official buildings, killing two police officers and injuring 11 others. The death toll resulting from the insurgency exceeded 3,500 by the end of 2008.

Algeria. Algeria is under the threat of militant groups of radical religious revivalism. Ninety-nine percent of the country's population are Muslims. A major conflict began in 1991 when the country's government cancelled a general election after its first round of results. These results showed that a radical Islamic political party, the Islamic Salvation Front (FIS), would win the election. The government in power feared that power in the hands of the FIS would end democracy in the country. After the cancellation of the election, the government banned the FIS and took into custody thousands of its leaders. This led to the emergence of several Islamic guerrilla groups who began to wage war against the government. Some of these groups eventually fought one another. The result was a series of massacres targeting entire communities and villages, as well as government forces. These massacres have claimed 150-200,000 human lives. Many measures taken by recent governments have, to some extent, controlled the chaotic situation. One guerrilla group, Salafist Group for Preaching and Combat, has publicly endorsed al-Qaeda. This group remains at large, fighting the government. Other fighting groups in the country may also be connected to al-Qaeda. In April 2009, there was a report that an al-Qaeda linked Algerian-based terrorist group had released two Canadian diplomats and two European women in exchange for four imprisoned Islamic militants. The same group also had threatened to kill a British tourist if Britain did not release a top-notch Islamist terrorist. Some suggest that this top-notch terrorist was Osama bin Laden's top European envoy. An end to the ongoing violence and the guerrilla wars in this country is still far, far away.

Somalia. Somalia has had civil wars since the time of insurrection against its pro-US Siad Barre regime in the mid-eighties. Ninety-nine percent of the country's population are Muslims, as in Algeria. After Siad Barre fell from power in 1991, a counter-revolution took place to reinstate him. The resulting violence increased and led to a state of anarchy in the country. In the process, a number of tribal leaders and warlords declared their own autonomous states within Somalia. These self-declared states include Somaliland, Puntland, Jubaland, Southwestern Somalia, and Gulmudug. Years of international mediation followed through an eight-country East African international agency, the Intergovernmental Authority on Development, resulted in a Transitional Federal Government (TFG). This transitional government first operated from Nairobi, Kenya, from 2004. In the midst of the continuing chaotic situation, the TFG managed to move into Somalia and establish a temporary seat of government in Baidoa; the country's capital Mogadishu was under the rule of the warlords belonging to a group called the Islamic Courts Union (ICU). The ICU's rule at the time was not limited to Mogadishu. It also had the coastal areas of southern Somalia under its control. Then, on the invitation of the TFG, US-backed Ethiopian troops intervened to assist the TFG to take full control of Somalia. The Somali troops from Puntland also supported the TFG in this move. However, the ICU leader, Sheik Hassan Dahir Aweys, declared, "Somalia is in a state of war, and all Somalis should take part in this struggle against Ethiopia" ("Somalis `at war` with Ethiopia" 2006, para. 2). In this situation, the ICU, the Somali Islamist umbrella group, and other affiliated militias rallied together against the TFG and its allied forces, starting a country-wide war within Somalia. Responding to this new situation, the al-Qaeda movement called upon Muslims worldwide to join the ICU in defeating both Ethiopia and the TFG in Somalia. In turn, this led to more involvement by the United States in the region. A Web-message of July 1, 2006, allegedly written by Osama bin Laden, called upon the Somalis to build an Islamic state and warned western states that al-Qaeda would fight against them if they intervened. Meanwhile, the UN maintained that a number of Arab nations, including Libya, Egypt, and Eritrea, were also assisting the ICU in this war. As of January 2009, Ethiopia had withdrawn its troops from Somalia. By this time, the TFG had lost some of the territory that was under its control, but it entered into a power-sharing arrangement with some Islamist splinter groups. The al Shabaab movement, a group separated from the ICU, refused to accept any type of peace deal with the TFG. As a result, this ICU splinter group continued to fight with the TFG forces. The African Union troops assisted the TFG forces in the ensuing fights. Between 2006 and 2008, the wars in this country killed more than 15,000 civilians, and wounded about 30,000 others. By 2007, there were 1.9 million civilians displaced from their homes in Mogadishu alone. In addition, thousands of combatants died on the fighting fronts.

Sudan. There is an ongoing civil war centred on the Darfur region in the northern part of Sudan. It began in 2003 with surprise attacks on government forces and installations in the region. Two major militant groups, the Justice and Equality Movement (JEM) and the Sudan Liberation Movement/Army (SLM/A), staged these attacks. Their main grievance was that the Sudanese government led by President Omar al-Bashir was oppressing black Africans in favour of Arabs in the Darfur region. All parties to the fight are Muslim, unlike in the Second

Sudanese Civil War in the eighties. The details of this earlier conflict follow later in this section.

The militant movements fighting the government forces in the Darfur region have primarily consisted of recruits from non-Arab ethnic groups in the country. The government forces and the Janjaweed, a militia group recruited mostly from Arab tribes, have conducted raids on towns and villages in the region, aiming to end the conflict. There are various estimates of the number of human casualties resulting from this civil war and the number of people dead, from either direct combat or from starvation and disease inflicted by the conflict, could be as high as several hundred thousand. At the same time, more than two million people fled their homes. The displaced live in refugee camps, within and outside the country, with inadequate water, food, and medicine. In February 2010, the government of Sudan signed a ceasefire agreement with the JEM, the dominant rebel group. This presented much hope for further peace. Many even thought that this ceasefire agreement would lead to a version of a semi-autonomic rule for Darfur, similar to the one proposed for the southern part of the country. These hopes collapsed abruptly when, in violation of the February 2010 agreement, the government raided and made air strikes against a village in Darfur. The JEM withdrew from the negotiation table. After that, it joined hands with the other fighting groups in Darfur and formed a new alliance, the Alliance of the Resistance Forces. The formation of this alliance made it more difficult for the government forces to suppress the rebels in the region. The government forces, in fact, even faced military defeat in some of the Alliance attacks that followed. A related report notes that Abu Bakr Hamid of the JEM has said in its attack of March 16, 2011, the Alliance "defeated government forces, seized weapons, vehicles and captured young soldiers" (*Vancouver Sun*, December 24, 2010, B7). The fight continues.

The Second Sudanese Civil War was a clash primarily between the Muslim north and the non-Muslim south. This particular civil war ended with a peace deal in 2005, and led to the partitioning of Sudan into two distinct states in 2011: Sudan and South Sudan. South Sudan is now one of the United Nations member states. These two newly partitioned states have engaged in border disputes, especially in the area around Abyei. South Sudan was particularly disturbed by a large build-up of Sudan's infantry, tanks, artillery, and warplanes in the area around El Obeid, some 400 kilometres away from Abyei. At the same time, South Sudan accused its northern counterpart of providing support and training camps for militant groups, enabling cross-border attacks into South Sudan, leaving the region poised for a new war with unresolved contentious issues.

Uganda. In Uganda, an insurgency led by a rebellious group called Lord's Resistance Army (LRA) continues with no signs of ending. The LRA leader Joseph Kony, an ethnic Acholic from the north of the country, was once a self-proclaimed spirit medium. He started the LRA rebellion against the government formed by the National Resistance Army (NRA) led by Yoweri Museveni, a south-westerner. This was after the overthrow of President Tito Okello, who was an ethnic Acholi, by the NRA in 1986. In time, the LRA became infamous for its record of abductions, rape, torture, mutilation, child soldiers, forced labour, and even massacres. Consequently, the International Criminal Court issued arrest warrants against LRA leaders in 2005. The rebellion had already claimed tens of thousands of lives because of direct combat, starvation, and disease. It had also displaced nearly two million people from their homes. This conflict was once identified by many as the second worst "forgotten" humanitarian emergency in the world, with the "Africa's World War" in Congo in first place. Later, the LRA signed a truce with the incumbent government, on the condition that its troops would leave Uganda in exchange for two assembly areas in southern Sudan protected by the Sudanese government. Parties remained cautious about the future of this truce.

Ivory Coast. Ivory Coast has had almost two decades of political unrest since a military coup overthrew the government in 1999. The military junta then rigged the elections held a year later, and declared its leader as the country's new president. This resulted in popular protests that finally forced him to step aside. In late 2000, a civilian government returned to power. Then, in September 2002, discontented members of the army launched a failed coup to oust the civilian government. Since then, the country has remained split in two: the Muslim north held by the rebels and the Christian south retained by the government. French troops arrived to help the government fight the rebels. The insurgents too received assistance from outside; former combatants of Liberia and

Sierra Leone reportedly poured in to fight with the Ivorian rebel forces. The confronting parties had ceasefires and made serious attempts to work together. Violence continued regardless, and the unity governments they tried to build did not bring the desired results. In March 2007, with the latest peace attempt, Ivory Coast President Laurent Gbagbo signed an accord with the main rebel leader Guillaume Soro to form a unity government. They agreed to reunite the country, integrate rebel forces into the national army, and to hold elections by the year's end. A month later, the rebel leader, Soro, who had controlled the northern part of the country for four years, took office as the prime minister of the new unity government. This raised hope for peace in the country. However, many obstacles blocked the path to peace. Demobilization and reintegration of the rebel forces in preparing them to join the regular army became particularly problematic. The government also had to postpone the intended election indefinitely due to citizen identification and voter registration difficulties. Meanwhile, the French military and the UN peacekeeping forces have been stationed in the country to do their best to maintain peace between the conflicting parties.

The presidential election, which was finally held in November 2010, further aggregated the situation in the country. The results released by the election authorities showed that Alassane Ouattara, who challenged the incumbent president Gbagbo, received 54.1 percent of the votes cast. Despite this, Gbagbo declared himself the winner, stating that the results released by the election authorities were invalid. In this situation, both were sworn in as the president of the country. This, in turn, led to widespread violent clashes between the two rival forces. The fighting continued for four months until the forces loyal to Ouattara arrested Gbagbo in April 2011. By then, the battles between the two groups had claimed more than 1,000 lives and uprooted a million people. The new Ouattara government now faced the dormant task of confronting the country's long-standing ethnic divisions and the worsening humanitarian crisis in the country.

Intrastate conflicts concluded. In addition to the abovementioned contemporary conflicts, the list below provides some details of intrastate wars concluded in recent decades, just as in the section on inter-state conflicts. It is not a complete list, by any means, but it includes the intrastate conflicts of major concerns ended in many regions of the world. Of course, like the inter-state conflicts and under certain conditions, any of these disputes might be renewed, with grave and disastrous results.

Intrastate war	Dates	Death toll	Comment
Separatist War in Sri Lanka	1983-2009	80,000-100,000	The Liberation Tigers of Tamil Eelam (LTTE) started the war in 1983, aiming to create a separate state in the north and the east of the country for its ethnic Tamil minority.
Nepalese Civil War	1996-2006	12,700	Maoist rebels vs. Government
Burundi Civil War and Tribal Massacres	1993-2006	300,000	Started with a coup d'état staged by military officers of the minority Tutsi tribe. Since the assassination of the first post-independence Hutu president in 1962, the country had a series of brutal tit-for-tat tribal massacres between the majority Hutus and minority Tutsis.
Iraqi Internal Conflict	2006-2008	200,000	Fight between Sunni and Shia factions of Islam.

Angolan Civil War (immediately after War for Independence	1975-2002	More than 500,000	A power struggle between two former liberation movements: the People's Movement for the Liberation of Angola (MPLA) and the National Union for the Total Independence of Angola (UNITA) - Marxist-Leninist and anti-communist, respectively
Indonesia Internal Fight	1990-2001	10,000	Between Christians and Muslims.
Sierra Leone Civil War	1991-2002	200,000	Started by a student revolutionary group.
Indonesia - Suharto Genocide	1966-98	800,000	Indonesian Communist Party members were the biggest group affected.
Congo (Brazzaville) Civil War	1997-99	Unknown	Partisans of two presidential candidates, ethnic overtones, outside involvement, oil a crucial factor.
UK - IRA Armed Campaign	1969-97	1,800	Fight for a united Ireland. Catholics vs. Protestants. Formally ended in 2005.
Guatemala's Civil War	1960-96	200,000	Grassroots, popular response to a rightist dictatorship and the US attempts to halt the country's drift to the Left.

Tajikistan's Civil War	1992-96	50,000-100,000	Rebels (democratic reformists and Islamists) seeking representation in government, ethnic overtones.
Yugoslavian Wars	1992-96	260,000	Ethnic conflicts & cleansing finally led to a number of new states. The Hague tried former president Slobodan Milosevic for war crimes.
Philippines Civil War	1972-96	Unknown	Minority Muslims vs. Government.
Pakistani Sunnis vs. Shiites	1995	1,300	Fight between Sunni and Shia factions of Islam.
North Korea – Political Repression by Communist Rule (Kim Il Sung)	1948-87	710,000-3.500,000	Concentration camps, labour camps, executions, forced mass campaigns, and others.
Rwanda's Civil War & Genocide	1990-93	900,000	Tribal competition for power. Prime Minister Jean Kambanda condemned to life imprisonment for genocide.

Mozambique's Civil War	1977-92	900,000	Post independence government of the Liberation Front of Mozambique (FRELIMO) challenged by a Rhodesian and South African funded group, the Mozambican National Resistance (RENAMO). War ended with a peace accord and democratic elections.
Peru's Civil War	1980-2000	69,000	Guerrilla wars by Maoist and other revolutionary groups against the government.
Nicaragua vs. Contras	1981-90	60,000	Nicaraguan Democratic Force and a number of other groups together fighting the government. Also US involvement.
Liberian First Civil War	1989-96	220,000	A form of communal violence against the government, tribal overtones, ended in an all-party interim government.
Liberian Second Civil War	1999-2003	150,000	Two rebel groups vs. government, foreign involvement, ended with a transitional government.

Cambodia – Political Repression by Communist rule (Pol Pot)	1975-79	1,700,000	Political repression by the communist government, slave labour and malnutrition resulted from an imposed version of an agrarian collectivization programme - about 21% of the country's population perished.
Ethiopia – Red Terror, Political Repression	1977-78	500,000	Response by communist Menghistu Mariam, who gained control over the military junta, Derg, to counter the revolutionary attacks, with mass killings of opponents. Later, in 2006, Mariam was convicted for his role in Red Terror.
Nigerian-Biafran War / (Yakubu Gowon)	1967-70	1,200,000	Separatist war initiated by the southeastern provinces of the country. It resulted primarily from the neglect of Nigeria's ethnic, religious, and linguistic needs by its departing colonialists, the British.

China – Political Repression by Communist Rule (Mao Ze-Dong)	1949-50	40-70,000,000	Political purges (1.2 million in Tibet 1949-50 included), Great Leap Forward (23 million, 1958-61), Cultural revolution (11 million, 1966-69), and others.
Indonesian Civil War – Political Oppression under Junta Rule	1965-66	250,000	An anti-communist purge after an abortive coup resulted in the elimination of the Indonesian Communist Party as a political force.
Germany – Genocide and Similar Mass Killings (Adolf Hitler)	1941-44	11-12,000,000	Six million Jews & others (Romani, the disabled, Soviet prisoners of war, homosexuals, and other religious and political opponents).
Soviet Union-Political Oppression by Communist Rule (Josef Stalin)	1932-39	3,000,000 [being debated)	Political repression, purge of opponents, annihilation of some nationals of foreign ethnic groups (including poles, Germans, Koreans, & Americans).
Turkey – Genocide (Ismail Enver)	1915-22	2,000,000	Armenians, Greek Pontiacs, Greek Anatolians, & Assyrians.

A Sober Reflection

The inter-state and intrastate violent conflicts examined in this chapter are many and varied. Most commonly, they appear in the form of border disputes and land claims, fights for oil, fights for rare minerals, acts of vengeance, acts of genocide, state terrorism, struggles against state discrimination, racial or tribal wars, religious wars, ideological wars, liberation struggles, and separatist wars. The list continues. Irrespective of how they appear, all such conflicts can be grouped into four primary categories: economic exploitation, social and political vendetta, abuse of state power, and identity-politics. For example, fights for oil and fights for rare minerals belong to the economic exploitation category. The 1980-88 Persian Gulf War, the 1990-91 Gulf War, and the 1998-2000 Eritrean-Ethiopian war are three such conflicts. The wars of vengeance, primarily fuelled by the past actions of relatives and ancestors of the conflicting parties fall under the category of social and political vendettas. The ongoing conflicts between Sunnis and Shiites, Israelis and Palestinians, and between Indians and Pakistanis are three such conflicts. In such conflicts, the historic feuds could be hundreds, or even thousands of years old. For example, the Sunni-Shiites vendetta originates from a violent conflict between two groups of Muslims soon after the death of Prophet Mohammed over 1,400 years ago. The two groups were at loggerheads over who should succeed Prophet Mohammed. The Shia group believed that leadership should stay within the family of the Prophet. Sunnis believed that it should fall to the person chosen by the elite of the community. The Sunnis prevailed, but the scuffle between the two groups led to bloody confrontations.

Acts of genocide and other forms of state terrorism belong to the category of abuse of state power. The genocide seen in Indonesia (1966-98) and the mass scale political repression by Pol Pot in Cambodia (1975-79) are two such cases. On the other hand, the conflicts that originate from the competing interests of divergent racial, tribal, ethnic, religious, linguistic, cultural, or ideological groups belong to the identity-politics category. This category includes the struggles between the Africans and Arabs of South Sudan (1983-2005), the Hutus and Tutsis of Burundi (1993-2006), the Catholics and Protestants of Northern Ireland, UK (1969-1997), and communists and anti-communists of Angola (1975-2002).

The conflicts of the identity-politics category essentially place peoples of different backgrounds, beliefs, or ideological identities at loggerheads. However, it is a feature not unique to this category. It dominates in many conflicts of the other three categories as well. For example, the India-Pakistan vendetta conflict has held Muslims and Hindus in a long-standing feud. The vendetta conflict between Israel and Palestine is between Jews and Arabs. And, in conflicts resulting from the abuse of state power, such as those of North Korea (1948-87) and Cambodia (1975-79), the conflicting parties were communists and anti-communists. The more the parties have fought each other, the more the prejudices, mistrust, and hatred, based on such identities, have grown. The same identity differences also characterize the relationships among the global powers, the very ones who are at the forefront of maintaining world peace.

It would be interesting to know whether a group of people with a particular racial, ethnic, religious, linguistic, cultural, or ideological identity is, in general, responsible for the violent conflicts in the world. The violent conflicts examined in this chapter certainly do not suggest this. Instead, one sees people of all different identities among both the slaughterers and the slaughtered. For example, the blacks, the whites, the browns, and the yellows have all resorted to brutal force causing deadly violence. Christians, Muslims, Hindus, Buddhists, and Hebrews have also done the same. Some have engaged in holy wars, testing the might of their respective gods, demons, and other beliefs. There also have been internal violent conflicts within some religious groups, occurring between different sects of the same religion. Others have occurred between the so-called 'moderates' and the 'fundamentalists' or 'extremists' of the same belief system. Then, among the perpetrators of violence, there have also been people from every political leaning. Some have had leanings to the left, while others stood to the right of centre. Warring peoples occupy all types of countries: developed or developing, industrial or agrarian, large or small, Western or Eastern. Some countries were monarchies or dictatorships. Others were even democracies. Geographically, the countries marred with violent conflicts are spread far and wide, in many regions of the world. Thus, it would be inappropriate to point the finger of judgement at any particular group of people of any kind of identity and characterize them as the perpetrators of violence in the world.

Media personnel everywhere have been busy reporting on major acts and threats of violence around the globe. They have done this through numerous radio and television newscasts, newspapers, and the internet. The newscasters have also informed the public of the varied ways in which communities, nations, and states have responded to these acts and threats of aggression. Ironically, not all have condemned every such act or threat; in certain situations, some have condoned them.

Because of the ongoing violent conflicts in the world, hardly a day passes without ground battles, air raids, suicide attacks, abductions, incarcerations, and victimizations affecting hundreds, if not thousands, of people around the globe. During major combats, both combatants and innocent civilians die. The combatants die in fighting in the battlefield. The innocent civilians, including women and children, succumb to the injuries caused by the crossfire. Some combatants rape and kill innocent women in their own homes and nearby streets and allies. Some armed men go in gangs and massacre complete villages and communities. As a result, peace-loving citizens of these areas live in fear, intimidation, and horror, 24 hours a day and seven days a week. Meanwhile, researchers say that the civilian casualties of major violent conflicts have risen from less than five percent during WWI to more than 75 per cent. The civilian death toll during WWII alone was above 40 million; this was more than 65 per cent of the total number of people who lost their lives in this particular war. The discussions on ongoing major conflicts and, in particular the inter-state conflicts earlier in the chapter, show that the chances for the occurrence of another global catastrophe on the scale of WWI or WWII are very real.

Chapter 3:
A Violent Conflict with No Borders

IN ADDITION TO THE violent conflicts in and about states described in the previous chapter, there is one form of aggression of greatest global concern. It is characterized by a series of bloody terrorist attacks across the globe. Some Islamic militant groups take responsibility for these assaults. These groups do not necessarily represent the world Muslim community as a whole. Some Muslims do not support or condone such atrocities. Over the years, violent events associated with Islamic militant hostility have continued to threaten peace around the world. Such events have occurred practically in all the regions of the world. The specific countries affected by these events are many in number. The United States, Columbia, Peru, the United Kingdom, Greece, Kyrgyzstan, and Russia are among them. Jordan, Kuwait, Saudi Arabia, and Iraq are also among them. Afghanistan, India, Pakistan, Indonesia, Morocco, Tanzania, and Kenya are also a few others.

These Islamic militant groups have carried out their attacks at varied places, targeting both military personnel and civilians. The venues of these attacks include embassy buildings, army housing facilities, military compounds, bars and restaurants, hotels, and shopping malls. Bus stops, trains, nightclubs, schools and universities, and even residential neighbourhoods are several others. The following ten selected Islamic militant attacks between 1996 and 2005 show the general nature of the attacks and the extent of violence caused by them:

1. the bombing attack on French Archbishop of Oran after a meeting he held with the French Foreign Minister on 1 August 1996, allegedly carried out by the Algerian Armed Islamic Group;

2. the bombing of US embassies in Kenya and Tanzania on August 7, 1998, killing 225 people;

3. the seizure of Israeli and Greek diplomatic facilities in France, Holland, Switzerland, Britain, and Germany by Kurdish militants in February 1999;

4. a suicide attack on the U.S. Navy destroyer USS Cole (DDG 67) on October 12, 2000, while it was refuelling in the Yemeni port of Aden, killing 17 American sailors and injuring 39 others;

5. the suicide attacks on the New York World Trade Centre and Pentagon in Arlington using hijacked aircraft on September 11, 2001, killing about 3,000 people and injuring more than 6,000;

6. the ramming of an explosive-laden boat into the French oil tanker Limburg on October 6, 2002, while it was anchored about five miles off al-Dhabbah in Yemen on;

7. the car bomb explosion outside the Sari Club Discotheque in Denpassar, Bali, Indonesia, on 12 October 2002 by a local militant group, killing more than 200 people, mostly from the United States and Australia;

8. the bombing of a Spanish restaurant, a Jewish community, a Jewish cemetery, a Belgium Consulate and a hotel by 12 suicide bombers on 16 May 2003, killing 43 people and wounding another 100;

9. the suicide truck bombing of the British Consulate and a British Bank in Istanbul on 20 November 2003, killing 27 persons and wounding at least 450; and

10. the bombing of three Underground trains and a double-decker bus in London, England, by a group of Islamic militants on 7 July 2005, killing at least 56 and wounding over 700 others.

The Islamic militant groups responsible for such deadly attacks claim that they are mere acts of *jihad*, in the cause of God. Accordingly, the people that these Islamic militant groups are fighting should be those who have acted against Muslims in some manner. However, the victims of the attacks include civilians who likely have had no past thoughts, words, or actions against Muslims. Many Muslims around the world do not agree that such attacks on innocent civilians constitute acts of jihad under the commands of the Quran. In this light, let us try to see who, in particular, has been targeted in the concerned Islamic militant attacks.

Primary Target

The citizens of the Western countries and the United States in particular have been the primary targets of these types of terrorist acts. There appear to be two main reasons for this. First, many living in Islamic countries believe that the West has been particularly unkind to Muslims. Some past events have led to such beliefs. The British unwillingness at the time of partitioning colonial India into two separate states to treat the Muslim-majority Kashmir region as part of Muslim-dominated Pakistan, instead of Hindu-dominated India, is an example in this regard. Another example is the British initiative, supported by the other western countries, to create the state of Israel for Jews within the former Arab-dominated Palestine territory. The apparent delay on the part of the United States and other western powers in responding to genocidal attacks on Bosnian and Kosovo Muslims during the infamous 1991-1999 Balkan conflict is yet another example. These and some other past events may have led to the belief among Muslims that the West has been particularly nasty to them. The creation of Israel appears to be the hottest issue among Muslims in general. Adding fuel to the fire, the West, and in particular the United States, has demonstrated its keen interest to protect and promote Israel ever since its creation. In the process, Israel has become a powerful state, seemingly more powerful than any combination of Muslim states in the region. The conflicts that have arisen between Muslims and non-Muslims because of the partitioning of Colonial India and the Palestine Territory have continued to grow over the years. In fact, these conflicts have now become major threats to world peace.

Second, the West appears to have stood in the way of serious efforts made by Muslim countries for the improvement of the lives of their peoples. This has allegedly happened in many areas of human endeavour. Ironically, one of these areas is the embrace of the path of democracy, the very same political path that the West preaches throughout the world. The reaction of the United States and its western allies to the Palestinian government of Hamas is a case in point. It came to power democratically through a general election held in 2006. The West simply wanted to overthrow this government, regardless. For this, they initiated a number of measures. These measures include painful trade and financial sanctions against the Hamas government and military support to its rivals.

At the same time, the United States and its western allies also have been blamed for taking the side of brutal dictators and executive monarchs in the Middle East. They have done so even at times when a local regional power had vowed to depose them. According to critics, the United States has done nothing to promote democracy or good governance even in countries, such as Saudi Arabia, Egypt, Jordon, and Morocco, where it had exerted much influence.

A third area of Muslim efforts allegedly thwarted by the West is socio-economic development. The economically and socially exploited Muslim countries have always tried to free themselves. Not only Muslim countries do that; non-Muslim countries in similar situations also do the same. However, when a Muslim country in the Middle East tried to do so, the western states were seen to gang up against such a move. According to critics, the mounting of a coup by the West, and in particular the United States and the United Kingdom, to bring back to power the West-friendly Iranian dictator Shah Reza in 1953 is a case in point. This was after the government of Iran, led by centrist democrat Mohammed Mossadegh, nationalized the foreign oil companies that were operating in the country; most of these companies were British. Critics point out that the Mossadegh government nationalized the oil companies to divert profits from oil to modernize the economy of the country hoping to uplift the living standards of its people. Then, when the post-revolution (1979) government of Iran ended its feudal, dictatorial Shah rule and introduced liberal democratic reforms, the entire West was not happy. It is true that all the Iranian post-revolution governments have openly criticized and worked against western imperialism and exploitation. It is also true that they run their country on Islamic principles, based on Sharia law. However, the critics of the West say post-revolution Iran is doing all that within a framework of democracy. For the West, however, post-revolution Iran has always remained a rogue nation.

MEANWHILE, THE CONTINUING UNFRIENDLY attitude of the West towards post-revolution Iranian governments appears to stand in blatant contrast to the type of friendly relationship it continues to enjoy with Saudi Arabia. This contradiction is primarily two-fold. First, Saudi Arabia is a monarchy, and not a democracy. Second, it also implements Sharia law, just like Iran. This contradiction surely questions the West's sincerity in its proclaimed interests in promoting democracy and human rights around the globe. According to critics, it also strengthens the belief that the West's interests in the region have more to do with its precious oil resources than anything else. The Middle East, in fact, has become a land of contention among major global powers ever since it discovered its oil resources. In their competition for access to the oil resources, major global powers, including the United States and the Soviet Union, have enticed the Middle Eastern countries with lucrative economic and military aid packages, defence treaties, and the like.

It is also noteworthy that the West has had a dual-facetted approach to Muslims in general and their way of life. The West's approach to Jihad clearly testifies to this. The West praised the jihadists who fought the Red Army during the Soviet invasion of Afghanistan. These jihadists were labelled as freedom fighters at the time. When the same jihadists later vowed to free Muslims in Saudi Arabia and Palestine from Western domination, the West re-labelled them as terrorists. Many Muslims perceive such dual-faceted actions of the Western countries, and the United States in particular, as crimes committed against their kind. Concerned Islamic militant groups have responded to this situation by fighting against the West in the cause of God.

It is possible that there is also unsettled and uncontrolled anger and enmity between Muslims and the West, the current home to Christendom, due to historic reasons. Within two decades of the death of Prophet Mohammed, the founder of Islam, in 632 AD, Muslim armies occupied Jerusalem and all the other 'Oriental Patriarchates' of Christians. In the following decades, Muslim armies moved across North Africa, crossed the Straits of Gibraltar, and occupied the Iberian Peninsula. Their further advancement came to a halt with their defeat at the battle of Poitiers in France in the year 732, one hundred years after Prophet Mohammed's death. This set the stage for a long period of confrontations between Muslims and Christians during the Western rule of the Byzantine Empire (395 – 1453). The 12th and 13th centuries were particularly nasty with almost constant warfare between the two groups, with both Muslims and Christians alternately on the offensive or defensive. During this period, there were nine major Christian expeditions (Crusades) to recover the Holy Land of Jerusalem from Muslims. Later, during the collapse of the Mongol Empire, which once stretched from Eastern Europe to the Sea of Japan, the Islamic forces managed to create three large Muslim empires: Ottoman Empire in Asia Minor (1299 – 1923), Safavid Empire in Persia (1501 – 1722), and Mughal Empire in India (1526 – 1858). These empires together covered nearly the entire Muslim world, and more. The Islamic civilization that thrived under these empires was unmatched on Earth; it produced the richest, the most creative, and the most powerful in every area of human endeavour.

The spread of this great civilization across the globe also resulted in the further spread of Islam among the people who belonged to other faiths. In the process, Muslims continued to remain a target of the people in the West, as the biggest force trying to invade and dominate them and their popular religion, Christianity. However, with the subsequent gradual decline of the three Islamic empires due to pressure from their external foes, the dynamics between the competing parties had significantly changed. The Islamic empires, instead of invading and dominating others, now became nations dominated by the Western, Christian powers. This in turn led to enormous anger and enmity directed at the West by the Islamic crusaders. The main western target for this anger and enmity today is understandably the United States, as it has emerged as the unchallengeable leader among the western countries, and the world.

PRIMARY SUSPECT

Meanwhile, the West has identified the al-Qaeda militant group, based in Afghanistan, as the main Islamic group responsible for the ongoing militant attacks. Many believe that the aim of this group is primarily three-fold. First, it wants to drive Americans and American influence out of all Muslim nations, especially Saudi Arabia. Second, it wants to destroy Israel. Third, it wants to topple pro-Western dictatorships in the Middle East. For his own part, Osama bin Laden, the Saudi Arabian born leader of the al-Qaeda movement, clearly expressed his strong objection to two things: the presence of American troops in Muslim countries and the US foreign policy on Israel. These objections, in fact, have led to many Islamic militant attacks against US citizens, both within and outside the United States. Those affected by these attacks include US politicians, diplomats, military personnel (those in combat missions in Muslim countries), scientists and professionals, international development agency personnel, and even tourists.

MOTHER OF ALL TERRORIST ATTACKS

The series of September 11, 2001 bloody attacks on the United States became the mother of all militant attacks, ever. They are commonly referred to as the 9/11 attacks. On that particular day, 19 Islamic suicide militants hijacked four commercial passenger jet airliners. They were en route to San Francisco and Los Angeles, originating from cities within the United States. The militants' aim was to crash the airliners into targeted high-profile buildings in the country. Two of the hijacked airliners crashed into the 110-floor twin towers (North Tower and South Tower) of the World Trade Centre in New York. The first of the two crashed into the North Tower at 8:46 a.m. The second hit the South Tower, seventeen minutes later, at 9:03 a.m. Thirty-four minutes after that, at 9:37 a.m., another airliner crashed into the Pentagon, the headquarters of the United States Defence in Virginia. Then, twenty-six minutes later, the remaining hijacked airliner crashed into a field in Shanksville in Pennsylvania at 10.03 a.m. Apparently, the militants wanted this airliner to crash into either the United States Capitol Building, the seat of government for the United States Congress, or the White House, the official residence of the United States President.

After the airplanes crashed into the World Trade Centre, its two towers were engulfed by flames and, within two hours, collapsed to the ground. The hundreds of people within the impact zones met with instant death. Those who were on floors above the impact zones did not have any way to run for safety; at least 200 of them jumped to their death from the burning floors. At the same time, 411 emergency workers, who tried to rescue the trapped victims or to suppress the fire, perished. Many paramedics and police officers who rushed to the scene also met with the same fate. In all, there were 2,993 fatalities caused by these horrible terrorist attacks, which lasted for only 77 minutes, The fatalities included all 19 hijackers, all 246 passengers on the four planes, 2,603 in New York City in and around the Twin Towers of the World Trade Centre, and 125 at the Pentagon.

These militant attacks on US soil shocked the world in two ways. First, they raised an instant global awareness of the degree of tension between the United States and the Islamic world. Second, the attacks showed the heightened danger associated with such acts perpetrated by the concerned Islamic groups. While the world was still recovering from the shock of these terrible attacks, the humiliated and injured United States determined that Osama bin Laden's al-Qaeda movement had engineered them. The government of the United Kingdom also came to the same conclusion.

Paradoxically, the very same Osama bin Laden had once established an Islamic militant movement, similar to al-Qaeda, with American help. It was known as Maktab al-Khidamat (MAK) and its intended purpose was to resist the Soviet invasion of Afghanistan in the late seventies. Osama bin Laden formed his al-Qaeda movement only after the Soviets withdrew from Afghanistan, in 1988. By that time, the US had no more interest in him. The Taliban government that came to power in Afghanistan in 1996 was, however, particularly friendly to Bin Laden; it allowed Bin Laden and his new movement to operate from Afghanistan. After the Soviets' withdrawal from that country, a number of events turned Bin Laden and his new movement against the United States. This resulted in two *fatwas* issued by Bin Laden against the US. A *fatwa* in Islam is a religious opinion concerning Islamic law issued by an Islamic scholar. Bin Laden issued his first *fatwa* against the US in 1996, and the second in 1998. Many Muslims believe that Laden was not qualified to issue *fatwas*, as he was not an Islamic scholar, as such. Nevertheless, the fatwas issued by Laden have clearly expressed his burning desires in the name of Islam. His 1996 *fatwa*, in particular, called for the withdrawal of the American soldiers stationed in his country of origin, Saudi Arabia. In the 1998 *fatwa*, he stated his objections to both the continued presence of US troops in Saudi Arabia and the US foreign policy towards Israel.

US War on Terror

In response to the horrific 9/11 attacks, the United States wanted to accomplish two tasks. First, it wanted to capture Osama bin Laden and destroy his al-Qaeda movement. Second, it wanted to hunt for and destroy all other militant groups of global reach. To meet these ends, the United States launched a global War on Terror (WOT). US President George Bush Junior (Jr.) chose to launch this global war at a joint session of US Congress on September 20, 2001. At this session, President George Bush Jr. explained, "Our war on terror begins with al-Qaeda, but it does not end there. It will not end until every terrorist group of global reach has been found, stopped and defeated" ("War on words" 2009, para. 6). In this or any of his subsequent addresses, President George Bush Jr., however, did not speculate as to when he would like to see his stated goals achieved. The WOT first appeared to be an easy task for him, and his country. This looked especially so, considering its military resources, mightiest in the world, and its formidable allies around the globe. What happened later, however, shows that this was not the case.

Afghanistan. In hunting down Osama bin Laden, the United States first demanded that the Afghan Taliban government deliver al-Qaeda leaders located in that country to US authorities. The demand went with a stern warning, "they will hand over the terrorists or they will share in their fate" ("George Bush: The Taliban must hand over" 2001, para. 11). Despite the threatening nature of this warning, the Taliban government refused to comply with the US demand. Instead, they simply asserted that there was no evidence in their possession linking the al-Qaeda movement to the 9/11 attacks. The Taliban government also said that the Taliban codes of behaviour required granting hospitality and asylum to Osama bin Laden, as he was a guest in Afghanistan. As the tension between the US authorities and the Taliban government was heating up, both the United Arab Emirates and Saudi Arabia withdrew their recognition of the Taliban government. This left the Taliban government with diplomatic ties with only one country – Pakistan. Then, on October 7, 2001, the Taliban government offered to try Osama bin Laden in an Islamic court in their own country. As this offer was not acceptable to the US authorities, they went ahead with their planned invasion of Afghanistan on the same day. The invasion began with both aerial bombing and ground resistance. The British joined the United States in the aerial bombing. The Afghan Northern Alliance, which was already in the field fighting the Taliban regime, took charge of ground resistance with logistical support from the United States and a number of other countries, India, Iran, and Russia among them. This was the beginning of the US-led WOT.

The events described above show that the main purpose of this war in Afghanistan was to capture Osama bin Laden, destroy his al-Qaeda movement, and to remove the Taliban regime that "harboured" him. In a videotape recording, bin Laden said that the United States would fail in Afghanistan and then collapse, just as the Soviet Union had. Al Jazeera, the Arabic satellite news channel, released the videotape. In the same recording, bin Laden also called for a jihad-war against the United States. However, on the seventh day of the bombing raid (October 14, 2001), the Taliban government offered to surrender bin Laden to a third country for trial, subject to one condition. The condition was that the US first stop the bombing and show evidence of bin Laden's involvement in the 9/11 attacks. Americans rejected this offer as well, and continued with their Afghan invasion.

The air raids by the United States and the United Kingdom during the first few weeks managed to destroy Taliban defences, causing Taliban forces to flee Kabul. By the time the Afghan Northern Alliance forces finally came to Kabul on 13 November 2001, most of the Taliban fighters had already fled the town. As a result, Kabul fell to the hands of the US-led invading forces and the Afghan Northern Alliance, with little resistance. The fleeing Taliban forces later regrouped in the country's Tora Bora cave complex. The heavy aerial attacks that followed in the area killed many Taliban fighters, decimating the Taliban's ability to fight back. Some key al-Qaeda leaders, including Mohammad Atef, were among those who died there. For the time being, the whereabouts of Osama bin Laden continued to remain unknown.

Meanwhile, the UN Security Council facilitated a number of meetings among traditional Afghan leaders. Through these meetings, the UN managed to strike an agreement among them for a process for the transfer of power from the Taliban government to a democratically elected one. The first step in the process was to inaugurate an Afghan Interim Authority of 30 members. This was done on December 22, 2001. The mandate given to the Interim Authority was for only six months. At the end of the six months, as required by the process, a two-year Transitional Authority took the place of the Interim Authority. Then, a presidential election in 2004 and a parliamentary election in 2005 paved the way to a permanent government. This process of power transfer also envisaged the role of the International Security Assistance Force, established by the Security Council of the UN. The intended purpose of the Assistant Force was to assist the Afghan Interim Authority. Later, in 2003, the North Atlantic Treaty Organization (NATO) took control of the Assistance Force.

While these government-restructuring efforts were continuing in Kabul, the surviving Taliban and al-Qaeda forces continued with their regrouping efforts. Together, they also planned their next move. In a considerably short period of time, the Taliban forces managed to recruit new trainees and to conduct mobile training camps for them. The al-Qaeda forces also may have done the same. Both groups conducted their training operations in Afghanistan as well as in Pakistan, especially in the Pashtun areas. Having regained their strength to some extent, the two groups launched a jihad-war against the newly formed Afghan government and the US-led coalition forces that supported it. The two militant groups have continued the holy war since, with raids, ambushes, and rocket attacks. At times, they have demonstrated their renewed strength by undertaking some daring missions. For example, on April 27, 2008, they made an attempt on the life of Afghan President Karzai. They did this by opening fire at an official ceremony held to commemorate the Afghan liberation from the eight-year Soviet occupation. The shooting boldly continued for about a quarter of an hour during the day's military parade. Then on June 13, 2008, Taliban fighters broke into the Kandahar jail, one of the largest prisons in Afghanistan, and liberated all 1200 prisoners held there; 400 of those liberated were Taliban prisoners-of-war.

The year 2008 was also the deadliest year up until then for the United States and its allies that took part in the WOT in Afghanistan. According to a related report ("User: Grant bud", n. d.), Taliban leaders claimed that they killed 5,220 foreign troops, downed 31 aircraft, and destroyed 2,818 NATO and Afghan vehicles during that year. They further claimed that their men killed 7,552 Afghan soldiers and police personnel in 2008. The overall casualties of the WOT in Afghanistan, to the end of October 2008, included more than 20,000 Taliban and al-Qaeda fighters, 4,300 Afghan Security personnel, 200 Northern Alliance soldiers, and 1,014 US-led coalition personnel. According to Goodspeed, another report released on November 18, 2009, suggested that, on average, the anti-government forces summarily executed three Afghans every four days

(*National Post*, November 18, 2009). The British aid agency Oxfam and 14 other non-government organizations operating in the country authored the report. The same report also suggested that the anti-government forces executed Afghans for their suspected association with the government or NATO forces. Further, the report said that the following year, 2009, was still worse. According to statistics collected by NATO forces, the country's insurgent attacks increased by nearly 60 percent in 2009. The resulting rapid deterioration of the country's security situation and the spiralling rise in NATO deaths led to a call for an additional 40,000 troops to join the 100,000 NATO troops already in the country. In response, the United States agreed to deploy 30,000 additional troops by June 2010. Despite the increase of US troops in Afghanistan, the Taliban continued to wage a brutal war with the US and NATO forces. Some of the later Taliban attacks have turned out to be most daring and deadly. For example, on August 6, 2011, Taliban militants shot down a US Chinook transport helicopter and killed 30 Americans. Among the dead were some Navy Seal commandos from the US military unit that killed al-Qaeda leader Osama bin Laden on May 2, 2011 in Pakistan. It was the deadliest day for US forces in the decade long war in Afghanistan. Then, on August 19, 2011, Taliban forces attacked some UK institutions established in Afghanistan. On September 13, 2011, the same forces launched rocket attacks against the US Embassy and the nearby NATO headquarters. The war continues.

After ten years of this ugly war in Afghanistan, the US has succeeded in capturing Osama bin Laden (in Pakistan) and in removing the Taliban regime that harboured him. However, the al-Qaeda movement Bin Laden founded is still a major threat of global militant attacks. At the same time, Taliban forces are continuing to engage in guerrilla warfare against the new Afghan government the United States and its allied countries helped establish.

Iraq. The United States extended the WOT to Iraq on March 20, 2003. Some factors related to the 1991 Gulf War appear to have triggered this move; there were no Iraqi attacks on Americans within or outside the US. After the 1991 Gulf War, the US had been seeking a regime change in Iraq. President George Bush Senior (Sr.), who reigned during the first Gulf War, directed the US Central Intelligence Agency to create conditions for this regime change. Later, the US Congress and President

William Clinton issued a resolution calling for the same. President George Bush Jr., who succeeded President William Clinton in 2001, started his campaign for the Iraqi government change, just ten days after taking his oath as President.

There was an alleged attempt by Iraqi President Saddam Hussein to have President George Bush Sr. assassinated in late April 1993, during a visit to Kuwait in his position as former President of the United States. In retaliation, the US government sent a cruise missile to hit a building in Bagdad on June 16, 1993; this building housed the Iraqi Intelligence Service. The US government did this under the specific orders of President William Clinton. At the same time, the enforcement of northern and southern Iraqi no-fly zones, infringing on Iraq's sovereignty, also became a huge contentious issue. The United States, the United Kingdom, and France were the enforcers. They, however, did not have any specific mandate from the UN for carrying out such work. All these contentious issues led to regular exchanges of fire between the Iraqi defence installations and the patrolling foreign forces. The number and intensity of these exchanges had been on an upward trend since 2001.

Despite the above, the US declared another reason for extending the WOT to Iraq. This other reason was the alleged failure of the Iraqi government of President Saddam Hussein to comply with the UN Security Council Resolution 687 of 3 April 1991. This UN Resolution mandated the destruction, removal, or rendering harmless of all chemical and biological weapons in Iraq. This also applied to all related subsystems, components, research work, and manufacturing facilities. In addition, the mandate applied to all ballistic missiles with a range greater than 150 kilometres, and related repair and production facilities in Iraq. The same UN resolution required international supervision for the intended deweaponization work. At the same time, it had laid down a specific process for all this to happen. According to the process, Iraq was to first submit a declaration of the locations, amounts, and types of all concerned items within a set timeframe. Then, a Special Commission appointed under the resolution would carry out on-site inspections, take charge, and supervise the deweaponization work. Further, this Special Commission would develop a plan for future monitoring and verification of Iraq's compliance. The implementation of the process did begin. By 1998, the UN weapons inspectors verified that the Iraqi government, in fact, had destroyed a large amount of the concerned items. Then, in the same year, the UN inspectors had to leave Iraq suddenly and unexpectedly due to the threat of imminent military action by the United States and the United Kingdom. A four-day bombing campaign followed the weapon inspectors' departure. The inspection did not resume until four years later, on November 27, 2002.

Meanwhile, major disagreements arose between the military and the intelligence sources of the United States regarding Iraq. The disagreements were primarily regarding the extent of the weaponry destruction in Iraq and the level of its compliance. The US government then sought authorization from both the US Senate and the UN Security Council for the use of American armed forces against Iraq. The US government succeeded in getting the required support from the US Senate in October 2002. However, it failed in its attempts to get a resolution passed to the same effect at the UN Security Council. Among the Security Council members, only the United Kingdom and Spain were ready to support the proposed US resolution. The members that opposed the resolution included Canada, France, Germany, and Russia. Notably, three of the countries that opposed the resolution were NATO members. The nations that opposed the US resolution were of the opinion that military intervention in Iraq would result in a major risk to global security. Their preference was to pursue disarmament in Iraq through diplomacy and discussions. There were also thousands of strong public protests by tens of millions of people across the globe against military action against Iraq. Then, in his presentation to the UN Security Council on March 7, 2003 (Blix 2003), the chief UN Weapons Inspector, Hans Blix, stated that his staff had experienced few difficulties in their work which had resumed in November 2002. He also added, "And certainly much less than those that were faced by UNSCOM [United Nations Special Commission] in the period 1991 to 1998 ... At this juncture we are able to perform professional, no-notice inspections all over Iraq and to increase aerial surveillance" (Blix 2003, paras. 2 & 3). In the same presentation, Blix also said, "No evidence of proscribed activities has so far been found" (Blix 2003, para. 9). Despite this, the US government said that diplomacy had failed and began to invade Iraq .

on March 20, 2003. The declared objective of the war was to get rid of weapons of mass destruction (WMD) from Iraqi soil.

After commencing the war in Iraq, however, the US officials added three more reasons for it. One reason was that President Saddam Hussein and his government were allegedly harbouring al-Qaeda. Another was that the Iraqi government was allegedly providing the families of Palestinian suicide bombers with financial support. The third was that the Iraqi government had a record of human rights abuses. The more the US officials talked about these reasons for launching the war, the more there was suspicion around the world that Iraqi oil could well have been the main reason. In any event, the US wanted a regime change in Iraq, just as in Afghanistan. The decision to invade Iraq, however, did not have the blessings of the UN. In an interview with BBC on September 16, 2004, the UN Secretary-General Kofi Annan categorically said, "I have indicated that it [US war on Iraq] was not in conformity with the UN Charter from our point of view, from the Charter point of view, it was illegal" ("Iraq war illegal", 2004, para. 10). According to other critics of the Iraqi war, the United States and the United Kingdom have acted like vigilantes in their pursuit.

The forces of the United States and the United Kingdom took the lead in launching the Iraqi invasion. Of nearly 300,000 active troops who would take part in the invasion, 250,000 were Americans. The United Kingdom and Australia had the next biggest troop numbers. Three dozen other countries also participated by providing troops, equipment, and services. This was the biggest war front led by the United States since the Vietnam War. The invading coalition forces cooperated with the local militant group, Kurdish Peshmerga. This group had been in existence since the Kurdish independence movement began in the north of the country in the early 1920s.

The Iraqi army was one of the largest armed forces in Western Asia at the time of the incursion. It fought valiantly, resisting the attacking forces, but the invaders were very well prepared to meet a high level of resistance both on the ground and in the air. As a result, after only 20 days of fighting, Bagdad fell to the invaders on April 9, 2003. This ended President Saddam Hussein's 24-year rule of Iraq. After another six days of fighting, many other strategic positions in the country fell to the invaders. These other places included President Hussein's home town of

Tikrit as well. At the end of the six days, the US-led coalition declared that the invasion was effectively over. By that time, more than 9,000 Iraqi combatants and over 7,000 civilians had been killed. The casualties on the invaders' side totalled 139 US and 33 UK military personnel.

The victorious US-led coalition forces established an interim governing body for Iraq and named it the Coalition Provisional Authority. They vested it with executive, legislative, and judicial authority to manage the affairs of the country. The Provisional Authority was to enjoy such powers only until the establishment of a democratically elected government. The Authority's first term was from April 21, 2003 to June 24, 2004. Soon it vested most of the governing powers in the local Iraqi Governing Council, beginning in July 2003. Later, in January 2005, the Authority held a competitive election for a transitional government. Its primary task was to draft a new constitution for the country. A referendum held in October 2005 ratified the draft constitution it had prepared. The Iraqis finally voted for a parliament of 275 seats for a four-year term at a general election held in December 2005. The newly formed parliament then elected a president for the country, along with two deputies, in April 2006. The constitution allowed the parliament to elect all three of them, as a Presidency Council, on one list. This election was possible only with a two-third majority support in the parliament. Once elected, the three had to make all decisions unanimously. The first Iraqi president elected under the new constitution was Jalal Talabani. The constitution gave power to the Presidency Council to veto legislation passed by the parliament. At the same time, it also gave power to the parliament to override the veto with a three-fifths majority.

The end of the Iraqi invasion in April 2003 was also the beginning of a new wave of guerrilla attacks in the country. These attacks were against the coalition forces as well as the new government they were helping to build. A number of reasons appear to have motivated the attackers. Some of the attackers may have had only one of these reasons to act; others may have had more. Strong affiliation with former President Saddam Hussein's regime and the imminent loss of social and economic status, caused by its downfall, were two apparent reasons. Tribal interests, strong opposition to foreign occupation, and vengeance for killing family and friends were three others. Islamists' obligation to God and fellow beings by way of jihad was yet another. It is also likely that the guerrilla attackers had access to hundreds of weapon caches that had been built up by the conventional forces of the Saddam Hussein regime. In time, the US intelligence services warned the coalition forces in Iraq of combatants from outside Iraq as well. Experts believe that they may have come from a number of other countries, including Russia (Chechnya), Philippines, Saudi Arabia, Iran, Italy, and Syria. These non-Iraqi combatants may have brought in additional weapons to carry out attacks against the coalition forces and the post-invasion Iraqi government. The local and foreign combatants together have used, and are continuing to use, guerrilla techniques, such as suicide attacks, car bombs, mortars, missiles, and rocket propelled grenades. There also have been serious attacks on water, electricity, and oil infrastructures in the country.

The guerrilla attacks in Iraq increased over time. In response, the coalition forces focused on, among other things, the capture of the leaders of the former Hussein regime. In July 2003, the coalition forces captured and killed former President Saddam Hussein's two sons, Uday and Qusay, and a grandson. In addition, the coalition forces managed to capture hundreds of other leaders of the Hussein regime; some of them were also killed. Then, on 13 December 2003, the coalition forces captured and arrested former President Saddam Hussein himself at a farm near his birthplace, Tikrit. He and seven co-defenders later faced trial in an Iraqi court for the murder of 148 Shia men in the town of Dujail two decades earlier, in 1982. Notably, this was when his regime was an ally of the United States and the United Kingdom. The trial convicted the former President of the alleged crimes. He was executed by hanging on December 30, 2006.

The guerrilla attacks during and after 2003 were particularly daring in nature. There is no direct evidence to suggest that Osama bin Laden or his al-Qaeda movement had led them at anytime. However, bin Laden's messages transmitted through the Al Jazeera network were supportive of them. For example, in his October 19, 2003 congratulatory message to Iraqis, he said, "Be glad of the good news: America is mired in the swamps of the Tigris and Euphrates. [George] Bush [Jr.] is, through Iraq and its oil, easy prey. Here is he now, thank God, in an embarrassing situation and here is America today being ruined before the eyes of the whole world." ("Iraq War and U.S.", n.d., para. 8)

In a subsequent incident of March 31, 2004, a group of guerrilla attackers ambushed and killed four private security contractors who had worked for the coalition forces. After killing them, the attackers dragged their burned bodies through the streets and hanged them from a bridge over the Euphrates River. In November 2004, as reported by the U. S. government (U.S. Department of Defence 2005), the coalition forces encountered in Fallujah the heaviest urban combat [that they have been involved in] since the battle of Hue City in Vietnam. This 2004 combat became a 46-day long war, and resulted in a death of 95 US soldiers and approximately 1,350 attackers. The death toll among civilians was low; most of them had fled the area before the combat.

Meanwhile, the Iraqis started to witness new internal conflicts after they voted for a parliament under the country's new constitution in December 2005. These new conflicts were among the different sects of Islam and took the centre stage among the guerrilla attacks in the country in the following years. Some of the resulting attacks were more daring and deadlier than any before. For example, on February 22, 2006, a group of terrorists bombed and exploded the al-Askari Mosque, one of the holiest sites in Shia Islam, causing severe damage to the mosque building. The violence that erupted on the following days claimed the lives of more than 160 people. Later, on November 23, 2006 several militants attacked the Shia Sadr City slum with suicide car bombs and mortars. This attack killed more than 215 people and wounded another 250. It was the deadliest guerrilla attack since the beginning of the war in Iraq. Shia militants avenged the attack with mortar rounds in a number of Sunni neighbourhoods. Later, on August 14, 2007, a much more deadly attack took place. It consisted of a series of suicide bombers who attacked a northern Iraqi settlement of a non-Muslim, Yazidi community in Qahtaniya. These suicide bomb attacks killed more than 800 civilians living there and set fire to more than 100 homes and shops in the settlement. Many believed that these attacks were an act of retaliation to the stoning to death of a teenage girl from the settlement for dating a Sunni Arab man and converting to Islam. The United States has blamed al-Qaeda for these major attacks.

The post-invasion Iraqi government did what it could to put an end to the ongoing violence in the country. For a time, however, the violence continued with on and off guerrilla attacks. The rising numbers of deaths of US soldiers in Iraq was evidence of the continuing violence. The death toll of US soldiers from January to September 2004 rose by 500 and from October 2005 to March 2008 by 3,000.

Then, the opposition to the coalition's occupation of Iraq gained momentum - both within and outside Iraq. Bowing down to public opinion, some coalition countries started to withdraw, beginning in 2004. Nicaragua was the first country to pull out that year, followed by Spain, Dominican Republic, Honduras, Philippines, Thailand, and New Zealand. In the following year, 2005, Portugal, Netherlands, and Hungary left, and Norway and Italy pulled out in 2006. Lithuania and Slovakia moved out in 2007. Then in 2008, 19 countries left. They include Georgia, Mongolia, Armenia, Kazakhstan, Poland, Latvia, Macedonia, Bosnia, and Singapore. The others were Azerbaijan, Tonga, Japan, South Korea, Czech Republic, Denmark, Ukraine, Albania, Moldova, and Bulgaria. By the end of January 2009, Estonia and El Salvador also had gone, leaving behind only four countries: the United States, the United Kingdom, Romania and Australia. The total deployment among the four countries at that time was approximately 150,000; almost 96 percent were Americans.

Meanwhile, the new government of Iraq began to undertake its security responsibility. In November 2006, however, the UN Security Council extended until the end of 2007 the mandate given to the multinational force in Iraq. The Security Council did this in response to a special request made by the Iraqi government. Then, in June 2007, the Iraqi Parliament voted 85 to 59 in favour of a resolution that stated that similar future government requests would require the Parliament's prior consent. Despite this, the UN Security Council further extended the coalition mandate up to the end of 2008, without prior consent of the Iraqi Parliament. Then, in December 2008, the United States government entered into a special agreement with the government of Iraq, subject to a referendum. This agreement required American forces to withdraw from Iraqi cities by July 31, 2009, but allowed them to remain on Iraqi soil until 2011. In the event that Iraqis turned down the agreement at the referendum, the American forces were required to withdraw completely by July 31, 2010. Following the agreement, the United States withdrew its troops from Iraqi cities by July 2009, as required. By the end of 2009, however, there were still about 120,000 US military members on Iraqi soil; this showed a total reduction of more than 40,000 troops since 2008. The withdrawal of US troops from Iraq continued in the following years.

Overall, the Iraqi invasion and the subsequent internal attacks affected the lives of millions of people. On May 6, 2010, Matthew Duss, Peter Juul, and Brian Katulis reported that the total death toll by then was between 110,663 and 119,380. The estimated number of coalition casualties by that date was 4,712. A staggering 93 percent of them were American. In addition, the Iraqi invasion and post-invasion violence have uprooted about 4.5 million Iraqi people from their homes. This is about 14% of the total population of Iraq. Almost two million of the displaced have migrated to neighbouring countries as refugees. Many believe that the total death toll of Iraqis should be much higher, as its civilian casualties have been significantly under-reported: Some estimates place civilian casualties of this war at over 600,000 (White, 2011).

Despite the staggering magnitude of the casualties of the Iraqi war, its contribution to the global WOT remains questionable. There are two main reasons for this. First, no evidence ever surfaced suggesting any collaborative relationship between the toppled Saddam Hussein administration and Osama bin Laden or his al-Qaeda movement. The 9/11 Commission investigation also testified to this. Second, the UN weapon inspectors never found any hidden stockpiles of WMD in Iraq, as claimed by the United States. This clearly shows that the assertion of President George Bush Jr. that Iraq had stockpiles of WMD was erroneous; US government officials later attributed this error to an intelligence failure. On December 1, 2008, with less than two months remaining in his term of office, US President George Bush Jr. explained his position on this intelligence failure in an interview with Charlie Gibson of ABC News. At this interview, he specifically said, "The biggest regret of all the presidency has to have been the intelligence failure in Iraq. A lot of people put their reputations on the line and said the WMD are a reason to remove Saddam Hussein. It was not just people in my administration; a lot of members in Congress, prior to my arrival in Washington D.C., during the debate on Iraq, many leaders of nations around the world were all looking at the same intelligence. And, you know, that's not a do-over, but I wish the intelligence had been different." (Spillius 2008, paras. 2 and 3)

There was, however, some evidence suggesting that the Hussein regime had begun to provide financial support to Palestinian families affected by the Israel-Palestine conflict. These were the families of Palestinian militants or civilians killed in Israel-Palestine clashes. Notably, the Saddam Hussein regime had started providing such support only a few months before the commencement of the Iraqi war. A world news report (BBC NEWS 2003) substantiated such evidence. It referred to an event where a Palestinian organization, the Palestinian Arab Liberation Front, distributed financial assistance to 21 or more Palestinian families. In narrating the story, it had also shown a picture of President Saddam Hussein and the then Palestinian leader Yasser Arafat. In addition, it had shown a number of banners in the background hero-worshiping them. One of the banners read, "Iraq and Palestine are in one trench. Saddam is a hero." (para. 2) Another said, "Blessings of Saddam Hussein" (para. 6). The same BBC report had further stated that the Palestinian speakers at the ceremony condemned both Israel and the United States for the ongoing Israel-Palestine conflict. In turn, they later dismissed the Iraqi assistance to Palestinians as support for terrorism. There was also evidence to show that the Saddam Hussein regime had given assistance to a number of militant groups fighting in countries neighbouring Iraq. Such groups include the Iranian dissident group Mujahedeen-e-Khalq and the Kurdish Workers Party of Turkey. The Saddam Hussein regime's assistance to fighting groups in Israel, or any other country near Iraq, was not, however, tantamount to providing assistance to fight against the United States.

Although Afghanistan and Iraq set the main stage for the WOT, the US later extended it to a number of other countries in Europe, the Horn of Africa, Asia, and the Middle East. The WOT activities of the coalition forces in Europe remain minimal. Their main WOT activity in Europe has been a naval operation that began as early as October 2001. Its purpose has been to prevent the movement of the militant Islamists and WMD in the Mediterranean Sea.

The Horn of Africa. The US extended its ongoing Operation Enduring Freedom to the Horn of Africa, as part of its War on Terror for two purposes. One purpose was to detect and disrupt the ongoing activities of the Islamic militant groups in the region. The other purpose was to monitor and stop suspect shipments from entering the region. As part of the same war, the US forces also became involved militarily in a Somali internal power struggle between the UN-backed Transitional Federal Government (TFG) of Somalia and the Islamic Courts Union (ICU). In this power struggle, the US was particularly concerned about the support that the ICU was allegedly getting from the al-Qaeda movement. Chapter 2 has already discussed this conflict in detail. For whatever reasons, the US did not extend the WOT in the Horn of Africa to Sudan, where nearly half a million people had died due to state terrorism.

Asia. The United States' involvement in defeating terrorism in Asia was not limited to Afghanistan. The other Asian countries where the US got involved in anti-terrorist activities include Pakistan, Philippines, and Indonesia.

Pakistan. The United States conducted joint raids with Pakistan in search of Islamist leaders of global reach who had sought refuge in that country. The US military and financial aid to Pakistan also increased significantly after the 9/11 attacks. During the three years up to the 9/11 attacks, such aid only amounted to approximately US$9 million. However, the corresponding amount received during the three years after the 9/11 attacks was as high as US$4.2 billion. The joint raids of the United States and Pakistan resulted in the capture of a number of high-profile Islamic militants who had global connections. These militants include the Saudi Arabian born Zayn al-Abidn Mohammed Hasayn Abu Zubaydah (March 2002), Ramzi Binalshibh (September 2002), and Khalid Shaikh Mohammed (March 2003). Zubaydah was the Operations Chief and a key financial backer of al-Qaeda. He was also in charge of its training camps. According to available information, Binalshibh was a militant expected to join the 9/11 attacks hijacking team. He, however, failed to do so as the US Immigration Services had turned down his visa application to enter the country; they had turned down his applications on three earlier occasions as well. Once, he had shared a room in Hamburg with the Egyptian-born Mohammad Atta, the ringleader of the 19 airline hijackers in the 9/11 attacks. Then, Khalid Shaikh Mohammed was the third-highest ranking officer in al-Qaeda and the head of its military committee at the time of his arrest. It was believed that he was in charge of planning the 9/11 attacks. In addition, he was allegedly involved in a number of other high-profile global terrorist operations. The infamous militant attack at the El Ghriba synagogue in Djerba, Tunisia, the USS Cole (US Navy destroyer) bombing, and the killing of Wall Street Journal reporter Daniel Pearl were three of these terrorist operations. Earlier, Chapter 2 explained how American forces captured and killed al-Qaeda leader Osama bin Laden on Pakistani soil on May 2, 2011. Pakistani forces had no hand in this operation.

Pakistan's role in the WOT was not limited to arresting high profile militant leaders hiding in the country. In addition, Pakistan engaged in direct campaigns against the al-Qaeda and Taliban forces operating within its jurisdiction. For example, in 2004, the government of Pakistan sent 80,000 troops to remove the al-Qaeda and Taliban forces operating in the tribal areas of its Waziristan region. In time, the Pakistani military had to deal with increasing Taliban and al-Qaeda resistance, especially in Pakistan's northern border area. This situation had come about after the fall of the Afghan Taliban regime. With the growing logistic and military support from the United States, the Pakistani forces succeeded in capturing and killing many of the fighting Taliban and al-Qaeda militants in the area. Despite this, the Taliban and al-Qaeda managed to stage a formidable resistance to the Pakistani government forces. This resistance slowly grew over the years, and took the form of a civil war by 2009. Many other Islamic militant groups operating in the country have joined the fighting Taliban and al-Qaeda forces. One such group is the Tehrik-e-Taliban of Pakistan that allegedly masterminded the assassination of former Pakistani Prime Minister Benazir Bhutto. The primary aim of these other groups is to secure independence for Kashmir. Together, the militant groups have managed to keep Pakistani government on its toes in its grim attempt to maintain the country's sovereignty.

In their terror attacks, the Islamic militant groups have committed many atrocities. They have blown up vehicles at busy public places, such as restaurants and markets. They have also shelled government employees' residences and international agencies. They have even managed to besiege the army headquarters of the country to the utter embarrassment of its military. In the process, they have killed thousands of Pakistanis, and uprooted millions of others from their homes. All this has happened since the infamous 9/11 attacks in the United States. The

West believes that the Taliban and al-Qaeda movements remain anxious to acquire Pakistani nuclear weapons, and, apparently, the chances for this are real. For example, Shaun Gregory, Director of the Pakistan Security Unit at the University of Bradford, says, "The challenge to Pakistan's nuclear weapons from Pakistani Taliban groups and from al-Qaeda constitutes a real and present danger" (Siddiqi 2010, para. 9). According to an earlier related report, the terrorist commander Mustafa Abu al-Yazid had said, "God willing, the [Pakistani] nuclear weapons will not fall into the hands of the Americans and the Mujahideen would take them and use them against the Americans" ("Al Qaeda leader Mutafa Abu al-Yazid" 2009, para. 2). Because of this situation, many believe that Pakistan has become the most dangerous and explosive place on the planet.

Philippines. The US War on Terror in the Philippines began with the deployment of a US Operations Command in that country in 2002. Later, the US extended its WOT involvement to other neighbouring countries, including Indonesia. The primary aim of the US mission in Philippines was to confront the Abu Sayyaf group, a consortium of about 5000 Islamist guerrilla fighters concentrated on the country's southern island of Jolo. These guerrilla fighters were operating in three main groups, under three different commanders. At times, they have shown conflicting interests. They all appeared to have had links with radical elements that controlled several South China Sea shipping lanes. Some of them had strong footholds in a number of islands and coastal cities in the region and there had been some incidents of hijacking and robbing of freighters in the area. The scale of the relationship between the Abu Sayyaf group and these other militant groups with al-Qaeda has not been determined. However, many believe that at least some of the groups in the area have links to the global al-Qaeda movement. The United States military has reported that they have removed over 80 percent of the Abu Sayyaf Group members from the region.

Indonesia. There were a number of post 9/11 terrorist attacks in Indonesia. The years 2002, 2004, and 2005 were particularly devastating. In 2002, there were three major attacks, all on the island of Bali. One of them was an explosion in an eating-place, caused by a bomb hidden in a backpack. Another was a remote controlled car bomb explosion in front of a commercial building, the Sari Club. The third was an explosion in front of the American consulate in Bali. The three attacks killed more than 200 people, and injured another 300 or more. The 2004 attack was a car bomb explosion outside the Australian embassy in Jakarta. It killed 10 Indonesians, and injured more than 140 others. The attackers had sent a mobile phone text message to the Indonesian authorities before the incident. The text message warned the authorities of such an attack, if they did not release from prison Abu Bakar Bashir, who was spending jail-time on charges of treason. Then, in 2005, there were two suicide bomb attacks, one in a food court in Jimbaran and the other in the main square of Kuta. The Indonesian militant group Jemaah Islamiyah was suspected of carrying them out. The authorities later suspected that the same group had carried out the attacks in Bali as well. Many new measures taken by the Indonesian government resulted in combating militant attacks within its territory. According to one report, sometime in June of 2007, Indonesian government commandos managed to capture Zarkasih and Abu Dujama, two of the most wanted men in the region. Zarkasih was an overall leader of the Jemaah Islamiyah group. Abu Dujama was the alleged head of the military wing of Jemaah Islamiyah. A few months earlier, the Indonesian police uncovered in central Java an arsenal of deadly bomb-making material. The materials that were uncovered included potassium, TNT, detonators, and ammunition for a grenade launcher.

The Middle East. The countries in the Middle East, other than Iraq, that joined the US-led WOT included Saudi Arabia, Palestine (the Gaza Strip and the West Bank), and Lebanon.

Saudi Arabia. The WOT in Saudi Arabia has had a special twist. This is because the continued presence of the US troops in the country has been the main reason for ongoing terrorist attacks within the country's boundaries. The American troops have been in the country since the Iraqi invasion of Kuwait. This US military presence, along with the US policy towards Israel, led to two *fatwas* calling for jihad against the United States. The al-Qaeda leader Osama Bin Laden had issued these *fatwas*, as discussed earlier. Many of the country's imams, who shared bin Laden's views, gave a boost to anti-American sentiments among its people. Imams hold leadership positions in Islamic communities. Conducting worship services in mosques and answering Islamic religious questions are among their routine duties. Through their powerful sermons in

Saudi mosques, the imams who shared Bin Laden's vision have spread their inflammatory messages. Even before the 9/11 attacks, the United States and its western allies had pressured the Saudi government to crackdown on such imams. The pressure on the Saudi government grew heavier after the 9/11 attacks. The US was particularly concerned because 15 of the 19 hijackers involved in the 9/11 attacks were from Saudi Arabia. The increased pressure on the Saudi government had no apparent results. Consequently, the frequency and the severity of the Islamist militant attacks on Saudi soil continued to rise after the 9/11 attacks. The primary targets of the post 9/11 terrorist attacks in Saudi Arabia were the country's security forces, expatriate workers, and tourists from western nations. The terrorists have used many tactics in carrying out their post 9/11 attacks. These tactics include shootings at short range, suicide bombings, placing bombs underneath vehicles, and striking residential buildings and complexes.

The first major post 9/11 terrorist attack on Saudi soil occurred on the eve of the US invasion of Afghanistan, on October 6, 2001. In this attack, a suicide bomber struck and killed one American citizen, Michael Gerard, and injured a Briton and two Filipinos outside a shopping centre in Al Khobar. Then, there were about two dozen major terrorist attacks in the following three years. These attacks killed more than 70 people, mostly westerners, and injured more than 200 others. Some of the attacks that occurred during the period 2001-04 caused much more devastation, and were much more daring than ever before. For example, in May 2002, a Sudanese national unsuccessfully attempted to shoot down a US fighter jet taking off from the Sultan Air Base. He did this with a shoulder-launched surface-to-air SA-7 missile, capable of reaching low-flying aircraft. A year later, nine suicide attackers exploded three cars loaded with bombs in residential compounds housing westerners (and others) in Riyadh. These suicide attacks killed the attackers along with 26 others. Then, on May 29, 2004, a group of gunmen scaled the fence of the Oasis compound in Al-Khobar. This compound had housed the employees of foreign oil companies. Having entered the compound, the gunmen took dozens hostage. After that, the gunmen separated the Christians from the Muslim hostages, shot the Christians, and managed to escape arrest. Nineteen foreign civilians and several Saudis succumbed to the shooting. Later, on 6 December 2004, six militants carried out a violent attack on the American consulate in Jeddah. In this daring attack, the militants breached the consulate compound's outer wall and engaged in a shooting rampage. They killed five consulate employees and wounded ten others. Those killed included a Yemeni, a Sudanese, a Filipino, a Pakistani, and a Sri Lankan.

Palestine. The United States did not extend its War on Terror to Palestine. However, Israel appears to have treated its bloody confrontations with the Palestinian militants in the Gaza Strip and the West Bank as part of the global WOT. Chapter 2 discussed the conflict between Israelis and Palestinians in detail. Palestinian militants have not targeted the United States or any of its western allies in their attacks. The entire West, however, appears to have an active role in the conflict, unequivocally supporting Israel. At the same time, the West also continues to treat Hamas as a terrorist organization; it is, after all, the main Palestinian organization in combat mode against Israel. Hamas, however, has had no apparent relationship with the al-Qaeda movement. The al-Qaeda leaders, in fact, have repeatedly condemned Hamas for not taking a more militant approach in dealing with Israel. In particular, al-Qaeda leaders have blamed Hamas for participating in elections and for accepting Saudi and Egyptian mediation in its internal conflict with Fatah. The al-Qaeda leaders also do not see why Hamas should stick to any kind of ceasefire with Israel. At the same time, Israel and its western protectors, including the United States, put their weight behind Fatah in the internal conflict with Hamas. In doing so, Israel and its western allies have not recognized Hamas' clear electoral victory which allowed it to form a government in Palestine. This internal conflict, in fact, has reduced the geographical jurisdiction of the democratically elected Hamas government to the Gaza Strip. Meanwhile, in August 2009, one pro-al-Qaeda cleric, Abdel Latif Moussa, unsuccessfully staged a violent coup to seize power over the Gaza Strip from Hamas. He said that the purpose of the coup was to declare himself "the Islamic Prince of the new emirate of Gaza" (Karon 2009, para. 2). Despite all this, Israel, together with the United States and its allies, has continued to treat Hamas as a terrorist organization. In this situation, violence continues to resurface between Israel and Hamas at the slightest provocation by either one of them. Both sides do not hesitate to use rockets and missiles in their cross-border fights.

Israel's war on terror in the West Bank is somewhat different in form; the Fatah-dominated Palestinian Authority controls the Palestinian affairs in the West Bank. The main threat to Israel from the West Bank comes from the suicide missions undertaken by its jihadists; Israel is not under the threat of rockets and missiles from the West Bank. Israeli troops try to manage the situation in the West Bank with safety barriers and checkpoints on all major roads, curfews, search and arrest missions, and the like. They also trace and attack the strongholds of potential jihadists. At the same time, the Israeli government continues to expand Jewish settlements in the area. Because of these actions, the Palestinians living in the West Bank feel they have become victims of an occupying army. Critics of the Israelis point out that the Arab children do not see a future for themselves in the prevailing situation. They have seen their lands taken away from their parents for new Jewish settlements, homes bulldozed, parents butchered, and sisters and mothers sexually assaulted and killed. As a result, these children tend to join the forces of suicide bombers. Meanwhile, the Israeli forces operating in the West Bank target Hamas militants as well. The main reason for this appears to be Israel's fear that Hamas will eventually transfer their rocket technology from the Gaza Strip to the West Bank. Israeli forces, in fact, claim that they have uncovered some evidence of this potential technology transfer.

Lebanon. The main target of the US-led War on Terror in Lebanon is the Hezbollah organization, a strong community-based organization and political party in Lebanon. This organization has waged wars internally with the Western-backed Lebanese government. It has also waged wars externally with Israel. The traditional allies of Hezbollah are Iran and Syria. Their support to Hezbollah in its war efforts has been a major concern to Israel and its allies in the West, including the United States. The possibility of Iran becoming a new nuclear weapons state has further increased the tension between the pro-western and anti-western forces in Lebanon, and in the entire region.

In this situation, the approach by the United States in its anti-terrorist campaign in the region has been primarily two-fold. First, it continues to rally its Arabic and western allies in support of Israel. Second, it builds resistance to Hezbollah forces within Lebanon by supporting the West-friendly Lebanese government and others who are at odds with

Hezbollah internally. The events in the region over the past decades provide clear evidence to show the strong support Israel gets from the United States and its Arabic and western allies. Their continued support to the West-friendly Lebanese government is also a foregone conclusion. However, the support given by the United States and its allies to militant groups at odds with Hezbollah internally remains secretive. Seymour Hersh, a regular contributor to The New Yorker magazine on military and security matters has commented on such secretive support. He is a United States Pulitzer Prize-winning investigative journalist and an author based in Washington, D.C. In a CNN interview, he once explained:

> The key player is the Saudis. What I [Hersh] was writing about was sort of a private agreement that was made between the White House, we are talking about Richard—Dick—Cheney and Elliott Abrams, one of the key aides in the White House, with Bandar [Prince Bandar bin Sultan, the Saudi national security adviser]. And the idea was to get support, covert support from the Saudis, to support various hard-line jihadists, Sunni groups, particularly in Lebanon, who would be seen in case of an actual confrontation with Hezbollah—the Shia group in the southern Lebanon—would be seen as an asset, as simple as that.. We are in the business now of supporting the Sunnis anywhere we can against the Shia, against the Shia in Iran, against the Shia in Lebanon, that is [Hezbollah leader Hassan] Nasrullah. Civil war. We are in a business of creating in some places, Lebanon in particular, a sectarian violence. (*Your World Today* 2007)

A SOBER REFLECTION

The discussion above shows how the conflict with no borders grew in both time and scope since the mid-nineties. There has been a long-standing social and political vendetta between the two conflicting sides, dating back to the seventh century AD. However, what triggered the present conflict was the alleged discrimination by the US-led West against the Muslim world in recent history. The Islamic militant groups engaged in the conflict insist that they are carrying out their acts of terror simply to fulfil their obligations to God and fellow beings. The more these militant groups come under attack, the more they resolve to fight. The United States and its allies, however, take the position that they have no choice but to combat these militant groups to bring peace to the troubled world. This has resulted in a vicious cycle of violent attacks and counter-attacks across the globe in a seemingly never-ending manner. In the process, this particular conflict has already become a major threat to world peace.

These Islamic militant groups have also become involved in some of the intrastate violent conflicts discussed in Chapter 2. Only in some of these conflicts, Muslims are at loggerheads with non-Muslims. In the other struggles, divergent factions of Muslims fight each other. For example, in the intrastate conflicts of Russia, India, and Thailand, Muslims are in direct conflict with non-Muslims. However, in those of Yemen, Lebanon, Palestine, and Algeria, different factions of Muslims fight one another. Chapter 2 indicated the involvement of these Islamic militant groups, especially the al-Qaeda movement, in intrastate conflicts of both the categories.

The ability of these Islamic militant groups to rally together to match a common enemy is remarkable; the stronger the enemy, the bigger the combined militant group they form. The great number of Islamic militant groups that came to Libya from other parts of Africa as well as Asia to fight colonial Italy in the early forties is a case in point. Then, the influx of Islamic militants from many parts of the world to fight the superpower Soviet Union in Afghanistan in the late eighties is yet another strong example. Today, the Islamic militants are rallying together to fight the only surviving superpower, the United States, and its allies. The struggles of these militants in Iraq, Afghanistan, and Pakistan have turned particularly deadly. In the process, the war in Iraq became a disaster for the United States and its allies. The war-alliance founded by the United States at the beginning of the war did not last long. Most of the allies left the war zone halfway through the war. Later, the United States also agreed to pull back its own troops. Then, in Afghanistan, the WOT has come to a stalemate. Many major moves made so far by the US-led NATO forces have had a disastrous effect. The war in that country continues, from one deadly episode to another, with no hope for peace in the foreseeable future.

The death of Osama bin Laden has not ended the al-Qaeda movement. Nor has it ended Islamic militancy in the world. In the short term, it has brought all Islamic militants, including Taliban forces, to a common front on a course of vengeance. In the long term, Osama bin Laden will remain a symbol of heroism in the hearts and minds of all Islamic militants to come. The al-Qaeda movement that he founded is also likely to continue to enjoy a special place among all Islamic militant movements. This is primarily because the Islamist cause gained momentum throughout the world after Osama bin Laden emerged as a leader. Robert Fulford explains, "Since [Osama bin Laden emerged as a leader] then, the life of the Islamist cause has improved. The Gaza Strip is now under the Islamist control of Hamas. Turkey and Lebanon have Islamist-friendly governments. Iran has remained an Islamist mainstay, with its satellite Syria. Islamist forces threaten a dozen countries, even Saudi Arabia. They spread terror as far as Chechnya, Thailand and the Philippines. Across the West, every nation has been affected." (Fulford 2011, para. 12).

Lately, Pakistan has become a beehive of Islamic militant activities. Islamic militant groups, including al-Qaeda and Taliban forces, are assembling there and are forming a common front to fight against the Pakistani government and the US-led western forces operating in the country. Pakistan is a country that has nuclear weapons. If ever the militant groups fighting the government secure access to these nuclear weapons, there is a good possibility that they would use them in their struggle against Western countries. Already, as stated earlier, Mustafa Abu al-Yazid, an al-Qaeda leader in the country has vowed, "The Mujahedeen would take them [Pakistani nuclear weapons] and use them against the Americans" ("Al Qaeda leader Mustafa Abu al-Yazid" 2009, para. 2). Thus, there exists a very dangerous situation in Pakistan. The death of Osama bin Laden at the hands of American forces on Pakistani soil has only made this situation worse because of two new developments. First, his death triggered growing, countrywide anti-US popular protests within Pakistan. Second, there appeared rising mistrust between the government of Pakistan and the United States, as, for almost a decade, Osama bin Laden had a safe haven in Pakistan close to one of its key military units. The Pakistan government is wary because of the secretive way in which the US forces captured and killed Bin Laden on Pakistani soil, without any Pakistani government involvement. Of course, no one could guarantee that the Mujahedeen would eventually succeed in carrying out their threat. At the same time, no one could also guarantee that it would never happen. Should the unthinkable happen the possibility for it to develop into a global nuclear fiasco is dead real.

The tension in the country, and the world, further escalated due to an incident that occurred on November 26, 2011. In this particular incident, NATO forces operating in neighbouring Afghanistan attacked two military border posts in north-west Pakistan, killing 24 Pakistani soldiers. It appears to be the worst incident of its kind since Pakistan pledged to collaborate with the US in its WOT. This incident sparked off a new wave of popular protests across Pakistan against NATO and the US, some threatening to wage jihad against the US. In the heat of all this, the Pakistani government ordered the US to leave an airbase in Baluchistan that had been used to launch American drone missiles against militants in the Pakistani tribal areas. At the same time, the government closed down the Pakistani border crossing used by convoys delivering supplies to NATO forces in Afghanistan.

This chapter, together with Chapter 2, now completes the answer to the first critical question raised at the end of the introductory chapter: *what are the major violent conflicts in the world today?* Together, the two chapters have given an account of all the major violent conflicts of the world today. The discussions of the individual conflicts showed the dreadful possibility for some of them, given the right conditions, to develop into a worldwide fiasco. This takes us to the second critical question raised at the end of the introductory chapter: *Is there any guarantee that none of the ongoing violent conflicts will deteriorate into a worldwide fiasco?* It needs an answer, here and now. The next two chapters, Chapters 4 and 5, aim to accomplish this task.

Chapter 4:
Global Attempts to Bring Order

Is THERE ANY GUARANTEE that none of the ongoing violent conflicts will deteriorate into a worldwide fiasco? The answer to this second critical question depends on two main factors. One is the degree of effectiveness of the global peace efforts to contain the concerned conflicts before any of them turns into a global fiasco. The other is the possible impact of the changing world dynamics on those conflicts. This chapter, in particular, investigates the former: the effectiveness of the global peace efforts. The next chapter, Chapter 5, will investigate the latter: the possible impact of the changing world dynamics on ongoing major conflicts. The specific observations made in these two chapters will lead to an answer to the aforementioned question. In investigating the former, this chapter first probes the global peace efforts made prior to WWI and then those made through the League of Nations during the period between WWI and WWII. After that, it examines in detail the global peace efforts made through the United Nations after WWII.

PEACE EFFORTS PRIOR TO WWI
Throughout history, most people have longed for lasting peace on Earth. However, wars have been a part of human civilization. As a result, to date, the world has seldom had a long period of unbroken peace. No one really knows when and where people first formed peace organizations. Recorded history shows how people formed peace organizations as far back as the time of ancient Greece. The city-states of the time had waged

war on one another. As a result, and with the hope to limit wars, the leaders of several city-states got together and formed an organization called the Amphictyonic League. Later, in the early seventeenth century, French diplomat Maximilien de Bethune developed a "Grand Design" for peace in Europe. It called for a body of representatives from all European countries. There were also three other significant contributions to peacemaking in the same century. One was a book entitled *On the Law of War and Peace* by Hugo Grotius, a legal expert of the Dutch Republic. It helped formulate a basis for international law. Then, there was the *Peace of Westphalia Treaty* that followed the Thirty Years War, 1618-48, in Europe. This treaty tried to bring peace to Europe by establishing a balance of power through a process of distribution of military and economic power among nations. The third contribution was a book entitled *An Essay Towards the Present and Future Peace of Europe* (1693) by an English philosopher, William Penn. In this book, Penn called for an international council to settle disputes among nations. Later, in the eighteenth century, Abbé Charles-Irénée Castel de Saint-Pierre (1658-1743), a French clergyman, wrote a book entitled *The Project for Perpetual Peace* (1713). This book called for a "Senate of Europe" composed of representatives from all the European countries. Eighty-two years later, in 1795, German philosopher Immanuel Kant published his *Perpetual Peace: a Philosophical Sketch*. It promoted a global approach to world peace through a community of nations.

The following century, the nineteenth, was a more exciting period of peace activism, with a significant number of new peace organizations and conferences. These peace organizations included the New York Peace Society (1815), the American Peace Society (1828), and the Universal Peace Union (1866). The peace conferences held during this century included those held in London, England, in 1843; in Brussels, Belgium, in 1848; in Paris, France, in 1849; in Frankfurt, Germany, in 1850; and in The Hague, the Netherlands, in 1899, which had a follow-up conference in 1907. The two conferences of 1899 and 1907, in particular, had taken place in response to a request made in 1898 by Czar Nicholas II of Russia for an international meeting to create a peaceful universal alliance and limit arms among nations. This request was very much in line with what Immanuel Kant proposed earlier in 1795. These two conferences helped establish the Permanent Court of Arbitration to handle legal disputes among nations, but failed in their primary goals of creating a peaceful universal alliance and limiting armaments. With this failure, the idea of a League of Nations took root among major international players.

Peace Efforts through the League of Nations

Some suggest that it was Edward Grey, a former British Foreign Secretary, who proposed the idea of a League of Nations with a set of global checks and balances for the very first time. Later, it reappeared as one of the *"Fourteen Points"* on which US President Woodrow Wilson based his vision of what he believed the world should be after WWI. In this "Fourteen Points" document, President Woodrow Wilson not only identified the need for a League of Nations, but also explained that all countries should belong to it. Among his other points, he advocated for voluntary reduction of weapons and armed forces by states, no more secret treaties among states, and self-determination for people who shared the same nationality. Another point he promoted was that no nationality should have the power to govern another.

League of Nations Covenant. The Treaty of Versailles, (the Treaty), the peace settlement after WWI which was signed on June 28, 1919, formally established the League of Nations and its organizational structure. The Treaty devoted its Articles 1 through 26 to this purpose exclusively, under the main heading "The Covenant of the League of Nations" (the Covenant). US President Woodrow Wilson was one of the three signatories to the Treaty, along with David Lloyd George of the United Kingdom and Georges Clemenceau of France. The Treaty had 440 Articles in total. The remainder of the Treaty covered territorial, military, financial, and general areas of agreement among the major powers that signed the document. These agreements outside the Covenant were primarily aimed at a number of post-WWI strategic arrangements: reallocating foreign land captured by Germany, reducing its military (army, air force, and naval) and financial strength, and forcing Germany to admit full responsibility for starting the war and the damages it had caused.

Forty-four countries initially signed the Covenant of the League of Nations. Thirty-one of them had taken part in WWI. Despite US President Woodrow Wilson's key role in the establishment and promotion of the League, the United States did not ratify the League Covenant or join in as a League member. This was due to disagreements over the issue between the Woodrow Wilson administration and the US Senate. After its first meeting in London on January 10, 1920, the League moved its headquarters to Geneva in November 1920. Experts believe that the establishment of the League resulted in the institutionalization of international affairs for the very first time. For example, David Kennedy of Harvard Law School said that birth of the League was "a unique moment when international affairs were institutionalized as opposed to the pre-World War I methods of law and politics" ("League of Nations", n.d., para. 6).

According to the League Covenant, the main goals of the League were to promote international cooperation and to achieve global peace. The League sought to attain these goals through a number of state undertakings, three of which were: the commitment to not resort to war, the practice of open, just and honourable relations between nations, and the acceptance of international law as the rule of conduct among governments. Maintenance of justice and respect for all treaty obligations in the dealings of organized peoples with one another was yet another state responsibility. Other salient features of the Covenant included the following:

- The League would have a permanent Secretariat, headed by a Secretary General. The League's actions would come into effect through the workings of an Assembly, consisting of representatives of its member states, and a Council. The Council would consist of representatives of the principal Allied and Associated Powers (permanent members), together with representatives of four other League member states (non-permanent members) elected from time to time.
- The decisions made at any meetings of the Assembly or the Council would require the agreement of all the members of the League represented at the meeting, unless expressly provided otherwise in the Covenant or in the terms of the Treaty.
- The members of the League would bear its expenses in a proportion decided by the Assembly.

- The members of the League would recognize the need to reduce national armaments to the lowest point deemed necessary consistent with national safety and enforcement would be carried out by common action of international obligations. The Council would formulate plans for such armament reduction based on the geographical situation and circumstances of each state. Such plans would be subject to reconsideration and revision at least every ten years. Governments would not exceed the limits of armament without the concurrence of the Council.

- Any war or threat of war, whether or not immediately affecting any of the League Members, would be a matter of concern to the whole League. The League would take action deemed wise and effectual to safeguard the peace of nations.

- In the event that a dispute between League Members was likely to erupt, they would submit the matter to arbitration, judicial settlement, or to inquiry by the Council, and agree in no case to resort to war until three months after they heard the outcome thereof.

- If a League Member resorted to war disregarding the Covenant, the League would consider it as an act of war against all other members of the League. This would result in immediate severance of all trade or financial relations between the covenant-breaking nation and the other League Members and the prohibition and prevention of all financial, commercial or personal intercourse between their respective nationals. In addition, there could be military intervention by the League.

- The League would not have armed forces of its own; the members of the League would severally contribute to the armed forces it might require.

- The League would establish a permanent Court of International Justice.

- The non-members of the League in a dispute would be invited to accept the obligations of the League membership. If such a non-member refused to do so, the League would deal with it as in the case of a non-complying member.

- The League Members would entrust the League with the general supervision of:
  - the execution of agreements with regard to the traffic in women and children;
  - the traffic in opium and other dangerous drugs, and
  - the trade in arms and ammunitions with countries in which the control of the traffic would be necessary in the common interest of League Members.
  - On disputes arising out of a matter solely within the domestic jurisdiction of a state, the Council would so report, but not make any recommendations. When such a matter was referred to the Assembly, it would apply actions and powers of the Council under the League Covenant.

In time, the League went through some changes to its membership and Council structure. The League started with 42 founding members, excluding the United States. Sixteen of the founding members later left the organization. One of them, the Kingdom of Yugoslavia, returned and retained its membership until the final closure of the organization. At the same time, twenty-one new states joined the organization; however, only five of them retained their membership to the end. In December 1939, the League expelled one of its member-states, notably the Union of Soviet Socialist Republics. At its peak, the League had 58 members. Meanwhile, the composition of the League Council also changed a few times. Its composition started with four permanent members (the United Kingdom, France, Italy, and Japan) and an equal number of non-permanent members (Belgium, Brazil, Greece, and Spain). The League later increased the number of non-permanent members to six in September 1922, and to nine in September 1926. Germany joined the League and became the fifth permanent member of the Council in September 1926. Later, after both Germany and Japan left the League, the number of non-permanent members further increased to 11.

The League created the Permanent Court of International Justice referred to in its Covenant. In addition, the League created a number of agencies and commissions. Their purpose was to deal with pressing international problems in a number of areas. A disarmament commission, health committee, League mandates commission, and an international labour organization were among these agencies and commissions. A central opium board, commission for refugees, slavery commission, and a committee for the study of the legal status of women were also among them. The League oversaw the operations of all the established agencies and commissions as well as the Permanent Court of International Justice.

At the time of a dispute, the League could do three basic things in the form of sanctions under its Covenant. First, it could facilitate conciliatory discussions on the dispute in an orderly and peaceful manner, and warn the state deemed the aggressor in the form of a verbal sanction. According to the warning, the aggressor had to either take the necessary corrective steps or face consequences. If the state considered the aggressor failed to respond to the verbal sanction, the League could introduce economic sanctions. If the economic sanctions also failed, the League could use military force (physical sanction) to implement its decision by force. In the application of these sanctions at times of major disputes, the League had great successes as well as failures.

Successes. Notable among the successes of the League was its ability to settle a number of international disputes. They included the 1919-21 border dispute between Albania and the Kingdom of Yugoslavia, the 1921 dispute between Sweden and Finland on the Aland Islands, the 1925 border clash between Greece and Bulgaria, and the 1926 conflict between Iraq and Turkey over the control of the former Ottoman province of Mosul. The League's involvement in these disputes helped avert potential wars between the respective conflicting parties. In addition, the League was successful in dealing with some major humanitarian catastrophes. A good example in this regard was the case of 1.4 million refugees created by the 1923 war in Turkey. Almost 80 percent of the refugees were women and children. Further, the League played a laudable role in the economic and social development of some states. For example, the League arranged loans and oversaw their spending in Austria and Hungary at their times of economic difficulties; they had become virtually insolvent after paying their WWI reparations. The League's assistance helped put them on the road to economic recovery. Then, in 1930, the League took timely action over forced-labour issues in Liberia. This led to the resignation of Liberia's president, vice-president, and numerous government officials. The League also instituted programmes to combat international trade in opium and sexual slavery.

Failures. The most notable failure of the League was its inability to settle a number of international disputes of major concern; in fact, the international conflicts it failed to settle far outnumbered those that it did settle. Following is a list of the conflicts that the League failed to settle. It includes the dates, the countries involved, and the nature of their related disputes:

	Dates	Countries in Conflict	Nature of dispute
1	1919	Poland and the Czech Republic	Border dispute over Cieszyn and Teschen regions, both rich in coal mines
2	1919	Italy and Yugoslavia;	Border dispute over port of Fiume
3	1920-21	Poland and Lithuania	Control over the city of Vilna
4	1920-21	Poland and Russia	Polish invasion of Russian territory
5	1923–25	France/Belgium and Germany	Occupation of the Ruhr by French and Belgium troops
6	1931-33	China and Japan	1931 "Manchurian Incident" and the 1932 Japanese invasion of Shanghai
7	1932-35	Bolivia and Paraguay	Control over the arid Gran Chaco region
8	1935-36	Italy and Ethiopia	Italian invasion of Addis Ababa
9	1939	Germany and Austria	German occupation of Sudetenland and Anschluss
10	1939	Poland and Germany	German invasion of Poland

Of the intrastate disputes, perhaps one of the League's greatest failures was its inability to intervene in the 1936-39 Spanish Civil War. It was a war between the government of Spain and a right-wing group in the country called the *Nationalists*, which included most of the officers of the Spanish Army. In this civil war, the League even failed to prevent foreign intervention; the Soviet Union had come to support the Spanish loyalists, while Germany (Adolf Hitler) and Italy (Benito Mussolini) had come to support the Nationalist insurrectionists. Overall, however, the biggest failure of the League was its inability to settle the 1939 dispute between Poland and Germany, which finally led to WWII.

Reasons for failures. Numerous factors contributed to the League's failures and the following six are the most dominant:

Ineffectiveness of economic sanction. The economic sanctions enforced by the League were ineffective since the member-countries were able to trade with countries outside the League. Economic sanctions could have been a viable option if most of the countries around the world had become League members. However, this was not the case. On its part, the League tried to represent all the nations, but its membership never grew beyond 58 at any time.

League's inability to use military force (physical sanction). The League never had a military force of its own. Instead, it depended on its members, especially those who were militarily strong, to provide armed forces for its use. There was, however, no legal obligation on the part of the member-states in this regard. Britain and France, the two most powerful League members, were reluctant to use military sanctions, or even economic sanctions. Their inaction in the face of growing German militarism under Adolf Hitler showed their lack of continued commitment to collective security through the League. This left the League with no ability to resort to military action against the violators of its Covenant. This inability became clear during the 1935-36 Italian (Benito Mussolini) invasion of Abyssinia (Ethiopia). When the invasion occurred, the League condemned it and imposed economic sanctions against Italy. These sanctions were largely ineffective. In the face of continued aggression, the League tried and failed to enforce military sanction. The British Prime Minister at the time, Stanley Baldwin, later observed that no one had military forces on hand to match an Italian attack. The League's attempts to get military support from the United

States, although it was not a member of the League, also failed as the US refused to cooperate with any League action.

Problematic League membership. The United States, the most powerful country in the world, declined to be a League member from the very beginning. At the same time, the League had not admitted Germany and Russia that had the potential to become great powers. The League refused to admit Germany because of its role in WWI, and Russia for its communist rule; the founding members of the League had not welcomed all states of communist rule. However, both Germany and Russia later became League members. Germany became a member in 1926, and the Soviet Union (Russia) joined in 1934. Their League memberships were, nevertheless, temporary. Germany (Adolf Hitler) pulled out in 1933. Later, the League had to expel the Soviet Union for its aggression against Finland in 1939. Meanwhile, the League also lost two other major powers, Japan and Italy. These two nations had served as permanent members of the League Council from its inception. Japan withdrew its membership in 1933 after the League expressed its opposition to the invasion of the Chinese territory of Manchuria. In a similar way, Italy (Benito Mussolini) withdrew from the League in 1937, after it condemned Italy's invasion of Abyssinia and imposed economic sanctions on the invader.

Bowing to the pressure of big powers. The League very rarely acted against Covenant violations of powerful nations. For example, the League did nothing when France and Belgium invaded Ruhr, the industrial heartland of Germany, in 1923. Then, in the same year, the League bowed down to Italy (Benito Mussolini) and changed its decision on an incident that occurred in a border dispute between Greece and Albania. In this event, an Italian team, appointed by the League to oversee a settlement between the two conflicting parties, had been murdered.

Difficulties and delays in making decisions. Decision-making with unanimous consent at both the League Assembly and the League Council was too difficult and time-consuming to be effective. Article 5 of the League Covenant specifically required unanimous consent in making decisions at these League bodies. League decisions on procedural issues and a few specified topics were the only exception to this requirement; a simple majority support was adequate for decision-making on such matters.

Lack of authority to ensure compliance by all League members. The League had no means to ensure due implementation of its resolutions by its members. As a result, most League members appeared to have had a higher priority to protect their own national interests, with no solid commitment to League resolutions.

PEACE EFFORTS THROUGH THE UNITED NATIONS

The failure of the League of Nations to prevent WWII became a major concern among the leaders of the Allied forces who fought against the Axis powers of Germany, Italy and Japan. While WWII was still in progress, the key leaders of the Allied forces began to discuss the need for a more effective global organization for peacekeeping and preventing wars. The key leaders who led these discussions were US President Franklin Roosevelt, British Prime Minister Winston Churchill, and Soviet Premier Joseph Stalin. These three leaders, in particular, met several times between 1941 and 1945 to plan and develop the needed new global organization. This finally led to the founding of the UN. As a follow up, representatives of 50 countries met in San Francisco in April 1945 to create a charter for this new peacekeeping organization. Notably, this was before WWII was officially over.

United Nations Charter. The designers of the UN Charter wanted to ensure that it would address the defects and omissions of the League Covenant; the League had failed to avoid WWII because of these shortcomings. At the same time, the Charter's designers wanted to assign a more extensive field of activity and responsibilities to the UN than those allocated to the League. It is also interesting to note that the designers of the League Covenant were first limited to five major powers and that they worked behind closed doors. In the beginning, the five countries were France, Italy, Japan, the United Kingdom, and the United States. Later, these five worked in liaison with nine other allied nations. The UN Charter, on the other hand, turned out to be the product of concerted efforts of 50 nations. According to the finalized charter, the declared aims of the UN include maintenance of international peace, development of friendly relations among nations, international cooperation in solving international problems, and harmonization of the actions of nations in the attainment of these common goals. The salient differences between the League Covenant and the UN Charter are as follows:

Flexibility in dispute resolution or containment of wars. The UN Charter is much more flexible than the League Covenant in finding ways to settle disputes and contain wars. The Covenant limited the means to resolve disputes to arbitration or judicial settlement (Articles 12 and 13) or a set procedure (Articles 15-17). The set procedure would automatically kick in when arbitration or judicial settlement was inapplicable. The Charter, on the other hand, provides endless options to explore (Articles 33-38) in resolving disputes and avoiding or containing wars.

Right of a state to start a war. The Covenant did not categorically make it illegal for a party (state) to a dispute, which had accepted the findings of a negotiating body, to start a war. This was especially so if the other party or parties to the dispute had refused to accept the same findings. As a result, a party that had accepted the findings of a negotiating body could claim that it had a legal right to go to war with a party that had refused to accept the findings. The UN Charter, on the other hand, makes it illegal for any nation to initiate a war under any circumstances. However, Article 51 of the UN Charter does guarantee the right to individual or collective self-defence. This only refers to a right to respond to an illegal armed attack, and not to initiate one.

Resources for collective military action. The League did not have a military force of its own and its Covenant did not provide any means to collect military resources from its members for a collective action when needed. With no legal obligation to supply military forces to the League, its member-states had shown reluctance in contributing to its collective military action. The UN also does not have a military force of its own. However, the UN Charter has provided, by its Article 47, a specific means to collect the military resources needed for collective action.

Reduction of armaments. The League Covenant included set procedures (Article 8) to reduce national armaments. The intended reduction was to the lowest point consistent with national safety. It was also to be consistent with the enforcement of international obligations by common action. The UN Charter falls short of such a set procedure for the reduction of national armaments. Instead, the Charter proposes a strategy for the establishment of a system for the *regulation* of armaments (Article 26) and *possible disarmament* (Article 47).

Practicality in the decision-making process. The League Covenant required both the Assembly and the Council of the League to make all their decisions by unanimous vote. Only decisions on procedural matters and a few specified topics remained an exception to this. This essentially gave every League member the power of veto on all major decisions regarding international peace. This, in turn, had made decision-making at the League very difficult. In contrast, the UN Charter allows all UN organs and subsidiary bodies to make their decisions by majority vote. The extent of the majority support a particular decision needs depends on the issue's merit. For example, for decisions on important questions, the UN General Assembly needs a two-thirds majority of the members present and voting. The rule of unanimity and the power of veto apply only to five major powers: France, China, the Russian Federation, the United Kingdom, and the United States. That too is only when they act in their capacity as permanent members of the UN Security Council. The UN Security Council, however, can make its decisions on procedural matters by a simple majority vote.

Scope of International Court of Justice. Under the League Covenant, a League member-state was not obliged to join the Permanent Court of International Justice. Under the UN Charter, however, every UN member automatically becomes a party to the statutes of the International Court of Justice.

Declaration regarding non-self-governing territories. The League Covenant (Article 22, Mandatory System) embodied the well-being and development of the peoples of colonies and non-self-governing territories as a sacred trust of civilization. The UN Charter has gone far beyond that. Its Article 1 states, "The development of friendly relations among nations based on respect for the principle of equal rights and self-determination of peoples." Then, Article 73 of the Charter shows the need "to develop self-government, to take account of the political aspirations of the peoples, and to assist them in the progressive development of their free political institutions." The achievement of independence by about 100 nations after WWII shows that these UN Charter aims have had significant results.

Promotion of human welfare. The League Covenant included provisions for the promotion of human welfare in a number of areas. These areas include conditions of labour, treatment of native inhabitants in territories, traffic in women and children, traffic in dangerous drugs, and trade restrictions in arms and ammunition. The UN Charter has gone beyond that, especially by establishing a special organ for assisting the UN member-states with a coordinated programme of economic and social development. This special UN division operates under the name of the Economic and Social Council. Many of its development projects in developing countries have had tremendous impact on the lives of their peoples.

Fundamental rights and freedoms of the individual. The League Covenant did not address the issue of individual rights and freedoms. The UN Charter, on the other hand, specifically promotes and encourages "respect for human rights and fundamental freedoms for all without distinction as to race, sex, language, or religion ...." (Paragraph 3 of Article 1).

Meanwhile, Article 2 of the UN Charter specifically requires the UN and its member-states to act in accordance with the following basic principles:

- The UN is based on the principle of the sovereign equality of all its members.
- All members, in order to ensure the rights and benefits resulting from membership for all, shall fulfill in good faith the obligations assumed by them in accordance with the present UN Charter.
- All members shall settle their international disputes by peaceful means in such a manner that international peace, security, and justice are not endangered.
- In their international relations, all members shall refrain from the threat or use of force against the territorial integrity or political independence of any state, or in any other manner inconsistent with the Purposes of the United Nations
- All members shall assist the UN in any action it takes in accordance with the present UN Charter, and shall refrain from giving assistance to any state against which the UN is taking preventive or enforcement action.
- The Organization shall ensure that states that are not members of the UN act in accordance with the Principles

of the United Nations so far as may be necessary for the
maintenance of international peace.

- Nothing contained in the present UN Charter shall
authorize the UN to intervene in matters that are essentially
within the domestic jurisdiction of any state or shall require
the members to submit such matters to settlement under
the present UN Charter. However, this principle shall not
prejudice the application of enforcement measures, deemed
necessary to restore international peace and security, under
Chapter VII.

The founding of the UN with its Charter gave renewed and greater
hope for peace in the troubled world. The UN has now become almost
a universal organization; its member-states now number 193. The newly
established South Sudan is its latest member. Kosovo, which declared
independence from Serbia on February 17, 2008, and Vatican City are
the only independent nations that have to date not become members.
Vatican City, created in 1929, has not chosen to become part of the
international organization. The current UN membership shows that
the entire world's militarily and economically powerful nations have
become willing parties to the course of the UN; this was not the case
with the League of Nations. At the same time, the above-described
differences between the League Covenant and the UN Charter show
that the latter offers more efficient and effective means to make timely
decisions and avoid or contain future wars. The latter also includes
many more provisions for establishing self-governance and supporting
the fundamental rights and freedoms of individuals throughout the
world.

Successes. During its first 65 years, the UN has made remarkable
accomplishments in fulfilling its goals and objectives. Most importantly,
it has succeeded in avoiding worldwide catastrophes similar to WWI or
WWII up to now. Some UN actions have helped reduce international
conflicts, solved most of the ones that ruptured, and brought peace to
many troubled nations. The Universal Declaration of Human Rights,
adopted by the UN in 1948, in particular, raised the consciousness of
human rights throughout the world in an unprecedented manner. The
UN has also tried a number of war criminals, given humanitarian relief to
those affected by human or natural disasters, and largely ended colonial

rule. Further, the numerous UN economic and social programmes have raised the living standards of people living in developing nations.

For the first 45 years of its existence, the UN was faced with an unprecedented power struggle between two superpowers: the Soviet Union and the United States. There were real worries that this power struggle would eventually lead to a new world war. The worst of such worries arose at the time of a Cuban missile crisis in 1962 and took the world almost to the brink of a nuclear war between the two countries. The deciding moment came when the United States gave an ultimatum to the Soviets. The ultimatum required the Soviets to remove their medium range (750 – 1500 miles capability) and intermediate range (3500 miles capability) missiles from Cuban soil by a set date, October 29th, to avoid an all-out American invasion of Cuba. The Soviets' last minute agreement to comply with the ultimatum, subject to UN verification, helped avoid the imminent war. The war containment efforts of the UN at this and other such critical times helped avert the rupture of another world war up to now.

At the same time, the UN peacekeeping and nation-building efforts also have made tremendous progress. For example, with its peacekeeping efforts, the UN has managed to preserve the peace in Cyprus since 1964. The UN has also preserved the peace between the nuclear powers of India and Pakistan for three decades since 1971. The RAND Corp Study (2005) found that the UN was successful in two of three of its peacekeeping efforts and seven of eight of its nation-building efforts. Then, one report suggested that in 2005, there were "18 peacekeeping missions in the world, with more requests for new missions than the United Nations can handle" (Water 2005, para. 4). Such a high demand for new peacekeeping missions clearly testifies to the success of the past and present UN peacekeeping efforts. In addition, the number of wars, genocides, and human rights abuses across the globe has been significantly reduced. According to a report by the Human Security Centre (2005), international activism, mostly spearheaded by the UN, has made this possible.

The War Crime Tribunal set up by the UN began trying war criminals. The Tribunal has already completed the trials of war criminals in the former Yugoslavia and Rwanda. At the same time, the International Court of Justice helped settle many international disputes on territorial issues, hostage-taking, and economic rights. Then, on its humanitarian relief front, the UN has helped more than 30 million refugees fleeing war, persecution or famine. In addition, the UN has also come to the aid of those affected by natural disasters, such as floods, earthquakes, and hurricanes.

Further, there was an increase in the number of nations securing freedom from colonial rule during the second half of the 20th century. In all, 80 nations with more than 750 million people gained independence since the founding of the UN in 1945. The UN did its part to help these new nations gain independence and stand on their own authority. This help came in many areas of human endeavour. The UN has been able to assist through its numerous economic and social development agencies and programmes. The United Nations International Children's Emergency Fund (UNICEF), the World Health Organization (WHO), the Food and Agriculture Organization (FAO), and the United Nations Development Programme (UNDP) are among these agencies and programmes. Also among them are the United Nations Educational, Scientific and Cultural Organization (UNESCO); the International Monetary Fund (IMF); and the World Bank.

Despite its record of significant successes, the UN is not without weaknesses and failures. What follows below is an account of its most notable failures.

Failures. The most significant failures of the UN are found in four main categories: its inability to control nuclear proliferation; non-compliance of its member-states; inaction and inadequate or delayed action by its Security Council; and unilateral global policing by powerful nations. Each one of these main UN failure categories warrants some explanation.

Inability to control nuclear proliferation. The utmost concern among the critics of the UN is its inability to control nuclear proliferation. Article 26 of the UN Charter requires the UN Security Council to formulate plans for the establishment of a system for the regulation of armaments. The Security Council is to do this with the assistance of a Military Staff Committee, referred to in Article 47 of the Charter. The wordings of the related section of this article talk about "the regulation of armaments, and possible disarmament." The Nuclear Non-Proliferation

Treaty (NPT), designed to regulate nuclear weaponry, was adopted in 1968. This treaty contains a preamble and 11 articles. Articles I, II, and VI describe the specific undertakings of UN member-states in regulating nuclear weaponry. Article 1, in particular, requires that each nuclear weapons state not transfer to any recipient any nuclear explosive devices or the control over such devices. The same Article also requires the nuclear weapons states not to assist, encourage, or induce any non-nuclear weapons state to manufacture or otherwise acquire nuclear explosive devices or the control over such devices. Then, Article II describes the reciprocal undertakings of the non-nuclear weapons states. Article VI requires that all parties to the Treaty undertake "to pursue negotiations in good faith on effective measures relating to cessation of the nuclear arms race at an early date and to nuclear disarmament." The same article also requires the concerned parties to negotiate on a "treaty on general and complete disarmament under strict and effective international control."

Ironically, by the time the NPT came into effect, the number of nuclear weapons states had grown from one to five. Only the United States had nuclear weapons at the time of the founding of the UN in 1945. Then, Russia (the former Soviet Union), the United Kingdom, France, and China became nuclear weapons states in 1949, 1952, 1960, and 1964, respectively. These five nuclear weapons states were also the only permanent members of the UN Security Council. The adoption of the Nuclear Non-Proliferation Treaty *after* all the Security Council's permanent members had become nuclear weapons states is a subject of discussion among the UN critics. Since the Nuclear Non-Proliferation Treaty came into effect, four more countries have become nuclear weapons states: India in 1974, Pakistan in 1998, North Korea in 2006, and Israel in or before 1979. India and Pakistan have never been members of the Treaty. North Korea was a member of the Treaty until it announced its withdrawal in 2003. Israel is also not a member of the Treaty. Although Israel allegedly joined the nuclear weapons states in or before 1979, it pursues a policy of strategic ambiguity with regard to its nuclear weapons status. At the same time, the US and Israel have charged that Iran and Syria have illegal nuclear weapons programmes. Both Iran and Syria flatly deny the charge.

Meanwhile, under a NATO nuclear weapons sharing security arrangement, the United States provided nuclear weapons for seven non-nuclear weapons states: Belgium, Germany, Italy, the Netherlands, Turkey, Canada, and Greece. Canada and Greece stopped receiving US nuclear weapons in 1984 and 2001, respectively. The Non-Aligned Movement (NAM), which was founded in April 1955 (118 member-countries as of 2007) sees any kind of nuclear weapons sharing as a direct violation of the NPT. Accordingly, it has called on all countries to refrain from nuclear weapons sharing "under any kind of security arrangement" ("Statement" 2005, para. 9). NATO, however, says that the nuclear sharing arrangements are compliant with the NPT. NATO's justification for this is that all US nuclear weapons located in Europe are "in the sole possession and under constant and complete custody and control of the United States" (North Atlantic Treaty Organization 2007, para. 10). Whatever the case may be, the number of countries having nuclear weapons is now 16, well spread across the globe. All this is evidence that the UN, in its present configuration, has no strength to prevent further nuclear proliferation in the coming years.

Non-compliance by member-states. Just as in the case of the League of Nations, the UN does not have any means to ensure proper implementation of its resolutions by the member-states. For some member-states, protecting their own national interests takes higher priority. They do not show a firm commitment to the UN. The lack of success in implementing numerous UN resolutions in the Israeli-Palestinian conflict clearly testifies to this matter.

Inaction and inadequate or delayed action by the UN Security Council. In many situations, the main, and perhaps the only reason for this failure is the lack of unanimity among the permanent members of the Security Council in its decision-making. However, reaching unanimity among these members is not always easy. When irreconcilable differences crop up among them, they take a long time trying to reach a unanimous agreement. In the interim, the Security Council will take no action on the issues in question. Such inaction on some issues can last forever. When decisions are finally reached in such situations, they are either too late or too little to resolve the issues at hand.

Because of the need for unanimity among the Security Council permanent members, any one of them can veto a resolution supported by all other members of the Council. It can even be a resolution supported by a vast majority in the UN General Assembly. Historically, the Security Council's permanent members have used their veto power more than 250 times. One report ("United Nations Security Council", n. d.) states that since the inception of the Security Council, China (ROC/PRC) has used the veto power six times, France 18 times, Russia/USSR 123 times, UK 32 times, and US 82 times. The majority of the Russian/USSR vetoes were in the first ten years of the Security Council's existence. Notably, this was during the Cold War period. Since 1984, there have been 63 vetoes: China and France three each, Russia/USSR 4, UK 10, and US 43. All this resembles a power game played by the Security Council permanent members on the stage of world politics.

As a consequence of this power game, and as expected, the UN has miserably failed in responding to some devastating situations. The US invasion of Iraq, the genocides in Rwanda and Darfur, the Srebrenica massacre, and the humanitarian crises in Somalia and Congo (Second Congo War) provide examples of this malfunction. The one that stands out most in this regard, however, is the unremitting violent conflict between Hebrews and Arabs in the Middle East. Given the status quo, there is no hope that this conflict will ever end peacefully.

Unilateral global policing by powerful nations. The most powerful nations in the world have at times unilaterally acted on international issues. In particular, they have done so without the blessings of the UN. The US invasion of Iraq in 2003 and the Russian war in Georgia in 2008 are two good examples in this regard. In some situations, the UN has authorized such unilateral action, especially by the United States, after the fact. This is certainly not the case in all such situations. For example, in both the US invasion of Iraq and the Russian war in Georgia, the UN did not give its authorization before or after the fact. At the same time, these powerful nations exercise their veto power at the UN Security Council, preventing globally acclaimed actions, and critics find their bias to be questionable. For example, according to John J. Mearsheimer ("United Nations Security Council", n. d.), since 1982, the United States has vetoed 32 Security Council resolutions critical of Israel. Notably, the total number of vetoes cast by all other Security Council permanent members during the same period was much less. It is very worrisome that one permanent member could veto so many resolutions critical of one country. It suggests that the United States has acted in its own national policy interests, rather than those of the international community. According to critics, the exercise of veto power in this manner is yet another form of unilateral action on global matters. By such action, the US, in fact, has made the UN subservient to American interests. The United States government, on the other hand, may consider itself superior to any international organization when solving world problems. A statement made by former US President George Bush Sr. on May 29, 2009 alluded to such US thinking. He made this statement in Vancouver at an interview with Frank McKenna, Canadian Ambassador to Washington. In this statement, President George Bush Sr. said, "The UN is a vital institution, but is not really meant for problem solving" (Maich 2009, para. 12).

Reasons for failures. A closer review of UN failures points to a number of contributory factors, which fall under two main categories. The first relates to the performance of the UN in general and the other relates to the structure and effectiveness of the UN Security Council. There appear to be four main contributory factors in the first category. The initial factor is that the UN does not have a military force of its own. Second, the UN is not able to take decisive action on its own. Third, the UN has neither the authority nor any specific arrangement to ensure compliance by its member-states. Fourth, the role of the UN is increasingly becoming subservient to American interests.

The contributory factors in the second category hinge on the apparent shortcomings of the Security Council's structure. These shortcomings appear in three main areas. First, the Security Council lacks true international representation. Second, each of the five permanent members of the Council enjoys the power to veto its resolutions. Third, there is no system to separate the legislative, executive, and judiciary powers of the Council in governing its operations. These shortcomings of the existing structure of the Security Council have led to the inefficiency and ineffectiveness of its operations in many critical areas.

In the absence of a true international representation at the Security Council, its decisions may not have been always in the best interests of the global community. At times, the national interests and political motives of the Council members have taken precedence in their decision-making. According to critics, "Protecting the oil-rich Kuwaitis in 1991 but poorly protecting resource-poor Rwandans in 1994" ("The Universal Declaration" 2009, para. 10) clearly testifies to this.

At the same time, many do believe that the permanent members of the Security Council often use their veto power in a questionable manner. In the first place, giving such veto power to a small group of members of the United Nations contradicts its basic principle of sovereign equality for all its members. With this veto power, a permanent member can halt any UN diplomatic or armed action overwhelmingly supported by the world community. This, in fact, has happened on many occasions.

A SOBER REFLECTION

Before WWI, there was no global effort in any meaningful way to avoid or contain international wars. A well-organized and institutionalized global effort for this purpose first came into being with the founding of the League of Nations after WWI, in 1919. The founders of the League hoped that there would not be any more worldwide fiascos similar to WWI. Sadly, what followed later proved that this hope was in vain. In time, the League left more number of international conflicts unsettled than the number it managed to settle. In the end, it failed to prevent WWII.

The founders of the UN that replaced the League after WWII did their part to prevent repetition of the types of failures experienced under the League. For this, they introduced a number of new measures. More flexibility in decision-making and dispute resolution was one of them. A more workable arrangement for the implementation of physical sanctions (military intervention) was another. Bringing all states under the scope of the International Court of Justice was yet another new measure. These and other strategies generally helped the UN to be more effective than the League in many areas of human endeavour.

However, one particular policy the UN founders introduced brought only negative results. This new policy was to establish a system for *the regulation of armaments* (Article 26, UN Charter) and *possible disarmament* (Article 47, UN Charter). This new system replaced the League's set procedure for the *reduction* of national armaments. The new system put in place by the UN only increased national armaments, instead of reducing them. At the same time, more nations started to develop the ultimate weapon, the nuclear bomb. Those who produced nuclear weapons also started to engage in secret arms races, each trying to have a bigger share of world domination. All this has now led to a looming global nuclear catastrophe, threatening the very survival of humankind on the planet. It is a catastrophe waiting to be triggered by someone, sometime. The UN has failed to prevent all these destructive developments. That is not all. The UN is also blamed for the inaction and inadequate or delayed action by its Security Council. Further, it is blamed for the uncontrollable unilateral action by major global powers. These and other UN failures have once again built up international tension to an alarming level.

Meanwhile, nuclear proliferation appears to continue regardless, in an uncontrollable manner. In the process, some of the parties involved in ongoing major violent conflicts have already produced their own nuclear weapons. Some others have assured access to such weapons owned by their nuclear allies. At the same time, those who are handicapped with no direct or indirect access to such weapons appear to be busy in trying to meet their shortfall, at any cost. This applies to the Islamic militant groups that are engaged in a violent conflict with the West, as well. Any attempt to use nuclear weapons by a party to any one of the concerned conflicts, no doubt, will trigger an outbreak of the looming global nuclear fiasco. Some of the concerned conflicting parties, in fact, have already threatened to do so. Amidst all this, the UN stands helpless, with no teeth to bite. Whether this situation will eventually ease out or further deteriorate will depend largely on the changing world dynamics. The next chapter will investigate this.

Chapter 5:
Changing World Dynamics

THE FORCES AND ACTIVITIES that influence global politics and balance of power characterize the world dynamics in question. A major shift in these dynamics could influence the relationships among nations and their ongoing conflicts, for better or for worse. In the process, a shift in world dynamics could prevent, delay, or even advance the outbreak of any looming global catastrophe. What has happened in the past in this regard can throw some light onto the future. For this reason, this chapter begins with an overview of the major shifts in world dynamics in the past, starting from the beginning of the modern era in the fifteenth century. The related historical information is given in two sections. The first section reviews the major shifts in world dynamics from the beginning of the modern era to the time of WWII. The second section follows suit, reviewing the major shifts occurred thereafter.

BEFORE WWII

The early European global explorations that began in the fifteenth century changed world dynamics in a significant manner. These explorations created new global maps, giving a new view of the world. At the same time, they helped European powers establish contact with other parts of the world and open direct trade links with them. In particular, the trade involving African and Asian exotic goods, such as gold, silver, precious stones, and spices became an extremely lucrative global business for the globetrotting Europeans. Hoping to thrive in this arena, several European powers took control of the trade of these items. In doing so, they waged wars against each other in distant lands, each trying to get a bigger share of this profitable market.

Then, the industrial revolution of the seventeenth and eighteenth centuries created an unprecedented surge in European demand for foreign goods in the form of industrial raw materials. This created new economic opportunities in the production and trade of these materials in countries where they originated. With the help of incoming raw materials, Europeans manufactured industrialized products in mass scale. The situation remained rewarding until Europe experienced a severe economic depression (the Long Depression) in the 1870s. This economic depression created a need to find new markets outside Europe for European products now being mass-produced. In this new economic situation, the European powers expanded the scope of their interest in foreign lands from mere trade control to formal colonial rule. Russia, Japan, and the United States also became industrialized and had similar interests. In time, they joined the strong, colonial European powers, including the United Kingdom, France, Portugal, Spain, the Netherlands, Germany, and Italy. As their technological powers and economies developed over the years, they all also began to develop modern weapons, such as machine guns and warships. In so doing, they engaged in an arms race, each hoping to be more powerful than the rest. At the same time, they formed defence alliances, each committing to support its allies at times of wars. Later, the world witnessed how WWI (1914–18) and WWII (1939–45) played out as military struggles among these alliances.

As shown above, the world system that dominated during the times that led to the two global wars was *multi-polar* in character. Polarity, in the context of world dynamics or systems, means the presence of one or more hubs or centres made up of major powers acting as poles, each enjoying a network of alliances of individual sovereign countries. Such alliances could consist of countries widely spread across the globe. They could also exist within a particular world region, such as Europe or the Middle East.

At the time leading up to the two world wars, there were alliances of nations but there was no real 'superpower' in the way we now understand. Four basic features characterize a superpower in the modern sense. First, it would have a distinct political system. Second, it would have an identifiable and distinctive approach to international order, for the well-being and safety of all countries. Third, it would be economically and militarily strong enough to act globally (beyond its borders) when necessary. This is to act in defence of its political system and the preferred international order. Fourth, there would be a network of foreign countries aligning themselves with it, as its allies. The allies of such a superpower may include one or more major global powers. Such global powers could also be acting as poles in separate polar arrangements.

A Major Shift after WWII

The conclusion of WWII brought another major shift in world dynamics: the United States and the Soviet Union emerged as two competing superpowers. They had two distinct political systems; the Soviet Union had a communist and socialist totalitarian system, while the United States had a liberal democratic system. They also had different approaches to global order. Both were economically and militarily strong enough to act globally. In addition, they enjoyed their own networks of allied countries. Thus, the two nations embodied the characteristics of global superpowers. This laid down a solid foundation for a 'bipolar system.'

Even before WWII ended, the Soviet Union had consolidated its power in Eastern Europe. The Soviet Union had first appeared as a union of four Soviet Socialist Republics. Later, it grew to fifteen union republics. Armenia, Azerbaijan, Byelorussia, Estonia, Georgia, Kazakhstan, Kirghiz, and Latvia were eight of them. Lithuania, Moldova, Russia, Tajik, Turkmen, Ukraine, and Uzbekistan were the remaining seven. The continued expansion of this union's influence in Europe became a major concern for the United States for two main reasons. First, the two superpowers had opposing political ideologies and systems. Second, on the economic front, the United States encouraged free trade throughout the world. The Soviet Union, however, thought that the exposure of their fifteen republics to trade with the West would eventually become a threat to their communist governing system.

Meanwhile, in 1947 Britain and France signed a defence pledge. They called it *the Dunkirk Treaty*. It provided Western Europe with a unified defence front against communist threats in the region. This defence front later expanded with the inclusion of Belgium, Luxembourg, and the Netherlands, under a new name, *the Treaty of Brussels*. This new Treaty came into effect on March 17, 1948. In September of the same year, in response to the Berlin blockade, this five-nation defence alliance further expanded to include more Western European countries and became *the Western European Union's Defence Organization*. This organization saw the need for the participation of the United States as well in order to counter the military power of the Soviets. After the US joined, the organization changed its name to *The North Atlantic Treaty Organization* (NATO) on April 4, 1949. The countries that came together under the NATO banner included the five Treaty of Brussels states plus the United States, Canada, Iceland, Portugal, Italy, Norway, and Denmark. More countries became NATO members in the following years, Greece and Turkey in 1952 and West Germany in 1955.

With the North Atlantic Treaty of April 4, 1949, NATO members reaffirmed their faith in the purposes and principles of the UN Charter. In addition, by the same Treaty, they expressed their desire to live in peace with all other peoples and governments. One basic understanding was that they would unite their efforts for the collective defence and preservation of peace. In particular, Article 5 of the Treaty states:

> The Parties agree that an armed attack against one or more of them in Europe or North America shall be considered an attack against them all and consequently they agree that, if such an armed attack occurs, each of them, in exercise of the right of individual or collective self-defence recognised by Article 51 of the Charter of the United Nations, will assist the Party or Parties so attacked by taking forthwith, individually and in concert with the other Parties, such action as it deems necessary, including the use of armed force, to restore and maintain the security of the North Atlantic area. Any such armed attack and all measures taken as a result thereof shall immediately be reported to the Security Council. Such measures shall be terminated when the Security Council has taken the measures necessary to restore and maintain international peace and security. (NATO 1949, para. 6).

Then, the communist states in Eastern and Central Europe formed their own defence front in 1955. It took effect in Warsaw, Poland under the title, '*Treaty of Friendship, Cooperation and Mutual Assistance.*' Later, the name was simplified and became known as the '*Warsaw Pact.*' The founding members were the Soviet Union, Poland, Rumania, Bulgaria, Czechoslovakia, Albania, Hungary, and East Germany. This coalition was an initiative of the Soviets to counter NATO forces. By this time, the Soviet Union was the only nation other than the United States that had developed nuclear weapons: the atomic bomb in 1949 and the hydrogen bomb in 1953.

The Warsaw Pact document is quite similar to the North Atlantic Treaty. For example, the Article 4 of the Warsaw Pact states:

> In the event of armed attack in Europe on one or more of the Parties to the Treaty by any state or group of states, each of the Parties to the Treaty, in the exercise of its right to individual or collective self-defence in accordance with Article 51 of the Charter of the United Nations Organization, shall immediately, either individually or in agreement with other Parties to the Treaty, come to the assistance of the state or states attacked with all such means as it deems necessary, including armed force. The Parties to the Treaty shall immediately consult concerning the necessary measures to be taken by them jointly in order to restore and maintain international peace and security. Measures taken on the basis of this Article shall be reported to the Security Council in conformity with the provisions of the Charter of the United Nations Organization. These measures shall be discontinued immediately the Security Council adopts the necessary measures to restore and maintain international peace and security. ("Warsaw Security Pact" 1955, para. 5).

Arms race. As far as international security went, Europe now had two camps, the East and the West, each having a superpower with nuclear power capability. The Western camp also had countries in the North Atlantic region, outside Europe. These countries included the superpower United States, Canada, and Iceland. Due to the very nature of the defence agreements of the countries in each camp, a potential war between any two countries, one from each group, could involve all the countries in both the camps, triggering a new world war. In this alarming situation, both parties did their best to arm themselves up to the hilt to face any eventuality, leading to a dangerous arms race. At the same time, the tensions between the two camps and the dread of the escalating arms race spread across the other countries in the world led to many questions about the adequacy of their own security capabilities.

Today, as stated earlier, there are eight countries that have tested nuclear weapons: the United States (1945); Russia (former Soviet Union, 1949); the United Kingdom (1952); France (1960); China (1964); India (1974); Pakistan (1998); and North Korea (2006). These countries treasure their individual stockpiles of nuclear weapons. There is also strong suspicion that Israel too has such weapons. Some also believe that Iran, and possibly Libya, Algeria, South Korea, and Taiwan, are pursuing their own nuclear weapons programmes. Then, a number of other countries could become nuclear weapons states very quickly. They only have to choose to become so. According to experts, these countries include Australia, Canada, Germany, Japan, South Africa, South Korea, and Ukraine. South Africa developed nuclear power in the past, but has since abandoned its nuclear programmes.

The United States and Russia have the biggest stockpiles of nuclear weapons; their numbers are comparable. According to a report (Kile et al. 2011) in the Stockholm International Peace Research Institute (SIPRI) *Yearbook 2011*, together the two countries own almost 95 percent of all the nuclear warheads in the world. In particular, the United States has approximately 8,500 warheads while Russia has approximately 11,000, with more than 20 percent of the stocks remaining active at either end.

Nuclear weapons are only one type of WMD. The other types include biological and chemical devices. The Biological Weapons Convention of 1972 banned the manufacture, stockpiling, and use of biological weapons. Accordingly, both superpowers abandoned the production and use of such weapons. However, there have been reports to the contrary. For example, Liza Porteus noted in her *Weapons of Mass Destruction Handbook* (2006) that Russia continued to have stockpiles of various types of biological weapons. At the same time, the United States was conducting laboratory studies on substances such as anthrax. Today's situation in this regard is not known.

Chemical weapons did play a role in both WWI and WWII. In WWI, Germany and the Allies used large-scale chemical gas attacks on the battlefield in 1915. Then, during WWII, Nazi Germany used poisonous gases, such as hydrogen cyanide and carbon monoxide, to murder millions of people in extermination camps. More recently, the United States used tear gas and defoliants in the Vietnam War (1959-75). However, the use of chemical weapons has been banned on two occasions, first by the 1925 Geneva Protocol after WWI and later by the 1993 Chemical Weapons Convention (CWC). While the Geneva Protocol banned only the use of chemical weapons, the CWC specifically prohibited the development, production, and possession of all chemical weapons. One hundred and forty countries signed and endorsed the CWC. Despite all this, both Russia and the United States possess stockpiles of sarin, a toxic nerve agent. At the same time, a number of other countries are reported to have sarin as well as other forms of nerve agents. The "dirty bomb" and the "E-bomb" are two other types of WMD. It is possible that many more types of WMD are now under development.

Cold War. The competition between the two superpowers, the United States and the Soviet Union, took the form of a serious power struggle, each wanting to dominate the other. The tension between them reached a peak when Greece and Turkey came under the threat of communist guerrilla movements in 1947. The guerrillas had the support of the Soviet Union and some of its allies. In reacting to the situation, US President Harry Truman warned the world against such threats. On March 12, 1947 he said, "It must be the policy of the United States to support free people who are resisting attempted subjugation by armed minorities or by outside pressure" ("Cold War 1945-1960," n.d., para. 19). It sounded like an American declaration of war on the Soviets. True to his words, American troops went in and defeated the communist guerrillas in both Greece and Turkey in the following year. Many believe that this was the beginning of the Cold War between the two new superpowers. It was a cold war, as neither of the superpowers fought the other directly throughout its period. It finally ended in the early 1990s.

Deterrence. Having similar size stockpiles of WMD, the two superpowers had a means of avoiding a war between them - through deterrence. Weapons stockpiled on each side invited an immense retaliation if attacked. This meant that if a war broke out between them, it would result in severe destruction to life and property on both sides. This would be very much so whosoever emerged as the winner. In any event, the two superpowers' allies would also take part in any war between them. Through numerous defence treaties, the allegiance of the allied countries to the superpowers called for such participation. Such defence treaties included the Warsaw Pact and the North Atlantic Treaty.

It is true that there were no wars directly between the two superpowers. However, they fought for their beliefs by supporting third parties at war. This happened at the times of the well-known Berlin blockade (1948-1949), the Korean War (1950-53), the Hungary Revolt (1956), Suez Crisis (1956), and the Vietnam War (1959-75). It also happened during the Cuban missile crisis (1962), the Six-Day-War in Middle East (1967), the Soviet invasion of Czechoslovakia (1968), the Yom Kippur War (1973), and the Soviet invasion of Afghanistan (1979-89). Every time tensions rose between the two superpowers, each party tried hard to prevent a direct war between them. They did so primarily because of the assured mutual destruction. This strategy of deterrence no doubt helped them avoid direct confrontations with each other for several decades, although the tension between them continued to grow.

Detente. In order to reduce the growing tension between them, the two superpowers adopted a strategy of detente in the early 1970s. This strategy required the de-escalation of tensions between hostile nations, through diplomacy and confidence-building measures. The United States put this strategy to use first by lifting its trade embargo on China. It had been in place since the beginning of the Korean War in 1950. However, the prospect of a new, friendly relationship between the United States and China were of great concern for the Soviets. By then, the Soviets had severed their relationship with China due to numerous conflicts that had arisen between them. China had become a nuclear power with its own successes in the development of the atomic and hydrogen bombs in 1964 and 1967, respectively. In response to the new situation, the Soviets themselves started to embrace detente as a means of achieving global security.

By the late sixties, it had also become strategically important for the US to build a friendly relationship with China. This was to counter the growing strength of the Soviets around the globe. Many incidents that occurred in the sixties had clearly demonstrated the rising power of the Soviets. The Soviet Union's direct involvement in the Cuban missiles crisis of 1962 was one such occurrence. The capture of the US Navy intelligence research ship, USS Pueblo, by North Korea, a Soviet ally, in 1968 was another. The crushing defeat of the 1968 anti-communist rebellion in Czechoslovakia at the hands of the Soviet troops was yet another.

In this situation, the United States may have tried to use the policy of divide-and-conquer to its advantage. Some reviewers believe that US President Richard Nixon and Secretary of State Henry A. Kissinger exploited the Sino-Soviet rift at the time. They had done so through a "triangular diplomacy," playing off the two most powerful communist states of China and the Soviet Union against one another. On their part, the Soviets certainly feared a potentially strong Sino-American alliance playing against them. At this time, both the Soviet Union and the United States were feeling the excessive economic burden of their ongoing arms race. Furthermore, the Soviet Union also wanted to adopt detente in order to increase Soviet trade with Western European countries and thus weaken the US dominance.

Even before the detente-era began, the leaders of the two superpowers had engaged in summit discussions. These discussions had helped them ratify a number of important treaties. These treaties included the Partial Test Ban Treaty (1963), the Outer Space Treaty (1967), and the Nuclear Non-Proliferation Treaty (1968). Many saw these treaties as the building blocks of detente. Critics, however, point out that the main purpose of these treaties was to limit the nuclear ambitions of third parties, instead of curbing the growing combat capabilities of the two superpowers.

Two other factors also may have influenced the United States to adopt the strategy of detente. First, the NAM member-countries increasingly used the UN as a forum to voice their concerns. The biggest concerns they had were the growing tension between the two superpowers and nuclear proliferation. From the early sixties, at world forums, NAM member-countries had brought up for discussion the issue of nuclear disarmament. Eventually these countries became the major force that propagated the 1968 NPT. The number of countries that have now signed this strategically important treaty stands at 189. They include all five permanent members of the UN Security Council, which possess nuclear weapons. Second, from about the mid-sixties, West Germany started to pursue its own form of detente (*Ostpolitik*). It was an attempt to resolve the differences it had with its neighbours. Their neighbours included East Germany, Poland, and the Soviet Union. This attempt helped West Germany normalize its relationship with East Germany. In addition, within a few years, West Germany could enter into bilateral treaties with Poland and the Soviet Union.

Meanwhile, during the detente period, the leaders of the two superpowers had held a series of special summits. The discussions at these summits led to a number of treaties between them. These treaties had two main purposes. One was to limit the production and possession of WMD. The other purpose was to reduce the adversary nature of their existing relationship. These treaties included the following:

- The Anti-Ballistic Missile Treaty of 1972;
- The Strategic Arms Limitation Treaties of 1972 and 1979;
- The Prevention of Nuclear War Agreement of 1973;
- The Intermediate-Range Nuclear Forces Treaty of 1987;
- The Strategic Arms Reduction Treaty 1 of 1991;
- The Mutual Detargeting Treaty of 1994;
- The Comprehensive Test Ban Treaty of 1996;
- The Strategic Arms Reduction Treaty 11 of 2000; and
- The Strategic Offensive Reductions Treaty of 2002.

The Strategic Arms Limitation Treaty of 1972, in particular, called for the peaceful existence of the two superpowers and the avoidance of military confrontations between them. It also required either party not to promote any claims of international spheres of influence. The Prevention of Nuclear War Agreement of 1973 committed the two superpowers to consult with each other during conditions of nuclear confrontation. The Mutual Detargeting Treaty of 1994 required that their missiles no longer automatically target each other and that the two powers no longer operate in a manner treating each other as adversaries. Then, in December 1989, the Soviet leader Mikhail Gorbachev and US President George Bush Sr. jointly declared that a long-lasting peaceful era had begun. They did so at a summit they held in Malta. On this occasion, Gorbachev also announced, "The world is leaving one epoch and entering another. We are at the beginning of a long road to a lasting, peaceful era. The threat of force, mistrust, psychological and ideological struggle should all be things of the past." (Kirshon 2009b, para. 1)

Paradoxically, the latter part of this detente period also became one of loosing prestige and hegemonic power for both the superpowers, more so for the Soviets. The downturn of the dominating power of the Soviet Union started with political reform movements within its own bloc. These movements started in Poland in 1980 with the founding of an anti-totalitarianism trade union under the name 'Solidarity.' It forced the ruling Polish government to recognize it. It did this by staging a series of strikes that soon gathered global attention. In response, the Polish government, under pressure from the Soviet Union, declared martial law, banned the Solidarity movement, and arrested its leaders. This did not scare away reformers in other countries within the Soviet bloc. With Mikhail Gorbachev's assumption of power in the Soviet Union in 1985, however, there came a change in the Soviet attitude towards the reformers within the bloc. This led to a new policy of seeking non-military ways to gain support for communist rule.

The year 1989 was particularly eventful in political reforms within the Soviet bloc. In Hungary, the Communist government instituted multi-party general elections. In Poland, the discussions held between the Communist government and the Solidarity movement, which had resurfaced, led to multi-party general elections. The Solidarity group later formed the first non-communist government since 1948 within the Soviet bloc. The reformers of East Germany replaced its government's leader, Erich Honecker, and opened their border with West Germany. Symbolically, they felled the infamous Berlin Wall. Soon after that, Czechoslovakia, Romania, Bulgaria, and Albania all became independent. Romania was the only country where the incumbent communist regime lost power through a rebellion. The reformers executed the country's communist leader Nicolae Ceausescu and his wife Elena during the rebellion.

Because of the political reforms in these countries, and what followed, the Warsaw Pact virtually ended by July 1991. The Soviet Union ended a few months later. In time, a number of new independent countries within the former Warsaw Pact group joined the NATO organization. By 2008, Russia and Bulgaria were the only former Warsaw Pact countries that had not obtained NATO membership. By the same time, three of the former Soviet Union Republics, the Czech Republic, Hungary, and Poland, also had joined the NATO organization.

The events that led to the loss of the global power and prestige of the United States largely occurred in the seventies. These events included the capture of the USS Pueblo by the North Koreans (1968), the Marxist revolution in Ethiopia that ousted the pro-western monarch Haile Selassie (1974), the Maoist Khmer Rouge Revolution in Cambodia (1975), and the Vietnam War that ended with a humiliating defeat for American troops (1975). The installation of a communist regime in Afghanistan (1978), the Iranian revolution, overthrowing the Shah of Iran (1979), the 444-day long hostage crisis in Teheran (1979), and the overthrow of the US backed Somoza rule in Nicaragua are four other such events. In the 444-day hostage crisis, Iranian militants stormed the American Embassy in Teheran and kept seventy Americans captive. All these events, spread across the globe, must have made even the American people believe that their country was gradually losing its power and prestige on the world stage. Nevertheless, these events certainly did not tarnish the United States' image as a superpower. The US, in fact, later managed to recover its lost glory and emerge as the only superpower in the world by the end of 1991, due to two main reasons. One of the reasons was the continued downfall of the Soviet Union's hegemonic power. The other was the anti-detente approach to global conflicts pursued by US President Ronald Reagan, who came to power in 1981.

ANOTHER MAJOR SHIFT IN THE EARLY NINETIES

The disintegration of the Soviet Union brought about another major shift in world dynamics in the early nineties. By this time, the memberships of both the NATO and the UN had risen to new heights. Russia had taken control of all the nuclear and other types of WMD, which had originally belonged to the Soviet Union; they still matched in number those under US control. Russia, however, no longer had far-reaching hegemonic power. The number of nuclear weapons states had increased to nine, and not all the nine were NATO members. Politically, the former Soviet bloc countries, including Russia, had begun to move away from communist totalitarian policies. China also had begun to act the same way; the first major anti-communist showdown in China took place in Beijing's Tiananmen Square in June 1989. The NAM organization now had only one superpower to deal with.

Many thought that the new, unipolar world system, with the world's mightiest liberal democracy (the United States) at its helm, would lead to a more peaceful world. The dynamics of the new, unipolar world order, however, have failed to testify to that. Instead, two decades of the unipolar era have made global peace more elusive than ever before. The specific concerns in this regard are primarily three-fold. First, all the old major conflicts continue with no apparent permanent solution on the horizon. Second, too many new violent conflicts have arisen since the Cold War, some with possible global impact. Third, the potential for further nuclear proliferation has become much more evident. At the same time, the world is witnessing a downturn in the US' supremacy and the emergence of some new global powers. Let us further examine these concerns and new developments.

Continuation of old conflicts. Many old conflicts, some inter-state and others intrastate continue in various parts of the world. The inter-state conflicts of most concern are those between Israelis and Palestinians, Israel and Iran, India and Pakistan, and between North Korea and its neighbouring adversaries. They have not only continued, but have also become increasingly difficult to solve. Out of all these continuing inter-state conflicts, the one between Israelis and Palestinians especially stands out in this regard. There are three main reasons for this. First, the Israeli government is reluctant to end its housing construction on occupied land and to accept the two-state solution to the conflict, which is supported by the world community. Second, the attempts of the PNA's President Mahmoud Abbas to consolidate his power in both the Gaza Strip and the West Bank, by decree, cannot be a move popular among Palestinians. This is especially so, considering the clear victory of Hamas over Fatah at the 2006 PNA general election. Third, there is outside involvement on both sides to the conflict. For example, in the recent violent confrontations between Israel and Hamas, the United States and its western allies put their weight solidly behind Israel. At that time, Iran put its weight behind Hamas. If a major decisive moment comes in a violent confrontation between Hamas and Israel, there is no guarantee that the other Muslim nations in the region are going to look away. It is unlikely that any amount of material or financial support given to the Fatah-led Palestine government by the United States and its allies could negate the profound animosity and hatred between Hebrews and Muslims in the region, and the world. Testifying to this are Iran's repeated threats to target Israel if the United States or any other country attacks Iran. In this situation, it is too dreadful to imagine what could happen at a major decisive moment in a future major violent confrontation between Israelis and Palestinians, especially if Iran too has developed nuclear weapons by then. It is possible that such an eventuality could engulf the entire Middle East in fire and trigger a new world war.

The continuing intrastate conflicts are many in number. Some of them, in fact, are deadlier than many inter-state conflicts. Somalia provides a good example in this regard, with more than 300,000 deaths due to its internal conflicts since the mid-eighties. There are other continuing intrastate conflicts with less human destruction. Such conflicts include the Kayin State conflict between Kayin and Myanmar (1948), the Basque Fatherland and Liberty separatist crisis in Spain (1959), the Colombian civil war (1964), and the communist and Islamic insurgency in Philippines (1969). The Kurdish militants' revolt in Turkey (1984), the Second Civil War in Uganda (1987), and the Kashmir and Jammu insurgency in India (1989) are a few other long-standing conflicts.

There is also a new twist in the power dynamics among the parties involved in many conflicts since the Cold War. The dissolution of the Soviet Union was a huge blow, especially for Arab countries that were hostile to the United States and the West. It clearly took away from them a superpower-friend and ally that could counter the power of the United States and its allies. It also reduced, if not stopped forever, a major source of economic and military aid to these states. This, however, had opposite results for countries in the region that enjoyed close ties with the United States and its friends. Israel, in particular, benefits most among such countries for two main reasons. One reason is the loss of the traditional Soviet support for its adversaries. The other reason is the continued support it can rely on from the United States and its allies. This new situation puts Israel in an especially advantageous position in the Middle East region. Many believe that this, in turn, poses a significant threat to the peace and stability of the Arabs, and in particular the Palestinians, living in the region.

New conflicts. The number of new violent conflicts that emerged after the Cold War is staggering. They spread across many regions of the world. The most notable among them include the following:

- Nagaland ethnic conflict in India (1993);
- Ogaden insurgency in Ethiopia (1995);
- Naxalite-Maoist insurgency in the East Central part of India (1996);
- Kivu conflict in the Democratic Republic of the Congo (started in 1997);
- Al-Aqsa (Second) Intifada crisis in Israel (2000);
- Second Chechen War between Russia and Ichkeria (2000);
- WOT in Afghanistan (2001);
- Maghreb insurgency in Algeria, Mauritania, and Morocco (2002);
- WOT in Iraq (2003);
- War in North-western Pakistan (2004);
- Baluchistan conflict with Pakistan (2004);
- South Thailand insurgency in Thailand (2004);
- Niger Delta conflict in Nigeria (2004);
- Fourth Civil War in Chad (2005); and
- Second Tuareg Rebellion in Mali and Niger (2007).

This list includes both inter-state and intrastate conflicts. The cumulative fatalities of some of them are quite high. For example, one report ("List of wars" 2008) suggests that the estimated number of fatalities of the Nagaland conflict up to the end of 2008 was 43,000. The corresponding number for the Chechen War was 90,000. The same report shows that the Kivu conflict in the Democratic Republic of the Congo (1998) and the war in Iraq (2003) have been the deadliest of the new conflicts. Their fatalities have been discussed earlier.

Nuclear proliferation. At least two countries, Pakistan and North Korea, have tested nuclear weapons since the Cold War ended. Pakistan tested its nuclear weapons in 1998. North Korea followed suit in 2006. These nuclear tests clearly testify to the continuation of nuclear proliferation under the current unipolar world order. Pakistan and North Korea, like all the other countries before them, covertly engaged in the development of nuclear weapons for years. Then, they surprised the world with the testing of their weapons in the open. The United States is the country that first surprised the world with the use of such weapons in the mid-forties. This was at the end of WWII. Today many countries, including the United States, suspect Iran of having a secret plan for the development of nuclear weapons. There is also suspicion that several other countries want to follow suit. At the same time, the NATO nuclear weapons sharing arrangement remains intact. This is in spite of the continued objection by the NAM member-countries to such nuclear weapons sharing arrangements. The only post-Cold War change to this NATO arrangement is the withdrawal of Greece in 2001.

In any event, further nuclear proliferation appears unavoidable. There are three main reasons for this. First, possessing nuclear weapons has become a proven strategy for strengthened, if not guaranteed, security for individual states. The significant change in the US attitude towards North Korea, soon after it declared its nuclear capability and its intent to strike its enemies, is a case in point. North Korea did threaten to attack Japan and the American installations and troops in South Korea. General Mirza Aslam Beg, former Chief of Army of Pakistan, explains, "The non-proliferation regime therefore is fast receding into the background. USA, by its display of force for eventual attack on Iraq – a non-nuclear nation – is promoting the idea that the only way to deter aggression is to acquire nuclear weapons and North Korea's example is becoming precedence – a kind of safety device. Nations, who did not nourish any such idea to make nuclear weapons, may now be thinking otherwise, and those in the process of acquiring these WMD may well expedite it earlier than expected." (Beg, n.d., para. 10)

Second, the intent of the ongoing international efforts to stop nuclear proliferation is questionable. The primary reason for this is the absence of a serious rationale explaining why the countries already possessing nuclear weapons should continue to have them. The fact that all the countries that now possess nuclear weapons developed them secretly only makes it more difficult for a non-nuclear weapons country to understand why it should not follow suit.

Third, the newly emerging major powers (to be discussed later) are likely to develop and enhance their nuclear arsenals to match those of the current nuclear giants: the United States and Russia. Out of the emerging major global powers, India and China are already nuclear weapons states. The other emerging global power, Brazil, is not a nuclear weapons state. However, it has been using nuclear energy for peaceful purposes for decades now. According to an August 12, 2008 Council on Hemispheric Affairs report ("Brazil's nuclear ambitions"

2008), the ongoing nuclear energy programme of Brazil proposes to enrich uranium only to levels less than 5 percent. The enrichment levels required to build nuclear weapons are around 93 percent. The same report, however, adds, "It is still worth noting that it would be relatively easy for Brazilian technology to quickly increase enrichment to those levels" (para. 5). Thus, Brazil has the capability to develop nuclear weapons, if it chooses to do so. At the same time, unlike in the case of Iran, no one seems to be watching Brazil's nuclear programme under the microscope. Brazil continues to remain as a US ally in South America. Brazil, however, has openly argued in favour of Iran's nuclear programme for peaceful purposes; Brazil says that Iran has a right to pursue such a programme. It further says that Iran does not deserve any punishment because of Western suspicions that it wants to develop nuclear WMD. With its powerful economy and nuclear capability, Brazil could potentially challenge the balance of power in the Western Hemisphere in the near future.

Meanwhile, the development of nuclear weapons by any one country has the tendency to force others, especially its adversaries, to follow suit. This, in fact, is what has happened from the very beginning. For example, the Soviets developed their nuclear weapons capability after America did. Then, India's nuclear weapons capability came after China's, Pakistan's came after India's, and so on. At the same time, some of the countries that enjoyed military support from the former Soviet Union and are no longer getting that support from any other source also may consider possessing nuclear weapons of their own. This is most applicable to countries that appear to remain adversarial to the United States and its allies. North Korea, Iran, and Syria typically come under this category. Iraq was also in the same situation, until Saddam Hussein's regime ended. When such a country manages to secure nuclear weapons, it can lead to reciprocal action by other non-nuclear weapons countries. For example, the development of nuclear weapons by North Korea may have raised interest in following suit among its adversaries, such as Japan and South Korea. These two and other adversaries of North Korea, however, have been traditional allies of the United States. The United States, no doubt, will come to their help in case of an attack from North Korea. Nevertheless, in the face of the changing dynamics of the balance of power in the world, whether South Korea and Japan would solely depend on external support when responding to a potential nuclear attack from North Korea remains in doubt.

At the same time, any two adversarial countries becoming nuclear weapons states could lead to a nuclear arms race between them. Such nuclear arms races would be strategically similar to the one between the United States and the Soviet Union during the bipolar era. It was also the only nuclear arms race at the time. The future situation could be different with a number of nuclear arms races spread across the globe. For example, there could be new arms races between India and Pakistan, India and China, China and Taiwan, North Korea and South Korea, Iran and Israel, and so on. At the same time, some nuclear weapons states, other than the United States, could begin nuclear sharing programmes with their respective friendly non-nuclear weapons states, similar to the one the United States practises under the auspices of the NATO organization.

Dwindling US power. By the time the Cold War ended, the United States had the largest worldwide network of alliances and the power to reign supreme. In the years that followed, it was not hesitant to exhibit that power to the rest of the world. In the process, it always wanted to have the final say on world matters. The rest of the world appeared to have accepted this situation. At the advent of the Gulf War, US President George Bush Sr. had even said, "whatever we say goes" (Beg, n.d., para. 1). The United States could maintain this position for many years due to three main factors: strategic international military establishments, such as the NATO organization based in Europe; US troops stationed in other countries, including South Korea, Japan, and Saudi Arabia; and the Coalition Forces positioned in Afghanistan, Uzbekistan, and Tajikistan.

In time, however, the hegemonic influence of the United States and its ability to thrive as a superpower has become questionable. There appear five main reasons for this. First, the United States has failed in its role in bringing peaceful solutions to outstanding major disputes around the world. These disputes include the one between Israelis and Palestinians in the Middle East, wars in Somalia, the revolts of Islamic militant groups against the West, and the ongoing crises in Afghanistan and Pakistan. Second, the strategies adopted by the United States in preventing nuclear proliferation have miserably failed. Pakistan and

North Korea becoming new nuclear weapons states during the unipolar era is a case in point. Third, the United States faced strong criticism and condemnation from the world community for acting unilaterally in international matters. In such actions, it met with strong opposition and outright humiliation. The humiliation it suffered at the withdrawal of most of its allies from its Iraqi war, in particular, was devastating. Fourth, the United States also has come under criticism for aggressively promoting its own social and political systems and values in the rest of the world. The strongest criticism in this regard has come from the Muslim world and the communist giants, Russia and China. Fifth, the 2008 global financial and economic crash has particularly troubled the United States and its traditional allies in the European Union. Because of the dropping value of the US dollar and the rise of a number of new economic giants, even the traditional allies of the United States appear to be distancing themselves.

In this situation, the United States seems to have neither the dominating hegemonic power nor the economic credibility to act as a superpower as it did before. Despite all this, however, the United States has the second highest share of the world GDP, second only to the EU. At the same time, the US also has the highest share of the world's military spending. As a result, there appears to be no other country to match its ability to influence the world, at least for the time being.

New global powers in the making. One of the most noticeable developments in the unipolar world is the emergence of a number of developing countries as major global powers of economic potential and international influence. The Peoples' Republic of China, India, and Brazil are the most significant in this regard. In a 2008 list of countries by nominal Gross Domestic Product (GDP), these three countries appeared within the first twelve; the International Monetary Fund prepared this list. The remaining nine countries within the first 12 were Russia, Spain, and the G7 nations. The G7 nations are the United States, Japan, Germany, France, the United Kingdom, Italy, and Canada. In economics, the grouping acronym of BRIC refers to the fast-growing developing economies of Brazil, Russia, India, and China.

India and China, in particular, have shown remarkable economic growth over the recent years. Their 2008 estimated economic growth rates were 7.3percent and 9.8 percent, respectively. It is interesting to note that the corresponding growth rates for the European Union, United States, and Japan were at 1.5 percent, 1.4 percent, and 0.7 percent, respectively. Germany had the highest 2008 growth rate among the G7 nations. Many analysts believe that India and China will continue to do comparatively better over the coming years. A Centre for European Reform report (Centre for European Union, n. d.) explains, "On current trends, in 2020, the US, China and the EU will have a little under 20 per cent of global GDP, while India will have almost 10 per cent and Japan about 5 per cent" (p.23). Meanwhile, the 2008 estimated economic growth rate of Brazil is 5.2 percent. It is the largest economy in South America.

All three newly emerging global economies also have comparatively strong military and population strengths. China's active troops outnumber those of any other country, just as its population does. The strength of active troops in India, which has the second largest population, comes third, trailing behind China and the United States. Brazil's active troops are not comparable in number. However, it has the largest army among the South American countries. According to the list of countries by population, Brazil has the fifth largest population, after China, India, the United States, and Indonesia.

In summarizing the ground realities of the present world, the Brazilian President Luiz Inacio Lula da Silva once said, "In 2008, they (the BRICK countries) represented 15 per cent of the global economy and, what is much more important, almost 100 per cent of global growth" (Downie and Paulo, 2009, para.6). He said this in an interview he held with the *Daily Telegraph*. In the same interview, he also pointed out that the April 2009 G20 summit held in London was proof enough that the G7 alone is no longer in a position to make decisions on behalf of the world community. In this situation, he added, the economically dominant G7 nations no longer have the moral authority to solve the world's problems.

G20 is a group of developing countries established on August 20, 2003. Its core leadership consists of Brazil, India, China, and South Africa, more commonly referred to as the G4 Group. The purpose of the G20 organization is to counter the protectionist trade policies of the world's main trading partners. At the same time, the G4 countries want to use this forum to articulate their initiatives of trade liberalization. By 2009, the G20 group expanded to 23 member-countries. Argentina, Bolivia,

Brazil, Chile, Cuba, Ecuador, Egypt, Guatemala, India, Indonesia, Mexico, and Nigeria are twelve of them. Pakistan, Paraguay, Peru, Philippines, South Africa, Tanzania, Thailand, Uruguay, Venezuela, Zimbabwe, and Netherlands are the rest. A report on the G20 nations (Multilingual Archive, n. d.) suggests that together they represent 60 percent of the world's population, 70 percent of the farmers, and 26 percent of world's agricultural exports.

Twenty-seven sovereign states have come together to form the European Union (EU). These countries are primarily located in Europe and represent over 500 million citizens. As one economic entity, these 27 states rank highest in a nominal GDP list of countries. Two of its member-states, the United Kingdom and France, are nuclear weapons states. Both are also permanent members of the UN Security Council. The EU's share of the world's military spending is around 20 percent.

Meanwhile, Russia retains its status as an enormous military power. It has also recorded economic growth numbers higher than those of the G7 nations over the last several years. In 2008, the estimated economic growth rate of Russia was 6.0 percent. Russia's share of the world's landmass is approximately 11 percent. It is the largest country among the fast-growing economies. Going by these and other related factors, many believe that Russia could swing back to superpower status in the coming years. Some say that it has already started to do so.

Future Possibilities

The discussions above show that there is yet again a major shift in world dynamics in the making. Three new developments in the international scene primarily characterize this new shift. The failed attempts by the United States and Russia to recover their dwindling influence and economic power after the Cold War is one such development. The emergence of some developing countries as potential global powers and the unification of the powers of 27 sovereign states under the European Union are the other two.

These developments clearly point to a gradual transformation of the existing unipolar world order to one of multiple poles. Unlike in the case of the bipolar or unipolar world order, the emerging multi-polar system will not have any superpowers, as such – at least for the first few decades. Each of the multiple poles, however, will have the ability to influence the future global politics and balance of power. In all, there appear to be six poles in the emerging new world order. The United States, no doubt, will remain as one of them. Russia will be another. Brazil, India, and China will be three more poles in the new world order. The EU will be yet another. Only time could tell whether the US and Russia will regain their superpower status. Irrespective of that, one or more of the other mentioned poles also could emerge as new superpowers.

Russia and China, in particular, have worked together towards a multi-polar world order for some years now. In the process, they also have entered into a number of bilateral strategic agreements. The intent of the agreements was to work in partnership to promote the establishment of a new world order. The Sino-Russian Joint Statement of April 23, 1997 clearly testifies to this. According to a related report, this statement categorically noted, "The two sides shall, in the spirit of partnership, strive to promote the multipolarization of the world and the establishment of a new international order. ... All countries, big or small, strong or weak, rich or poor, are equal members of the international community. No country should seek hegemony, practice power politics or monopolize international affairs."(Stroupe 2006, paras. 6-8)

The same statement suggested that in another joint statement, dated December 10, 1999, the two parties proposed to do three specific things. Pushing forward the establishment of a multi-polar world based on the UN Charter and existing international laws in the 21st century was one of them. Strengthening the UN dominant status in international affairs and peaceful resolution of international disputes through political means were the other two. The statement also pointed out that the negative momentum in international relations had continued to grow. In explaining this, it listed what the two countries saw as the main defects of the existing unipolar system. There were six main defects in all. The forcing of the international community to accept a unipolar world pattern and a single model of culture, value concepts, and ideology was one of them. Weakening of the role of the UN and its Security Council, the seeking of excuses to amend the purposes and principles of the UN Charter, and the reinforcement and expansion of military blocks were three others. The replacement of international law with power politics and the acts of jeopardizing the sovereignty of independent states, using the concept of 'human rights are superior to sovereignty' and 'humanitarian intervention' were yet two other defects. The subsequent joint statements of the two countries clearly showed their irrevocable commitment to a new, multi-polar world order. For example, according to Joseph Stroupe (2006), in a special joint statement of July 1, 2005, the two countries reiterated their common stand to abide by the propositions to build a multi-polar world and a new international order, as enunciated in their April 23, 1997 statement. Meanwhile, some European leaders also called for a strong multi-polar world to counterbalance the United States' role as the sole superpower.

Among the six specific poles of the emerging new world order, there appear two distinct political systems. The United States (the currently surviving superpower), the EU, India, and Brazil have political systems based on liberal democratic values and principles. The political systems in Russia and China continue to be based on authoritarian values and principles. It is true that these two countries have transformed their communist economies to market economies. However, this has not resulted in the transition of their political systems to liberal democracy, despite worldwide expectations to the contrary.

Many of the countries other than the six major global powers appear to share the same two distinct political systems, one liberal democratic and the other authoritarian, one way or the other. At the same time, there also appears increasing interest among some Muslim countries to establish a completely different political system. It is a system based on Islamic principles. According to leading Islamic thinkers, the emphasis in this regard is primarily three-fold: enforcement of Sharia (Islamic) law; pan-Islamic political unity; and elimination of non-Muslim, military, economic, political, social, or cultural influences in the Muslim world. Sharia law is an integral part of Islam. The noted non-Muslim influences appear to compete with the Islamic way of life and values. Thus, the Islamic political system under consideration could be unique. Saudi Arabia, Iran, and Somalia are already practising Sharia law. Many believe that Indonesia is also doing the same, though only in some parts of the country. Iran and Saudi Arabia, in particular, are also economically and militarily strong countries.

The approach of any of the six major global powers (poles) to peace in the world could be anything between two ultimate modes of behaviour, one preferred and the other not preferred. In the 'preferred' ultimate mode, the major global power (pole) would first recognize, accept, and respect the existing socio-political diversity among states. Similarly, it would also recognize, accept, and respect the existing (regional or worldwide) international institutions. Then, it would try to work with the existing international institutions in resolving disputes among states, while promoting global peace at all times. In this approach, the major global power would not envisage the total embrace of its own social and political values and principles by all the other states in the world. Such a major global power would appear in the world scene more as a facilitator, a trouble-shooter or a go-getter - rather than a regulator or a global police officer. The special agreements between Russia and China for a new world order appear to see the wisdom of such an approach. In the 'not preferred' ultimate mode, the major global power would have less tolerance for socio-political diversity among states. At the same time, it would treat its own interests above that of international institutions. Such a major global power would engage in selling its own social and political values and principles to the rest of the world. In the process, such a global power would appear as a global police officer or a regulator. In the past, many countries have strongly criticized the United States for this kind of behaviour.

As for the ability of the six major powers to act globally, none of them appears to have this ability as of now. The United States and Russia remain as the strongest military powers on the planet. They still lack the economic credibility and hegemonic power to act globally. In the past, however, they both had repeatedly demonstrated their ability to act globally. The chances for these two powers to regain that ability in the coming years or decades are real. At the same time, the chances for the other concerned major powers (China, India, the EU, and Brazil) to follow suit are also equally real.

The relationships of the six major powers among themselves and with others could become a critical factor in shaping the emerging new world order. The rivalry between the United States and Russia (former Soviet Union), in particular, has not ended with the end of the Cold War. Their relationship, in fact, appears to have worsened since. There are three main reasons for this. First, the Russian "regional interference" for the control of the oil and gas resources of the Central Asian and Caspian Regions and in the former Soviet Republics has particularly angered the Americans. Second, the US plans to install Missile Defence Systems in Poland and Czech Republic have equally angered the Russians. In response to such US defence plans, Russia, in fact, has stepped up missile development with regular flights of strategic bombers. For this, it had to abandon the implementation of the Conventional Forces in Europe Treaty. The third reason is the 2008 Russian war in Georgia.

Meanwhile, the United States has continued to pursue a policy of economic engagement with China for some years now. It is safe to assume that the US will continue with this policy. Before the 2009 presidential election, Barack Obama and his colleagues had specifically expressed their desire to do so. For example, the Obama administration's Secretary of State Hillary Clinton then said, "Our relationship with China will be the most important relationship in the world in this century" (Reid, 2009, para. 4). At the same time, the US relationships with the EU, India, and Brazil have always remained cordial and friendly. The 2007 US-India nuclear agreement, in particular, is a clear testimony for the US' desire to continue to work with India on matters of common interest. The leading nations of the European Union have always been the closest allies of the United States. Brazil too has been an ally of the United States for many years. As well, the closeness of the current relationship between Russia and China is evident from the special agreements they have entered into for ending the current unipolar world order.

The relationship between China and India is, however, uniquely different. They have locked themselves in a border dispute for decades. The 1962 war between them was a flare up of this dispute. Then, the special assistance given to Pakistan in its nuclear weapons and missile programmes by China has made its already strained relationship with India worse. On top of all this, India is now claiming that China is seeking to surround India with naval facilities at strategic locations in the Indian Ocean. These sites include Sitter (Myanmar), Hambantota (Sri Lanka), and Gwadar (Pakistan). At the same time, China is concerned that India has implemented a 'Look East policy' and has become closer to a number of other countries in the East Asia region.

Among the relationships of the six major powers with others, the ones with the countries suspected of having secret nuclear weapons programmes could be of special interest. Such countries include Iran, Libya, Algeria, South Korea, and Taiwan. Iran, in particular, is not likely to collaborate with the United States or the EU, at least not in the near future. The main reason for this is the strong bond the United States and the Western countries continue to have with Israel. At the same time, Iran is not likely to enjoy a friendly working relationship with India on global matters. This would be especially so in areas where India strategically differs from its archenemy Pakistan. The standing of Iran with Russia and China could be different. This is due to the historic ties Iran has had with them. It is difficult to say whether the newly liberated Libya will have the same interests in developing nuclear weapons as the overthrown Gaddafi regime. In any event, Libya and Algeria also are likely to have closest relationships with Russia and China among the six global powers. There appear three main reasons for this: closer political systems, closer geographic locations, and past and present special ties through bilateral and international agreements. Then, both South Korea and Taiwan are likely to continue with their strong ties with the United States and the EU.

The relationships of the six global powers with the Muslim world in general are also of special interest. Muslim countries in general have closer ties with Russia and China than with the United States, the EU, or any other global power. There are three main reasons for this. First, the common resolve of Russia and China for a multi-polar system is not based on a vision of a single model of culture, value concepts, and ideology. Theirs is more receptive to the peaceful co-existence of different cultures. Second, the United States and the EU countries were, and still are, not favourite countries of the Muslim world in general. In contrast, Russia and China appear to enjoy much closer, friendlier relationships with many Muslim countries. The special invitation to Russian President Vladimir Putin to speak at the Organization of the Islamic Conference of October 2003 is a clear testimony to the closeness of Russia, in particular, to the Muslim world. This conference was a gathering of 57 Muslim states. President Putin, in fact, was the first head of a non-Muslim majority state to speak at this organization. The timing of the invitation was also particularly significant; Russia was waging a long-running war in Chechnya at the time. Third, Russia and China have worked in collaboration with many Muslim countries in a number of strategic areas. They did this even after the end of the bipolar era. The nature and extent of this collaboration in the areas of defence and nuclear energy programmes appears particularly significant. For example, China allegedly transferred equipment and technology to the nuclear weapons and ballistic missile programmes of Pakistan. China is also the largest defence supplier for Pakistan. At the same time, some believe that Pakistani scientists are now behind the secret nuclear weapons programmes in other Muslim countries, especially Iran and Libya. North Korea, which enjoys friendly relations with China, is also allegedly assisting Iran in its nuclear programmes. As well, Russia signed a special civil nuclear cooperation agreement with Libya in 2008. Under the agreement, Russia is helping Libya in the design and construction of nuclear reactors. Russia is also helping Libya in the supply of nuclear fuel. Russia has a similar civil nuclear cooperation agreement with Iran as well. These two countries have a common interest in limiting the political influence of the United States in Central Asia. Meanwhile, Algeria has had its traditional ties with both the former Soviet Union and China. These ties in the area of military supplies are especially significant. Today, Algeria is the primary leading military power in North Africa.

All the above points to the possibility that the emerging multi-polar world order would strengthen over the years. It would be a world order dominated by six major powers: the US, the EU, Russia, China, India, and Brazil. None of them would have the level of hegemonic power or the economic credibility to act as a superpower, at least for the time being. In time, however, it is possible that one or more of them could eventually gain superpower status. This, however, would take at least a few decades from now. In the interim, the world would witness the consolidation and further deepening of the emerging multi-polar world order in the years ahead.

Ironically, the major changes to world dynamics and the state of the world order since WWII (1945 to date) appear quite similar to those that occurred in Europe during the period from 1815 to 1945. Both periods in question started with a bipolar era. Great Britain and the Austrian Empire dominated the former bipolar era (1815-59), while the United States and the Soviet Union dominated the latter (1945-89). In both situations, the competing superpowers had two distinct political systems. Then, in both cases, a unipolar system replaced the bipolar order. This happened in each case after one of the competing superpowers lost its hegemonic power. Special occurrences during the unipolar eras that followed in the two periods also look incredibly similar. For example, in both cases, the party that lost superpower status moved from its traditional authoritarian rule towards democracy. At the same time, a new type of union of states emerged in Europe: a unified Germany in the earlier case and the European Union in the recent one. Then, in both cases, a multi-polar world order emerged at the end.

The above shows a historic pattern in the changing world dynamics. If this pattern is anything to go by, the presently emerging multi-polar world order could only end up in an era of mass murder and genocide. This, in fact, was what happened in the earlier case. The multi-polar world order at the time deepened the tensions among the powerful nations of the day and set the world stage for two world wars: WWI and WWII.

At the same time, the world today is by no means short of violent conflicts that could trigger a new world war. Chapters 2 and 3 showed how the conflicts between Israel and Palestine, India and Pakistan, North Korea and its adversaries, and between Islamists and the West are set to do the trick this time around, given the right conditions. It is more than likely that once any of these conflicts, or any other for that matter, triggers a global war, the world will end up in a nuclear holocaust. The dire consequences of such an end are beyond anybody's power of comprehension. Right now, the world appears to be at the mercy of the power-balancing game of the present major global players; one single step by any one of them in the wrong direction could trigger this global nuclear catastrophe. This is a very dangerous situation, especially considering the amount of nuclear weapons already spread around the globe.

In the interim, nuclear proliferation is likely to continue, maybe even faster than ever before. In the process, a number of countries who are suspected of covertly developing nuclear weapons could become nuclear weapons states. If Iran becomes one of these new nuclear weapons states, it would create a number of new fault lines in the geopolitical landscape of the already volatile Middle East, and the world. This clearly calls for an early, if not immediate, resolution of the present major crises in the Middle East in particular. In the absence of early resolutions to these conflicts, especially the one between Israelis and Palestinians, the chances of resolving them would become much more difficult and complex with further consolidation of the new world order. Then, the chances for nuclear weapons coming under the command of unauthorized sources also remain high. At the same time, the NATO nuclear weapons sharing programme, which has provided US nuclear weapons for seven 'non-nuclear weapons states,' is likely to stay or even grow further. This could lead to counter nuclear-weapons-sharing-programmes initiated by some of the major powers not involved with NATO, such as China and Russia. Such a move would result in more stockpiles of nuclear weapons spread across the globe in an unprecedented manner.

What is clear from all the above is that the world is slowly but surely getting closer to a global nuclear catastrophe. Any of the existing major violent conflicts could trigger it at an opportune time. In this situation, no one in his or her right mind could give a guarantee that none of the ongoing violent conflicts in the world would deteriorate into a worldwide fiasco. This completes the answer to the second critical question asked at the end of the introductory chapter, namely: *is there any guarantee that none of the ongoing violent conflicts will deteriorate into a worldwide fiasco?* Having so completed the answer to the second critical question, now it is time to look at the third critical question asked at the end of the same chapter: *if there is no such guarantee, what needs to be done to prevent such an eventuality,* meaning a worldwide nuclear fiasco? The next chapter will attempt to answer it.

Chapter 6:
Avoid the Looming Danger

THE PREVIOUS CHAPTERS SHOWED the extent of existing threats to world peace, culminating in a looming global nuclear catastrophe. A number of these chapters also showed the dire capability of some of the existing conflicts to trigger it. Of course, even a completely new conflict could do the same. If somehow materialized, this global fiasco could literally incinerate the major cities of the world and destroy the planet's ecological base. This, in turn, could have devastating effect on humans as well as other species living on the planet. The annihilation of all forms of life on our planet is an awful possibility. The decimation of the human population, taking us back to our Stone Age, is an assured consequence.

There are many talks, seminars, weapons reduction programmes, bilateral and multinational agreements, UN resolutions, and much more that aim at the existing threats to peace. However, the situation is only getting worse by the year. This shows that if we continue to depend on the status quo, we may not avoid the unthinkable. It is time to think creatively to find a way to prevent the possible outbreak of the looming global catastrophe before it becomes too late. This is what this chapter will do.

There are two main areas where action is necessary to prevent the outbreak of the impending catastrophe. First, the global tension should not be allowed to build up to a tipping point. Second, the existing global checks and balances, kept through the UN to protect the world from wars, need to be made stronger and more effective.

To prevent any further increase in global tension, the human activities that have been building up global tension to the present level must end. These activities are primarily four-fold: unilateral global policing by powerful nations, the US-led War on Terror, nuclear proliferation, and the continued dependence on the outdated 'an eye for an eye' approach to conflict resolution. The unilateral global policing and the US-led WOT should end forthwith. Nuclear proliferation too must end, along with total destruction of existing stockpiles of nuclear weapons. Further, the archaic 'an eye for an eye' approach to conflict resolution should be a thing of the past. Those who are attempting to resolve ongoing conflicts should start afresh by adopting non-violent means of reaching their goal. At the same time, the United Nations Organization needs to be reformed or replaced to make the existing global checks and balances stronger and more effective. What follows is a detailed discussion of these specific measures under the following five headings:

- End unilateral global policing.
- End the War on Terror.
- Destroy all weapons of mass destruction.
- Adopt non-violent means of conflict resolution.
- Reform or replace the United Nations Organization.

These measures constitute a five-fold course of action that could prevent the outbreak of the threatening global nuclear catastrophe.

END UNILATERAL GLOBAL POLICING

Unilateral global policing by any major power clearly shows its blatant contempt for the international community. Such global policing panics the world, disorients the prevailing world order, and raises global tension instantly. Unilateral global policing also claims lives. Past incidents of such policing have created a dangerous precedent. The 2003 Iraqi war waged by the United States, the mightiest power in the world, is a classic example in this regard. The 2008 Georgian war launched by Russia provides another case in point. As Chapter 4 explained, neither the

United States nor Russia ever received UN authorization to wage these wars.

The validity of both these wars clearly remains questionable. At the end of the Iraqi war, US President George Bush Jr. made the ludicrous statement that an intelligence failure caused this war. In the 2008 Georgian war, Russia launched a large-scale ground-and-air-based military attack against Georgia. It did this to support the forces of the separatist movements in South Ossetia and Abkhazia. After defeating the Georgian forces, Russia officially recognized the groups separated from Georgia. Russia's actions received the condemnation of the international community. The United States, the UK, France, Poland, Sweden, and the Baltic States were among the countries that protested against Russia's open aggression. US President George Bush Jr. warned Russia, "Bullying and intimidation are not acceptable ways to conduct foreign policy in the 21st century" (Gerstenzang 2008, para. 1). It is certainly a meaningful statement from a US President who had used the same unacceptable practices in conducting US foreign policy. The infamous Iraqi war was just one such instance.

Both the Iraqi and Georgian wars occurred since the world moved away from a bipolar era to one dominated by a single superpower. The surviving superpower, the US, initiated one of the wars. The country that ended the bipolar era by losing its superpower status, Russia (USSR), initiated the other. This former superpower still enjoys the same military capabilities as before, although it has lost its hegemonic power. Such wars of unilateral global policing could occur in a multi-polar world as well. For example, the 1950 invasion of Tibet by China, the 1971 invasion of East Pakistan by India, and the 1979 invasion of Afghanistan by the Soviet Union all took place during the bipolar era. Such wars initiated by a major power in a multi-polar system could generally end up in more violence and destruction than in a unipolar system. This could happen, especially if one or more of the remaining major powers in the multi-polar system resort to military means to stop such a war.

The act of waging a war against a sovereign nation by another, whether a major power or not, is a blatant violation of international laws. It is the moral duty of every nation, no matter how powerful, to work within the framework of these laws. In particular, the most influential countries must play an exemplary role in ensuring that these laws are upheld and complied with. It is unconscionable for major powers to force their policies and wishes onto the less powerful by any means.

END THE WAR ON TERROR

US President George Bush Jr., who launched the WOT in September 2001, wanted it to continue, "Until every terrorist group of global reach has been found, stopped and defeated" ("War on words" 2009, para. 6). President Barack Obama, who took over from him in January 2009, took steps to shift direction in some aspects of the war. For example, he gave orders to close down Guantanamo Bay and the CIA's secret prisons run by the previous administration. He also gave orders to end harsh interrogating practices. He did not even like the term 'War on Terror.' In its place, his administration started to use the term 'overseas contingency operations.' These and other changes managed to create an impression in the minds of many people that President Obama ended the WOT. In reality, however, this has not happened. The United States' continuing expenditure on WOT operations testifies to this. For example, a US Congressional Research Services report, prepared by Amy Belasco (Belasco 2011), suggests that the United States' estimated funding for WOT operations has remained at more than 100 billion dollars annually since 2009. The request for 2012 is staggering: 131.7 billion dollars. Many thought that the capture and killing of al-Qaeda leader Osama bin Laden by US forces in 2011 offered an opportunity for President Obama to end the WOT. Even some American experts shared this view. However, the Obama administration chose to take advantage of Bin Laden's death to further strengthen its resolve to continue with the WOT. As an example of numerous statements testifying to this resolve, US Secretary of State Hillary Clinton expressed her view, "Even as we mark this milestone [Bin Laden's death], we should not forget that the battle to stop al-Qaeda and its syndicate of terror will not end with the death of Bin Laden. Indeed, we must make this opportunity to renew our resolve and redouble our efforts" (Engelhardt 2011, para 10). This shows that the WOT has become a way of life for the United States.

However, what the US should do is voluntarily withdraw from the WOT, rather than extending it further. There is a multitude of reasons for this. Most importantly, the WOT is illegal. According to the United

States' own legal definition of terrorism, the WOT is not a war on terror or terrorism. The US legal definition of terrorism only refers to violence and intimidation used to coerce a government or community *by a sub-state group*. This implies that the target of a US war on terror should be a sub-state group. This was certainly not the case. Instead, the United States started its WOT in 2001 by invading a sovereign foreign state, Afghanistan. Then, under the same pretext, the United States invaded another sovereign foreign state, Iraq, in 2003. It is also against international law for any country to invade other sovereign states. Thus, it is clear that the United States has blatantly violated both national and international laws in initiating and pursuing its WOT.

The War on Terror is also senseless. People wage wars against enemies. However, terror or terrorism itself is not an enemy; it is only a tactic used by an enemy, and is a violent symptom of underlying animosity and hatred. Waging a war against terrorism to end terrorism is similar to an attempt to cure a severe throat infection by taking an aspirin to alleviate the fever that the infection has caused. The aspirin may get rid of the fever. However, this would only be for a few hours. Repeating aspirin doses every few hours may help keep the fever down for an extended period. Unfortunately, during that time, the throat infection that caused the fever would worsen by the hour, perhaps to an incurable state. Such band-aid approaches only cover up the symptoms of problems and do not mitigate the underlying issues. In this example, instead of aspirin doses to fight the fever, what is required is a cure for the throat infection. The cure could be an antibiotic. If the throat infection were cured, the fever would disappear for good. In the same manner, one could control terrorism effectively, not by waging a war against terrorism, but by finding a meaningful resolution to its underlying cause.

In investigating the root cause of terrorism, there are two critical questions to answer. First, who is carrying out these acts of terrorism? Second, why is that party committing such acts? After the 9/11 terrorist attacks, the US government apparently did ask itself these questions, searching for answers. Immediately after the disastrous event, President George Bush Jr. singled out Osama bin Laden and his al-Qaeda movement based in Afghanistan as the party responsible for these attacks. Then, in one of his policy statements on the WOT, he said, "Today's war on terror is like the Cold War. It is an ideological struggle with an enemy that despises freedom and pursues totalitarian aims.... I vowed then that I would use all assets of our power of Shock and Awe to win the war on terror. And so I said we were going to stay on the offence two ways: one, hunt down the enemy and bring them to justice, and take threats seriously; and two, spread freedom." ("War on Terrorism", n.d., para. 17)

The United States, in fact, did ask itself the two critical questions in investigating the 9/11 incidents. It determined answers to both of them. Then, it concluded that Osama bin Laden and his al-Qaeda movement were the perpetrators of the attacks. And the reason for the attacks was the deeply divided difference between the ideological beliefs of the two parties. To address the root cause of the attacks, the United States could have involved all relevant parties in a peaceful, non-violent process. Instead, it chose to start a global war on terror. It started this war by sending its mighty forces, the mightiest in the world, to Afghanistan, to hunt down Bin Laden and his al-Qaeda movement on their own soil. As demonstrated in our aspirin example, the US-led WOT will fail to address the real issue at the root of the concerned acts of terror. As a result, the WOT will not bring a lasting solution to the ongoing acts of terror. This also means that the WOT, launched by the United States and supported by its allies, will continue until they themselves end it voluntarily.

The dismal futility of the War on Terror is easily seen. After ten long years, the US did manage to capture and kill the al-Qaeda leader Osama bin Laden, but his surviving followers remain a major threat to peace and security, especially in the West. During these ten years of war, the WOT helped forcibly replace the Taliban government that had sponsored and harboured the al-Qaeda movement with one friendly to the US and its allies. The new government, however, is failing to end the violent opposition it faces from the deposed Taliban forces. This is very surprising, considering all the help the new government is getting from the US-led NATO forces stationed in the country. Today, the people of Afghanistan witness more violent activities in their country than before the WOT. This clearly shows that there is no military solution for the Afghanistan conflict.

American authorities now understand at least military means alone will not bring a solution to Afghanistan. That may be why US General David Petraeus said (McCormack 2009) at the February 8, 2009 Munich

Conference on Security Policy that there is no purely military solution in Afghanistan. Petraeus was the author of the US Army and Marine Corps counter-insurgency field manual (FM3-24). He was also the commander of all US forces in the Middle East, including Central Asia. Then, almost at the same time, Steven Harper, the Prime Minister of Canada made a statement in a CNN interview (Foot 2009) that the Taliban in Afghanistan cannot be defeated. Later, in 2011, Canada ended its WOT combat operations in Afghanistan. Now it appears that the fallout of the WOT in Afghanistan includes the resurgence of Taliban forces, a record-high drug production, and re-armed warlords. This, in turn, has threatened the well-being and rights of innocent Afghan citizens. Afghan citizens, in fact, have been victims of wars for more than three decades now. Since the time of the Russian invasion in the eighties, millions have died, and millions more have fled their homes. In addition, these wars have destroyed their social fabric and the infrastructure of the country.

What about the situation in neighbouring Pakistan? At some point, the United States extended its WOT to Pakistan. This led to the movement of many Taliban and al-Qaeda militants from Afghanistan to Pakistan. Ever since, Pakistan has experienced more violence in the country than ever before. The Taliban and al-Qaeda forces now operating in Pakistan have also entered into a "holy alliance" with the local militant groups, as has been discussed earlier. This alliance of Islamist militant groups is trying to topple the Pakistani government. The main grievance of these groups is that the government continues to collaborate with the United States in its WOT. They hope to replace the present Pakistani government with an Islamic one. If ever the groups succeed in their attempt, they will also have direct access to a readymade nuclear arsenal.

In 2009, there was a much-publicised terrorist attack on the visiting Sri Lankan cricket team's bus. It killed seven Pakistanis, six police officers, and the civilian bus driver. It also injured eight of the visiting Sri Lankan cricket players. In his comments on the incident, Rifaat Hussain, a professor of defence and security studies at Quaid-i-Azam University said, "Whoever did this wanted to send a strong message that no area in Pakistan is beyond their reach ... I fear they may follow up with something more grisly and devastating" (*Vancouver Sun*, March 4, 2009, B5).

Meanwhile, Pakistan went through a political crisis. It started with President Asif Ali Zardari's dismissal of the provincial government in Punjab, following a decision made by the country's Supreme Court. By this decision, the Supreme Court had disqualified the former Prime Minister Nawaz Sharif, who led the provincial government, from holding any elective office. This decision applied to his brother as well. The Sharif brothers believed that President Zardari was behind the Supreme Court decision. This led to a series of demonstrations organized by the political party led by the Sharif brothers against the Pakistani government. These demonstrations took place in cities across Punjab. In his newspaper column, Jonathan Manthorpe summed up the ongoing power struggles in the country and said, "There is a three-cornered fight for power in Pakistan these days that include control of the country's stock of nuclear weapons" (*Vancouver Sun,* March 4, 2009, A1).

What about the WOT in Iraq? So far, it has not achieved any of its stated objectives. The only exception is the removal of Saddam Hussein's government from power. There has been no evidence found suggesting that former President Hussein was holding WMD as alleged. There has also been no evidence to suggest that he had a direct link to Osama bin Laden or his al-Qaeda movement. Further, there was no evidence suggesting he had killed even a single American citizen within, or outside, American borders. Although the war has turned out to be a sham, its cost to Iraqis is shocking. Hundreds of thousands of Iraqis have died and a staggering 16 percent of the country's population had to flee from their homes. That is not all. The country has now become a haven for many foreign Islamic militant groups. There is also much more sectarian fighting now than during the period of Saddam Hussein's regime. As Kim Sengupta reports (2004), a 2004 study, conducted by the International Institute for Strategic Studies, London, has concluded that the occupation of Iraq (by US-led forces) had become a potent global recruitment pretext for jihadists. The same study has also found that the Iraqi invasion has galvanized al-Qaeda and perversely inspired insurgent violence in that country.

Most of the countries that joined the United States in its WOT in Iraq have left the country. Practically all of the remaining forces are Americans. Most of the Iraqis want all Americans to leave as soon as possible. Some of these Iraqis had even supported the invading US troops. In a poll conducted in 2006 ("Iraqi public on the US presence" 2006) seven out of ten Iraqis wanted US-led forces to withdraw from Iraq within one year. At the same time, 78 percent said they believed that the presence of US forces was provoking more conflicts than those being prevented. The sentiments of the international community were the same. For example, in a 2007 BBC World Service poll of more than 26,000 people in 25 countries ("World view of US role" 2007), 73 percent of the global population disapproved of the US handling of the WOT in Iraq. In another BBC poll in the same year ("Most people want Iraq pull-out" 2007), two-thirds of the world population believed that the US should withdraw its forces from Iraq. Meanwhile, according to the findings of a 2006 Pew Global Attitudes Project survey ("America's image slips" *2006*), the majorities in 10 of the fourteen countries surveyed said that the war in Iraq had made the world a more dangerous place. These countries included France, Germany, Jordan, Lebanon, China, Spain, Indonesia, Turkey, and Pakistan.

What has resulted from the WOT launched by the United States is particularly counterproductive to its own declared goals in two main areas. First, the WOT consolidated opposition to the United States. Many believe that both the al-Qaeda and Taliban groups played roles in seeing this happen. The conclusions of a 2005 report of the Oxford Research Group on global conflicts testify to this. A March 2005 special summary of this report says that it concluded, "Al-Qaeda and its affiliates remain active and effective, with a stronger support base and a higher intensity of attacks than before 9/11. ... Far from winning the 'war on terror,' the second George W. Bush [Jr.] administration is maintaining policies that are not curbing paramilitary movements and are actually increasing violent anti-Americanism("Share the world's resources," n. d., para. 2)

Second, the WOT has helped recruit terrorists. The WOT in Iraq, in particular, has helped anti-American militant-recruiters to meet and enlist Islamic militants from many countries. In explaining this situation, a research paper that the British Military Defence published in the South African *Mail & Guardian* said, "The war in Iraq...has acted as a recruiting sergeant for extremists across the Muslim world. ... Iraq has served to radicalize an already disillusioned youth and al-Qaeda has given them the will, intent, purpose and ideology to act. ("War on Terrorism", n.d., para. 4)

Critics believe that this has helped spread jihad activities all over the world. According to two New York University (School of Law) researchers, Peter Bergen and Paul Cruickshank, this, in fact, has resulted in "a sevenfold increase in the yearly rate of fatal jihadist attacks, amounting to literally hundreds of additional terrorist attacks and thousands of civilian lives lost" (2007, para.6). Echoing these observations, a 2007 report of the US National Intelligence Estimate said, "The Iraq conflict has become the cause célèbre for jihads, breeding a deep resentment of US involvement in the Muslim world and cultivating supporters for the global jihad movement" ("Classified Key Judgments" 2006, para. 9).

At the same time, by launching its WOT the United States also set a bad example of resorting to force in resolving conflicts. According to critics, the WOT appears to have influenced a number of other countries, marred by inter-state and intrastate violent conflicts, to follow suit. For instance, in the midst of rising international condemnation, the Israeli government justified its attacks on the Gaza Strip in 2008 as mere acts of war on terror. Then, several other countries began to act in the same manner. They all have defended their use of force as a means to resolve conflicts by seeking refuge in the US WOT policy. The leaders of some of these countries have even said publicly that they, in fact, were following in the footsteps of US President George Bush Jr.

Meanwhile, the United States has faced criticism for its double standard in fighting its WOT. A number of reasons have led to this criticism. America's lack of action in response to the fund-raising activities of the Irish Republican Army (IRA) on American soil is one such reason; the IRA raised funds on American soil even during the height of its violent activities in Northern Ireland. Then, America's inaction on the Pakistani government's alleged support of Taliban operatives is another reason. Pakistan has allegedly supported Taliban operatives both during and after the US invasion of Afghanistan. The main allegations against Pakistan came from none other than Afghan President Hamid Karzai. In his allegations, President Hamid Karzai had even characterized Pakistan as the central front in the war against terrorism.

The WOT initiated by the United States has not made any place on Earth safer than before. On the contrary, in the places where the war was, or still is, in operation, violent acts are continuing, with more frequency and vigour. A vast majority of those who have succumbed to them are civilians, including women and children. However, the WOT has helped America and its allies in two main areas. First, it has replaced some regimes that were hostile to them with ones that are prepared to work with them. Second, the allied forces, primarily American, are now active in more parts of the world than before. In other words, the WOT has given America, the dwindling superpower, the new position of imperialist master in the changing world. However, this has given more reasons for adversarial forces to fight against it, reversing the very purpose of the WOT.

Overall, it is abundantly clear that ending the WOT without delay will be in the best interest of all the concerned parties, including the United States. It is an illegal and senseless war. The more the US-led forces fight the Islamic radical groups, the more the Islamic radicals commit themselves to their cause. If the United States and its allies continue with the WOT, the world could end up as one big battlefield in the coming years.

Destroy All Weapons of Mass Destruction

Working toward a world free of Weapons of Mass Destruction appears to be the only way to stop the growth of these arsenals. The challenges to the current strategies for controlling and regulating these weapons, especially nuclear weapons, are too many to overcome.

Of all the known nuclear weapons states, only the United States and Russia have engaged in arms-control measures. They demonstrated success with a series of bilateral arms control treaties that sought to limit the increase of nuclear weapons held by each of them. The first two agreements were the Strategic Arms Limitation Talks (SALT) and the Anti-Ballistic Missile Treaty (ABM) of 1972. The SALT produced an interim agreement on the limitation of strategic nuclear weapons. The ABM Treaty restricted the number of anti-ballistic missile systems and launches. Then in 1979, the two parties agreed on the SALT II treaty. The intent of this treaty was to establish limits on certain categories of strategic arms. Both nations later withdrew from the ABM to move forward with their individual ballistic missile defence programmes. The United States withdrew in 2002, and Russia followed suit in 2004.

Their Intermediate Nuclear Forces treaty (INFT) of 1987 focused on the reduction of the number of arms between them. It helped remove all the intermediate-range nuclear warheads and delivery systems from Europe. Since then, the two powers have held strategic arms reduction talks in 1991, 1993, 1999, 2002, and 2010. The talks in 1991 and 1993 ended with two treaties. The Strategic Arms Reduction Treaty (START) was one of them. START II was the other. Each treaty sought further reduction in the number of nuclear warheads and delivery systems. START II also sought to eliminate certain categories of warheads. These categories included land-based intercontinental ballistic missiles (ICBMs). The 1999 talks were a failure due to major disagreements over renegotiation of the 1972 ABM treaty. The subsequent talks in 2002 ended with a new treaty: the Strategic Offensive Reduction Treaty (SORT). This permitted each party to hold between 1700 and 2200 warheads. It also permitted the two parties to put into storage, instead of destroying, the rest of the warheads they possessed. According to the treaty, either party could withdraw from it at three months notice. Then in 2010, the two countries signed a new treaty on the reduction of strategic offensive weapons, replacing the START I treaty, which had expired in December 2009. The new treaty required that each party reduce their number of nuclear warheads to 1,550. Deployed and non-deployed delivery vehicles could not exceed 800 on each side. The Russian and US presidents, Dmitry Medvedev and Barack Obama, pledged to work with the legislators of their respective countries to ensure the timely ratification of this new treaty.

During and after the period of bipolar world order, the international community also entered into a number of arms control agreements. Their purpose has been to prevent more states developing nuclear and other types of WMD. The treaties address a host of issues related to all types of WMD, missile technology, and nuclear testing. The agreements that do not exclusively relate to nuclear WMD include the Biological and Toxic Weapons Convention of 1972, the Missile Control Regime of 1987, and the Chemical Weapons Convention of 1993. The Missile Control Regime of 1987, in particular, sought to control the production and export of missiles capable of carrying chemical, biological, and nuclear weapons.

The agreements that exclusively relate to nuclear WMD include the Limited Test Ban Treaty (LTBT) of 1963, the Nuclear Non-Proliferation Treaty (NPT) of 1968, and the Comprehensive Test Ban Treaty (CTBT) of 1996. The NPT is the key treaty covering nuclear proliferation in particular. Almost all the states have signed this treaty, with the notable exceptions of India, Pakistan, and Israel. As stated earlier, North Korea signed the treaty, but later withdrew from it. The LTBT (1963) restricted the testing of nuclear weapons to underground trials. The CTBT (1996) sought to ban all nuclear test explosions. It is incongruous that some states have not yet signed a number of these important agreements. Notably, the nations that need to put the CTBT into action, including the United States, have still not signed it.

Meanwhile, there is increasing pressure on non-nuclear weapons states to possess nuclear and other forms of WMD. There are two main reasons for this. First, the on and off talks among the states possessing nuclear and other forms of WMD clearly show that such weapons are still useful. The discussions between the United States and Russia that have the biggest stockpiles of WMD, in particular, are of especial significance. Second, the non-nuclear weapons states that once enjoyed a group safety guarantee under the Soviet defensive umbrella have now become acutely vulnerable, as stated before. This second reason, in fact, is most persuasive in tempting a non-nuclear weapons state to build its own nuclear weapons. This is especially so, if one is also faced with a longstanding hostile relationship with an equally, or more powerful state. Pakistan and North Korea provide two good examples in this regard. North Korea has a long-term hostile relationship with its neighbour South Korea, which is a close ally of the United States. Pakistan has a similar hostile relationship with neighbouring India, which had carried out its first nuclear test in 1974. Both countries, North Korea and Pakistan, developed their own nuclear weapons after the disintegration of the Soviet Union. If this state of affairs remains, more non-nuclear weapons states are likely to become nuclear weapons states in the coming years. Japan has already suggested that, should the United States withdraw its defence nuclear umbrella, it would feel obliged to become a nuclear weapons state. More countries possessing nuclear weapons could also lead to new arms races spread across the globe. For some time now, Israel and its western allies have been accusing Iran of having a covert programme for developing nuclear weapons. While the accusations persisted, Iran fuelled its first nuclear power plant and became a peaceful user of nuclear energy in October 2010. It maintains that it has no plans to develop nuclear weapons. Adversaries, including Israel and the United States, think otherwise. Because of this situation, the UN Security Council demanded that Iran suspend its nuclear enrichment activities altogether. When Iran refused to do so, the Security Council imposed sanctions against it. Iran continues to maintain its position that its ongoing nuclear programme is only for peaceful purposes (power generation). It further says that it is pursuing the programme in direct consultation with the appropriate international agency, the IAEA. The NAM countries that support Iran's nuclear programmes for peaceful purposes also have called on the Security Council and Iran to work for a solution through the IAEA.

Meanwhile, people in Arab countries appear to be particularly interested in Iran's nuclear programmes. The Anwar Sadat Chair for Peace and Development at the University of Maryland conducted a survey in 2008 to gauge the public opinion among Arabs on Iran's nuclear programme. This survey, conducted in six Middle East countries: Egypt, Jordon, Lebanon, Morocco, Saudi Arabia, and the UAE, concluded, "In contrast with the fears of many Arab governments, the Arab public does not appear to see Iran as a major threat, Most believe that Iran has the right to its nuclear programme and do not support international pressure to force it to curtail its programme. A plurality of Arabs (44%) believes that if Iran were to acquire nuclear weapons, the outcome would be more positive for the region than negative." ("Arab public opinion, Al-Qaeda & the long war" 2008, para. 21).

Some radical groups among Arabs openly support the proposition of Iran having nuclear weapons. For example, according to a 2006 report by the Middle East Media Research Institute, Anwar Raja, the Lebanon based representative of the Popular Front for the Liberation of Palestine, demonstrated open support at a public rally in Damascus. At this rally, he categorically stated that Palestinian people are in favour of Iran having a nuclear bomb, not just energy for peaceful purposes.

As well, non-Arab Muslim countries have shown their support for Iran's nuclear programme. All along, the world's most populous Muslim-majority nation, Indonesia, has supported Iran's nuclear programme for peaceful purposes. In its role as a non-permanent member of the UN Security Council, Indonesia abstained from a vote on a UN resolution to impose a third set of sanctions against Iran in March 2008. The second largest Muslim population in the world, Pakistan, is also equally supportive of Iran's nuclear programme. Pakistan is already a nuclear weapons state. Some suspect that it is helping Iran to develop nuclear weapons. In referring to Pakistan's position on Iran's nuclear interests in 2005, the former chief of staff of the Pakistani Army, Mirza Aslam Beg, said, "I would certainly not like my future generations to live in the neighbourhood of a 'nuclear capable' Israel.... Countries acquire the (nuclear) capability on their own. Because it is threatened by Israel, Iran will do the same." (Beg, 2005, para 1).

The biggest objection to Iran's nuclear programme understandably came from Israel and its US-led Western allies. Their concerns regarding Iran's nuclear programme led to IAEA inspections of the Iranian nuclear facilities in 2003. The results of these inspections have not revealed Iran's actual possession of nuclear weapons. The inspections, however, led to new proliferation concerns. These new worries arose primarily from the possibility that one of the key scientists who helped develop nuclear weapons in Pakistan was now sharing nuclear weapons technology with Iran, and other Muslim countries. These other Muslim countries include Iraq, Libya, Syria, and Saudi Arabia. If the alleged involvement of a Pakistani scientist in transferring nuclear technology was true, it leads to an important question: was he doing that on his own accord or as part of a Pakistani state-sanctioned nuclear proliferation network? On its part, the Pakistani government, which had collaborated with the United States on its global WOT, has categorically denied any involvement in Iran's nuclear programme at state level.

Meanwhile, it appears that the dual-faceted behaviour of the United States in its dealings with other countries has played a role in promoting the need for nuclear weapons among non-nuclear weapons states. Historically, the United States has been benign to nuclear-weapons states. At the same time, it has been haughty and arrogant to others. The 1990 proclamation by US President George Bush Sr., "Whatever we say goes" (Beg, n.d., para. 1) at the advent of the Gulf War clearly showed the pompous, arrogant behaviour of the United States towards other countries, particularly the weaker ones with no nuclear weapons. Later, President George Bush Jr. generally continued with the same behavioural style during his two consecutive terms of presidency. During his second term in office, however, there was a dramatic change in the behaviour of the United States towards North Korea. This was after North Korea declared its nuclear weapons capability and the intent to strike American troops and installations in South Korea, Japan, and beyond, if provoked. The United States showed the same change of behaviour towards Russia, when it invaded Georgia in 2008. According to critics, this kind of dual-faceted behaviour of the United States has helped promote among non-nuclear weapons states the idea that the only way to deter aggression is to acquire nuclear weapons.

This shows that if the situation remains unchanged, the world is likely to witness six major developments concerning weapons of mass destruction. First, the United States and Russia may further reduce their WMD stockpiles. They, however, would try to maintain their status as the owners of the two biggest WMD arsenals. Second, the newly emerging global powers, such as China and India, may strive to raise their arsenal strengths to claim a bigger share of control in the changing world. Third, some of the present non-nuclear weapons states, especially those threatened by one or more adversarial nuclear states, could covertly develop nuclear weapons in the coming years. Fourth, there may still be other new cases of nuclear proliferation, with the help of nuclear scientists from states already possessing nuclear weapons. Fifth, new arms races would develop between rival nuclear weapons states and among the main global powers in the changing world. Sixth, there would be no justification why a non-nuclear weapons state should not think of developing nuclear weapons when they see that those already developed by the present nuclear weapons states are considered to be 'authentic.' These potential developments clearly point to the irrefutable fact that the destruction of all weapons of mass destruction is the only solution to stop the spread of such deadly weapons across the globe. In any event, the dire consequences of past nuclear plant disasters, especially the ones in Chernobyl, Ukraine, in 1986 and in Fukushima, Japan, in 2011, have shown that nuclear power and human beings cannot co-exist.

ADOPT NON-VIOLENT MEANS OF CONFLICT RESOLUTION

The world has already witnessed how an isolated violent conflict in one corner of the world could gather momentum and develop into a world war. Surely, no sensible person would like to see the repetition of that history in any form, ever. Avoidance of such disasters is possible only if we can manage to prevent the build up of global tension to a tipping point. For this, it is essential that the parties to ongoing and future conflicts not use the infamous 'an eye for an eye' approach to conflict-resolution. It is a proven recipe for more squalor and death. Only an approach based on non-violence can constitute a recipe for *'live and let live.'* Therefore, we should only depend on non-violent means in resolving inevitable conflicts among humans. It is a challenge all humans must face and endure. The consequences of the failure to meet this challenge effectively could result in human disasters of unprecedented scale.

The key to conflict resolution by non-violent means is primarily four-fold. First, there should be an irrevocable commitment to non-violence on the part of the conflicting parties. Violence should never be a justifiable means to resolve a conflict. The theories of 'just wars' should be a thing of the past, and only of the past. Once the emerging multi-polar global order is established, it could spin the world back to the old days of competing polar groups of states and the practice of deterrence. This would invariably make non-violence a strategic necessity in resolving major conflicts. However, the commitment to non-violence *as an act of deterrence* is conditional to the extent of the restraint exercised by the conflicted parties. On the other hand, a commitment to non-violence through a genuine desire to *'live and let live'* is not so conditional. Approaches to resolve conflicts with such a commitment only would stand the test of time.

Second, in resolving a conflict, the primary focus should be on the present and the future, and not the past. Learning the historic context of a conflict would undoubtedly help better understand its current dynamics and the avenues open for its resolution. The past, however, should not lay down a template for the future. Parties involved in many major conflicts draw strength from history for their respective positions. This history may be modern, medieval, or ancient. This is evident in many ongoing conflicts, most predominantly in the conflict between

Arabs and Israelis. Too much focus on the history of a conflict can be unproductive, since that history may have not been consistent over time. The opposing parties may have different periods in history that support their respective arguments. Any party's historical argument in a conflict may ignore the historical occurrences that favoured its opponent. At the same time, many new things may have happened since those historic times, making the current situation much different. In resolving a current conflict, therefore, the primary focus should always remain in the present and the future. The specific factors related to the present that need attention should include the factual grievances, future aspirations, and areas of common interest for the conflicting parties. As for the future, it is necessary for all concerned parties to demonstrate and agree on new ways of living together in peace and harmony - as friends and neighbours. For this, it is necessary to think of win-win solutions to conflicts. Such solutions could guarantee the rule of law within a framework of enhanced democracy. Future economic and social ventures of common interest would be particularly attractive to all the parties involved in any conflict.

Third, there should be a successful political solution to any major conflict, like the ones discussed in Chapters 2 and 3. No such major conflict would end for good without a successful political solution. Some believe in military solutions to violent conflicts. History, however, shows the futility of such beliefs. The current example of the War on Terror launched by the United States, the mightiest power in the world, is a case in point. In such military attempts, even if a party to a conflict emerges as a clear winner on the battlefield, the issues of the dispute would remain unresolved. There is the potential for the defeated party to regain strength and reappear on the battlefield some time later. In any case, a military victory by one conflicting party over another would only bring a 'solution' of subjugation, and not of mutual acceptance. What the world needs is not solutions of subjugation of one group of people by another, but solutions for all groups of people to co-exist in a framework of lasting peace.

Fourth, there are some important lessons to learn from both the failures and the successes of earlier experiences in conflict resolution. Chapter 4 discussed in detail the failures and successes of the League of Nations and the UN in their attempts to resolve international conflicts. The same chapter also discussed the reasons for the failures of these two international peace organizations. The victors of WWII founded the UN with a view to overcoming the problems and difficulties experienced by the League of Nations. As expected, the UN did make progress in meeting this challenge in some areas, but not in all. For example, the UN, like the League of Nations, has failed in securing compliance from all its member-states in implementing its resolutions. At the same time, the UN has failed to deliver in a number of new areas of concern. These new areas include, but are not limited to, nuclear proliferation and unilateral global policing by global powers. The current world situation warrants complete reform or even replacement of the UN to guarantee lasting peace to our future generations. There will be a separate discussion on this later in this chapter.

Meanwhile, the failures and successes of past attempts to resolve intrastate conflicts also provide good lessons for the future. The successes in resolving conflicts that led to internal wars in South Africa and the United Kingdom, in particular, are extremely noteworthy. The process of reconciliation under the Truth and Reconciliation Commission of South Africa has a lot to offer. It provided a legal process for people to speak their truth and for perpetrators to go on trial. In the process, it helped keep the country together at a turbulent time and pressured those concerned, both within and outside the country, to end apartheid. Meanwhile, the factors that contributed to finding a solution to the Northern Ireland crisis in the United Kingdom are many. Peter Hain, Secretary of State for Northern Ireland, once listed the key factors among them in a speech he delivered at the Chatham House on June 12, 2007. He is also a former UK Secretary of State and an author of numerous books and political essays. The key factors he listed in this speech include the following:

- The need to create space and time free from violence, in which political capacity can develop;
- the need to indentify key individuals and constructive forces;
- the importance of inclusive dialogue at every level, wherever there is a negotiable objective;
- the taking of risks to sustain that dialogue and to underpin political progress;

- alignment of national and international forces;
- the need to avoid or resolve pre-conditions to dialogue; and
- the need to grip and micro-manage a conflict at a high political level, refusing to accept the inevitability of it.

Past efforts to resolve these and other major conflicts within states offer lessons in three main areas. First, it is important that all parties to the conflict have representation at the conflict resolution and reconciliation table. This would give an opportunity for all the affected parties to uncover what is important about the issues that need attention. Second, the contribution of participants who seek to gain something from the talks for those whom they represent is very unproductive. Such participants are not there to make a sincere effort to understand the points of view of others or to negotiate with them. Their contributions at the talks would be limited to making statements they think their supporters would want to hear. Any amount of talk involving such participants would not help bring about a meaningful solution to a conflict. This, in fact, was what happened in Canada's attempts to change its constitution through the Meech Lake Accord of 1991 and the Charlottetown Accord of 1992. In explaining the situation, Nick Leonen, a former Member of the Legislative Assembly of British Columbia, Canada, says, "Those who took part in the decision-making process [of the two Accords] came to the table representing particular interests, and were there to get something for those whom they represented" (Herath 2007, p. 20).

Third, conflict resolution and reconciliation talks can fail due to communication weaknesses on the part of the participants. Such weaknesses appear primarily in two main areas. First, when emotions among the participants are high, they attack each other, instead of the problem they are supposed to resolve. This prevents participants from seeing the problem beyond emotion. In turn, it results in attacks or discussions about mere symptoms of the problem that needs to be resolved. Second, the participants almost never advocate positions good for all. Instead, they try to stress how the conflict could be resolved by addressing the concerns of only those whom they represent. It is true that in almost all ongoing conflict resolution forums, the participants go to the table representing only one segment of the conflicting parties.

Every such participant, however, needs to look at the conflict in a holistic manner and advocate solutions for the good of all.

If any of the above failing features dominate, then the conflict resolution and reconciliatory talks will not bring about desired results. Instead, such talks could radicalize attitudes all round, add to the mistrust among the competing parties, and bring further misunderstandings to their respective positions. All this will only prevent future agreements among the involved parties, further escalating the conflict in question.

REFORM OR REPLACE THE UNITED NATIONS ORGANIZATION

There was a recognized need to reform or replace the League of Nations because of its proven failures even before WWII. The leaders of the major global powers at the time, however, looked at this need, with the seriousness it deserved, only after WWII began. This shows that they had to first witness a widespread bloody war before responding to that need. May be this is how humans generally behave. For example, all the major improvements to natural disaster response programmes around the world have come about only in the aftermath of some unprecedented catastrophic events. The manner in which countries have developed their earthquake and flood response programmes clearly illustrates this. In the same way, today's world leaders may not think of the need to reform or replace the UN with the seriousness it deserves until, perhaps, another world war has begun or even ended. Meanwhile, the ground realities stand naked in front of them. The most poignant reality is the inability of the UN to meet effectively the growing challenges to world peace in the current world. This shows the urgent need to reform or replace it. The time has come for the current world leaders to step up to the plate and respond to this urgent need *now*, without procrastination.

The victors of WWII founded the UN in the mid-forties to address the global issues seen and foreseen at that time. However, the state of the world today is very different. A number of new developments that occurred after the founding of the UN have resulted in significant changes to the world's geopolitical landscape. Continued nuclear proliferation, a special violent conflict between some Islamic radical groups and the West, and the emergence of new global powers are among these new developments. The founders of the UN surely did not envisage such future developments, at least to the extent that we see them today.

Currently, there appear to be a number of fault lines in the operations of the UN. Chapter 4 has already discussed them as reasons for UN failures over the years. The most concerned fault lines of the UN include the questionable structure and decision-making processes of its organs, its inability to prevent and stop unilateral global policing by major powers, and its failed armaments reduction and regulation programme. The UN's inability to ensure compliance by its member-states is yet another major fault line. Chapter 4 also discussed how the UN failures have made the world once again dangerous and insecure with a looming global disaster. Any serious attempt to avoid this catastrophe needs to include whatever measures necessary to remedy the existing UN fault lines.

Remedying the present UN fault lines is possible. It calls for strategic changes in six critical areas. The structure and the decision-making processes of the UN organs, the regulation and disarmament of weapons of mass destruction, and the extent of the commitment of UN member-states to implement UN resolutions are three of these critical areas. The funding arrangements for the UN, the UN's military capability, and the prevention of unilateral global policing by major powers are the other three. Strategic changes in all these areas should take into account both the rights and the obligations of all sovereign states.

Some of the needed strategic changes invariably call for amendments to the existing UN Charter. Article 109 of the Charter describes the process for pursuing any amendments thereto. According to this Article, an amendment to the present UN Charter is possible only with the support of two thirds of the members of the UN, including all permanent members of the Security Council. Any amendment so supported also needs to go through a process of ratification; the signatory states need to ratify the amendment in accordance with their respective constitutional processes. After the ratification, the amendment takes effect. All states need to look at the needed strategic changes with full preparedness to compromise and sacrifice, where necessary, for the sake of the common good of the global community. In particular, the five permanent members of the Security Council (China, France, Russia, the United

Kingdom, and the United States) need to step up to the plate and show leadership in pursuing the needed changes.

If any of the permanent members of the Security Council stands in the way of this reform, the global community could consider replacing the UN with a new international organization. Any new organization must have the ability to meet effectively the current and future challenges of the world. The global community should not wait to make this move. In a way, such a move offers a far easier approach to the same ends. In any event, no one should wait for another world war to start thinking about the need to reform or replace the UN. It is already an outdated organization. The world needs a reformed UN, or a new international organization in its place, not in another sixty years, but *now.*

This completes the discussion on the five-fold course of action that could prevent the looming global catastrophe. This course of action calls for urgent, positive response by all the countries around the globe. The countries that possess WMD, particularly those that are also permanent members of the UN Security Council, have a much bigger role to play. It is a crucial moment in the history of humankind where these countries should step up to the plate and show leadership in meeting the challenge posed by the looming global catastrophe. It is a challenge too risky to ignore or to delay in finding solutions. All states must face the challenge together, *now.* This completes the answer to the third critical question raised at the end of the introductory chapter: *what needs to be done to prevent such an eventuality?*

Avoiding wars is a good thing. It is, however, difficult to believe that the mere avoidance of wars will guarantee lasting peace on the planet, as the world's history of wars could repeat itself. At the same time, peace in its true sense is much more than the mere absence of war. As the present occupants of the planet, we certainly would like to pass on a world of real, lasting peace to our future generations. This brings us to the next and last critical question posed at the end of the introductory chapter: *is there anything more to be done to ensure lasting peace on the planet?* The next chapter will attempt to answer it.

Chapter 7:
Lasting Peace on Earth

CHALLENGES

THE WORD 'PEACE' MEANS many things. According to the *Oxford Dictionary of English* (Stevenson 2010, 1306) peace refers to "freedom from disturbance; tranquility" or "a state or period in which there is no war or a war has ended." *Random House Webster's College Dictionary* (Steinmetz 1997, 958) gives some additional meanings to peace. They include "freedom from civil commotions; public order and security," "a state of harmony between people or groups; freedom from dissension," and "freedom from anxiety, annoyance, or other mental disturbances". In the context of political discussions, people in general, including politicians, have interpreted the meaning of peace as the absence of war. This explains why all ongoing peace efforts, both within and among nations, primarily aim at avoiding wars. Avoiding wars, no doubt, is an essential part of any peace building process. However, the avoidance of wars alone may not result in lasting peace in any jurisdiction.

For example, the five-fold course of action described in the previous chapter would prevent the outbreak of the nuclear catastrophe that is threatening the world. It would do so by further strengthening the existing global checks and balances administered though the United Nations and by reducing global tension. However, the mere avoidance of this disaster would not necessarily end existing conflicts. The odds are that the existing conflicts will continue until the involved parties end them peacefully. At the same time, new, similar conflicts could emerge. This is inevitable, as long as the causes of such conflicts continue to exist. In time, any or all of these conflicts could result in the same level of violence and global tension as now. Thus, a need may arise for yet another attempt to prevent a global fiasco. In fact, there were two such attempts in the 20ᵗʰ century. The failure of both these attempts resulted in the outbreak of WWI and WWII. We can only hope that future such attempts will not fail. Even if they succeed, humans would still live with uncertainty, with global disasters threatening to explode from time to time.

Clearly, while avoiding any future wars, we also need to address the causes of major human conflicts if we are interested in long-term peace on the planet. If not, people will always remain in a state of hostility, with or without wars. In any event, we should not be complacent about living under the continued threat of global wars. Our future generations deserve much better than that. We want them to live in a world of lasting global peace, free from tension and violence. For this, it is fruitless to continue to depend on the ongoing political or military manipulations of global powers. Instead, we should trust ourselves and depend on the ability of humans to address the causes of major human conflicts. Once humans gain that ability, there would be no wars. In that desired world, people around the globe would use their inherent forces of mutual understanding, respect, love, and compassion - instead of mutual suspicion, fear, disrespect, and hatred - to live together as one family. The onus is on us to do what it takes to transform our present troubled world to one of lasting peace.

For this transformation, we must first identify the root causes of major violent conflicts among humans and a way to overcome them. A re-examination of the past and present major conflicts with a view to understanding the primary driving forces behind them can be a convenient starting point in this task. Any attempt to do this on every past and present major violent conflict on an individual basis would run for not one, but many books. Therefore, for practical reasons, let us concentrate on the four basic categories of major violent conflicts identified at the end of the second chapter (A Sober Reflection). The understanding is that these four conflict categories represent the essence of all major violent conflicts. Economic exploitation and social or political vendetta are two of these four categories. The abuse of state power and identity politics are the remaining two.

Economic exploitation. Historically, rich and powerful countries colonized the poorer and weaker ones, typically for economic reasons. This happened in a rampant manner from the late 15th to the 20th century, as discussed in Chapter 5. During this period, a number of European states established colonies in far away continents, including South America, Africa, and Asia. Portugal, Spain, France, and Great Britain were the main colonizers of the time. These and other European powers extracted and marketed the colonies' natural resources, for their own benefit. The colonists also used the fertile lands in their colonies for commercial farming. The farmed products were sold in the global market - for profits.

While gaining these and other economic benefits, the colonizers also spread their political and religious beliefs. However, the colonizing powers had typically looked for colonies for economic gains. Colonization as such is now an outdated practice. However, today, many powerful nations meet the same exploitative ends through numerous neo-colonial strategies. With or without active colonization, the world has witnessed many major violent conflicts driven by economic exploitation, pursued by powerful nations. The Gulf War of the early nineties and the Congo (Brazzaville) Civil War (Chapter 2) offer two recent examples. In each of these cases, the desire to secure access to scarce oil resources was the primary driving force in the conflict.

Greed or the intense, selfish desire for wealth and power causes the conflicts of economic exploitation. The rich and powerful exploiting nations exhibit a 'me first' attitude when it comes to the use of world resources. The stronger a nation becomes, the more it strives to take control of everything around the world. However, natural resources, renewable or not, are not unlimited. The non-renewable resources will definitely run out eventually. The renewable resources will also end if their rate of extraction exceeds their renewable rate.

The demand for natural resources is not likely to slow down anytime in the future. Increases in world population invariably call for more and more resources. Enlarging economies also have the same effect. The global population increased from 2.55 billion in 1950 to more than 6 billion in 2000. This is an increase of more than 100 percent in 50 years. The world population, in fact, passed the seven billion mark in November 2011. Some experts believe that the world population will not continue to grow at the same alarming rate. Their world population estimate for 2050 is around 9.0 billion, showing only a 50 percent increase for the first 50 years of this century. Nevertheless, it shows a continuous upward trend in world population. At the same time, enlarging economies, including the BRIC countries, have created an unprecedented growth in demand for scare natural resources, both renewable and non-renewable.

This situation clearly warrants a coordinated approach to the extraction and use of the scarce natural resources of the world for the benefit of all nations. In any event, at the current level of globalization, economic failures in any one nation could lead to economic hardships in many others. All this clearly shows the strategic need for all nations to work in cooperation, caring for each other's requirements and sharing what is available in an equitable manner. Only such an equitable means of sharing world resources among nations can put an end to wars on the economic front. For this, all nations should seek international economic cooperation in a true spirit of *caring and sharing.*

Social or political vendetta. In conflicts of social or political vendetta, typically relatives or descendents of a group of people who have been wronged or murdered try to take vengeance on the wrong doers or killers of their relatives. All four ongoing major inter-state conflicts discussed in Chapter 2 offer great examples of this characteristic. The major conflict without borders between some Islamic militant groups and the West described in chapter 3 is another. At the same time, some of the intrastate conflicts, such as the Kivu conflict in Congo (Chapter 2), also provide examples of this type of conflicts.

A conflict caused by vengeance would normally continue with violent attacks and counter-attacks, generation after generation. Every child born to any of the sides in such a conflict would become a potential target of enemy attacks right from birth. It is generally believed that children are born free. However, this is not true with the children born to families involved in these conflicts. Once born, these children grow up in an environment of hatred filled with prejudice, suspicion, fear, and cruelty. After becoming adults, they take the place of their parents in the hate-conflict to which they were born. Thus, the conflict continues generation after generation.

It is important that the parties involved in such conflicts understand that hatred can never appease hatred. History does not provide a single example to suggest otherwise. No one should ignore this reality. Great philosophers of the past have reminded us of this truth. For example, the Buddha, who lived more than two thousand five hundred years ago, had said, "Hatred is never appeased by hatred in this world. By non-hatred alone is hatred appeased. This is a law eternal." (Dhammapada, Chapter 1, Verse 5)

People entangled in conflicts of social or political vendetta should not continue to live in the past, preoccupying themselves with historic issues, however contentious they might have been. Instead, those involved in such conflicts must make an effort to live in the present by making peace with the enemy for the sake of their future generations. After all, no one can undo the past. Any attempts to prove who was right or wrong in the past would only revive old wounds, making peacemaking with the enemy more difficult. Parties to such conflicts should connect to each other empathetically. No one will be able to do this if one treats its enemy groups as mere terrorists. In the event a party to a conflict treats its enemies as mere terrorists, it will remain part of the problem, not the solution. When warring parties succeed in their attempts to connect to each other empathetically, they will have the readiness to *forgive and forget* the contentious past, no matter who did what, when, and why. This willingness could contribute to the peaceful resolution of conflicts caused by social or political vendetta. *Forgive and forget*, indeed, is a time-honoured and universally proven principle. There is no reason to believe that it could fail us in the future.

The abuse of state power. States have the power to enact legislation, enforce laws, implement policies, settle disputes through courts, and use armed forces when deemed necessary. In using these powers, however, all states also have a responsibility not to go beyond the limitations provided by their governing laws. Nations are governed not only by the laws they themselves have enacted. They are also governed by international laws adopted by the UN on behalf of the global community. The primary purpose of global laws is to save the world from the scourge of war and to protect the fundamental rights and freedoms of the individual.

The abuse of state power, disregarding governing laws, national or international, only leads to a state of anarchy.

Despite this, some despotic rulers abuse their power to accomplish some unpopular missions. In doing so, they typically begin by taking control of the media and putting the police force to immoral use. When these intimidating measures become inadequate, they look for other means to fulfil their goals. The official institutions they turn to include the state intelligence services, armed forces, and even the judiciary. In the process, despotic rulers often make harsh changes to existing legal codes, and permit and encourage torture, killing, and the destruction of property belonging to those they label as "state enemies."

In conducting activities abroad, these rulers primarily depend on their hired agents, state intelligence services, and security forces. For resources outside their official institutions, they often turn to special death squads, veterans, and those engaged in underworld operations. While making use of all such avenues, these rulers manage to cover their blatant brutality by publicly professing adherence to good governance. It is simply hypocrisy. At the same time, such rulers also resort to dubious ways to remain in power for life, while also promoting their own kith and kin to replace them once they are gone. For this, they employ tactics to delude the people they govern, using false promises, wrong notions, and numerous other acts of deceit. Unfortunately, all this leaves the victims of such state power abuses with only one strategy to respond: *fight back*. In turn, this only makes the existing conflicts with such despotic rulers more difficult to solve. These conflicts often deteriorate into genocide or other forms of mass murder and outright wars.

History provides many examples of rulers who have abused state power. Adolf Hitler of Nazi Germany, Josef Stalin of Russia, Mao Ze Dong of China, Kim IL Sung of North Korea, Pol Pot of Cambodia, Ismail Enver of Turkey, and Suharto of Indonesia are several examples from the past. They all established policies aimed at the deliberate destruction of those identified as their enemies. These rulers were also infamous for the use of their armed forces and police, outside the law and against their own citizens. The ruling junta of Myanmar, Muammar Muhammad al-Gaddafi of Libya, and Robert Mugabe of Zimbabwe are examples that are more recent. The global checks and balances implemented through the UN have had only limited success in restraining or controlling the abusive use of state power by these and other despotic rulers.

Greed for power and delusion appear to be the primary factors that contribute to the abuse of state power. To remain in power, rulers obsessed with this greed have no shame or fear of doing anything outside the standards of good governance. Deluded, such rulers may feel that they have absolute power and are not responsible to anyone in what they do. As a result, they may also think that they can do anything, anywhere within their jurisdiction. They may also believe that they are above the law, nationally and internationally. However, state power is not an open-ended phenomenon. It is subject to a series of checks and balances, such as national and international laws, public opinions, established moral codes, and periodic democratic elections. They do impose some limits to state power in numerous ways. Rulers of states have a responsibility to respect and work within the confines of these limits in a trustworthy and reliable manner. The world will continue to witness conflicts resulting from abuse of state power as long as rulers shun away from this responsibility. Thus, the solution lies in the preparedness to *act responsibly in a trustworthy and reliable manner* on the part of the rulers.

Identity politics. The term identity politics refers to political activities designed to advance the interests of people who unite around a common identity. There are several factors that define such identities: race, ethnicity, tribe, religion, language, culture, and ideology. Any group of people could identify with one or more of these attributes. The competing interests of different identity groups often result in conflicts, within or among states.

In such conflicts within states, typically some groups claim discrimination by those in power. At worst, such conflicts end up in civil or separatist wars and crimes of genocide perpetrated by those who rule. Any one of these affinity groups could be the discriminator or the discriminated. Chapter 2 provided many examples of major conflicts within states caused by identity politics. The countries affected by such conflicts in the recent past include Russia, Turkey, Yemen, India, and Sri Lanka. Among them, we also find that Myanmar, Thailand, Sudan, Ivory Coast, and Burundi have each experienced the deadly consequences of identity politics. Generally, the conflicts of identity politics within states begin with the adoption of discriminatory laws and policies. Typically, a government that is dominated by a majority identity group adopts such laws and policies for the advancement of that particular group - at the expense of others. This brings groups of other identities, the minority groups, into conflict with the government. Such situations could exist even under governments elected through democratic processes, as we now know. India and Sri Lanka offer two examples in this regard.

In such situations, the affected groups first seek remedies to the discriminatory laws and policies through peaceful means. These means include negotiations with the government, sit-in protests, and public demonstrations. When peaceful means end with no results, the affected groups face a dead-end. At this point, some of the affected parties seek remedies through violence. Such violence normally takes the form of civil wars or separatist wars - as witnessed in the above-mentioned countries. The more the discriminating government uses its military power to suppress the violence, the more the affected groups commit themselves to fight. In the process, some of the affected have at times emerged as suicide attackers, in readiness to give up their own lives for the sake of their fight against discrimination and oppression. No power on Earth would be able to stop them from attack.

On the global scene, Iran and a few other countries claim that they have become victims of discrimination by the United States and its western allies. Iran, in particular, says that the entire West is discriminating against it because of its unique, Islamic political ideology. The Islamic groups that take responsibility for the major violent conflict without borders (chapter 3) have a similar claim. They, in fact, say that the West has discriminated against the entire Muslim world. These Islamic groups insist that their ongoing fight against the western countries is a mere response to that situation.

The identifiable differences among humans, based on race, ethnicity, tribe, religion, language, culture, and the like, are not going to disappear. The world and its people will always remain diverse. According to the Cambridge Academic Content Dictionary, race refers to "any group into which humans can be divided according to their shared physical and genetic characteristics" (Heacock 2009, 770). The same dictionary says ethnic means "relating to or characteristic of a large group of people who have the same national, racial, or cultural origins, and who usually speak the same language" (Heacock 2009, 314). The term tribe generally refers to a group of people organized largely based on kinship. Accordingly, there must be at least a few races and many ethnic and tribal groups.

People around the globe speak many languages and practice many religions. According to a Linguists report (O'Neil 2006), humans speak 5,000 – 6,000 languages. Another report (Lewis 2009) lists the largest of these languages in descending order of population of first-language speakers. It names Chinese, Spanish, English, Arabic, Hindi, Bengali, Portuguese, Russian, Japanese, and German as the first ten languages, in that order. Then, Javanese, Lahnda, Telugu, Vietnamese, Marathi, and French appear as the next five. A 2007 study ("Major Religions" 2007) lists 21 religions, each claimed by more than one-half million people worldwide. The first six religions ranked by the number of adherents, shown within brackets, are Christianity (2.1 billion), Islam (1.5 billion), Hinduism (900 million), Chinese traditional religion (394 million), Buddhism (376 million), and primal-indigenous (300 million). The same report classifies 16 percent of the world population (1.1 billion) as 'nonreligious.'

There are also numerous cultural variations among humans. An amalgamation of many different features of a community characterizes its cultural identification. History, art, music, dance, cuisine, and costume are among these features. Customs and traditions, language, and other community-specific tangible and non-tangible aspects are also among them. At the same time, no two people, communities, or nations may fully agree on the ideological front, political or otherwise. These multi-racial, multi-ethnic, multi-tribal, multi-religious, multi-linguistic, multi-cultural, and multi-ideological features of the human society only make it widely sophisticated, diverse, and magnificent. Every state across the globe has its share of this human heritage. Indeed, it is a heritage worth celebrating.

It is true that any group of people anywhere on the planet will always cherish their own identities, such as race, ethnicity, tribe, religion, language, culture, ideology, and the like. It is simply a universal phenomenon. This, however, does not necessarily suggest that any one group of people of a particular identity will have an inborn sense of dislike or hatred towards those of other identities. In the end, all humans have the same basic needs and aspirations. Moreover, children born to parents of any identity are equally precious. All this implies that it should be easy for every living human being to open one's heart to the wellbeing and happiness of all the others on the planet. However, the politicians who indulge in identity politics do not make it that easy.

These politicians make relentless efforts to thrive on the identifiable differences among the people as a means to come to power, and to hold on to power. They first sow seeds of hatred and animosity among the groups of different identities. After that, they begin to champion the cause of some of the identity groups against those of the others, promoting fear and suspicion among all. In the process, people begin to define their relationships by their identifiable differences. This, in turn, leads to discord and conflicts among the differing groups. Some conflicts turn bloody and claim lives, as seen earlier in the book. Unfortunately, however, the more there is hatred, suspicion, discord, and violence, the more the people tend to empower the very politicians who created the rifts. Once in power, such politicians gladly adopt discriminatory laws and policies in favour of the groups of people whom they represent. Such acts of discrimination, in fact, could have adverse effects beyond the jurisdiction of the state that creates them. US President Barack Obama referred to this unfortunate reality in the context of the deteriorating relationship between the United States and the Muslim world. He did so in his historic June 4, 2009 Cairo address. In this speech, he said, "So long as our relationship is defined by our differences, we will empower those who sow hatred rather than peace, and who promote conflict rather than the cooperation that can help all of our people achieve justice and prosperity. This cycle of suspicion and discord must end." (McCain 2009, para. 14)

No doubt, it is essential to end the empowerment of those who sow seeds of hatred and promote fear and suspicion among humans based on their identifiable differences. For this, people must first start celebrating, instead of despising, the diversity among them. After all, it is an asset, and not a liability. It is easy to understand this by looking at the animal species on the planet. They do not look alike, sound alike, or behave alike. Would it not be better that way? Of course, it would be better that way. Humans all over the world enjoy this animal diversity. Governments and private organizations around the world spend colossal amounts of money every year to save endangered species from extinction. In addition, they run and maintain massive zoos, exhibiting different animal species. At the same time, scientists around the world spend their time and money researching the finer details of the intricacies of their lives. Every little secret of their lives, unveiled through such research, gives immense joy to all humans. This situation should equally apply to the diversity among humans. We, humans should and must find time to understand, appreciate, and celebrate the intrinsic diversity among us.

In exploring human diversity, one could also discover some fundamental values all humans share. Freedom of thought, freedom of conscience and religion, freedom of speech, freedom of peaceful assembly, and freedom of choice of employment are some of these common values. The right to education, the right to own property, the right to work, and the right to rest are a few others. A standard of living adequate for the health and wellbeing of oneself and family, free participation in the cultural life of the community, and the ability to take part in the government directly or through freely chosen representatives are three others. These and other fundamental human values, in fact, constitute the foundation of freedom, justice, and peace in the world. This also means that the parties to inevitable conflicts among humans could rely on these common values as a basis for resolving them in a peaceful manner. When the common human values become a basis for resolving a conflict, every party would be able to look at the competing positions of all other parties in an empathetic manner. This, in turn, could help the conflicting parties find peaceful solutions in a mutually acceptable manner.

The UN Charter of June 1945 first listed the fundamental common human values. The Charter referred to them as *human rights and fundamental freedoms* for all, without distinction as to race, sex, language, or religion. Then, the same common values reappeared, this time in detail, in *the Universal Declaration of Human Rights* adopted by the UN in December 1948. These fundamental human rights and freedoms are equally applicable to all nations and states, irrespective of their varied social or political cultures. In emphasizing this point in his Cairo address, President Obama said, "I do have an unyielding belief that all people yearn for certain things: the ability to speak your mind and have a say in how you are governed, confidence in the rule of law and equal administration of justice, government that is transparent and doesn't steal from the people, the freedom to live as you choose. These are not just American values. They are human rights. And that is why we will support them everywhere. (McCain 2009, para. 61)

His specific reference to the fundamental human rights and freedoms as a basis for a fresh dialogue between the United States and the Muslim countries shows the relevance and the significance of these common human values in resolving major conflicts in the world.

The UN adopted the Universal Declaration of Human Rights in December 1948 by a vote of 48 in favour, 0 against, with eight abstentions. Afghanistan, Argentina, Australia, Belgium, Bolivia, Brazil, Burma (Myanmar), Canada, Chile, China, and Columbia were among the states that voted in favour of the Declaration. Costa Rica, Cuba, Denmark, the Dominican Republic, Ecuador, Egypt, El Salvador, Ethiopia, France, Greece, Guatemala, Haiti, and Iceland were also among them. The remaining countries that voted in favour include India, Iran, Iraq, Lebanon, Liberia, Luxembourg, Mexico, Netherlands, New Zealand, Nicaragua, Norway, Pakistan, Panama, Paraguay, Peru, Philippines, Thailand, Sweden, Syria, Turkey, the United Kingdom, the United States, Uruguay, and Venezuela. The abstentions were Yugoslavia, South Africa, Saudi Arabia, and the Soviet Bloc states. The Soviet Bloc states include Byelorussia, Czechoslovakia, Poland, Ukraine, and the USSR. A close review of the list of the states that voted in favour shows that they include states of majority populations belonging to all major religions, including Christianity, Islam, Hinduism, and Buddhism. Afghanistan, Egypt, Ethiopia, Iran, Iraq, Lebanon, Liberia, Pakistan, Syria, and Turkey, were among the Muslim majority states who voted in favour of the Universal Declaration.

Many notable academics and religious leaders praised the adoption of the Universal Declaration of Human Rights. For example, soon after its adoption, the Lebanese philosopher and diplomat Charles Malik called it "an international document of the first order of importance" ("Universal Declaration", 2011, para. 27). Then, on October 5, 1995, Pope John Paul praised it as "one of the highest expressions of the human conscience of our time" ("Universal Declaration", 2011, para. 27). At the same time, there were occasional reaffirmations of commitment to the Universal Declaration of Human Rights and its principles by many states in different regions of the world. For example, the Asian states reaffirmed their commitment to the principles of the Universal Declaration as well as the UN Charter with their Bangkok Declaration of 1993. Then, a December 10, 2003 statement, issued by Marcello Spatafora on behalf of the European Union, said that the Universal Declaration "placed human rights at the centre of the framework of principles and obligations shaping relations within the international community" ("Universal Declaration", 2011, para. 27).

Despite such praise and support for the Universal Declaration, there has been some criticism in relation to some of its contents. According to the critics, the Universal Declaration does not adequately address important issues in four main areas: cultural and religious context of Islamic countries; property rights; education; and freedom of thought, conscience, and religion.

Some Islamic countries, in particular, took the position that the Universal Declaration failed to take into account the cultural and religious context of Islamic nations. The concerned Muslim countries include Iran, Saudi Arabia, Sudan, and Pakistan. They said that Muslims could not implement the Declaration without "trespassing the Islamic law" ("Cairo Declaration" 2007, para. 3). As a follow up, the foreign ministers of 45 member-states of the Organization of the Islamic Conference adopted a separate human rights document on August 5, 1990 to serve them as a guiding document in matters of human rights. The Conference adopted it under the name '*The Cairo Declaration on Human Rights in Islam.*' Ten months later, the Organization of the Islamic Conference officially resolved to support this Cairo Declaration. Its critics, however, point out that it limits the rights enshrined in the Universal Declaration and the International Covenants. For example, they say that the Cairo Declaration guarantees equal dignity, but not equal rights for women. Because of such rights limitations, the critics say that the Cairo Declaration does not appear to be complementary to the Universal Declaration.

Critics of the Universal Declaration in the area of property rights argue that the property rights through forceful extraction, for example taxation, negate other peoples' inalienable rights. According to the critics, the Declaration has not addressed this important issue. The criticism in the area of education centres on Article 26 of the Universal Declaration. According to this Article, elementary education shall be compulsory. In the opinion of the critics, compulsory education violates the right of a person to follow his or her own interests, say in alternative education or to go without schooling. The issue criticized in the section covering freedom of thought, conscience, and religion is that the right to conscientious objection to military service is omitted. Organizations and groups such as the Amnesty International and War Resisters International would like to see that right included in the Universal Declaration.

The above examples show that the 1948 Universal Declaration of Human Rights is no longer valid as a 'universal' document. The contentious issues in these areas call for in depth discussions at the UN General Assembly. All UN member-states need to carefully consider all the issues in question, with a view to arriving at an improved document of universal human rights truly acceptable to the global community. It is a UN task already long overdue. An improved document would have not only worldwide acceptance, but also across-the-board applicability in conflict resolution both within and among nations.

Until an improved universal declaration comes into effect, all states need to continue to use the 1948 Universal Declaration of Human Rights document to its fullest potential. Every UN-member state is obliged to respect and implement its provisions effectively without fear or favour. At the same time, UN-member states also have an obligation to repeal their own laws and regulations found inconsistent with the intent and purpose of the UN human rights declarations. This should apply to their state constitutions as well.

Despite the need to do more work to arrive at a truly universal human rights declaration, the fact remains that there are some fundamental human values shared by all humans. No one disputes that. The very existence of these common values makes it easier for humans to acknowledge and celebrate the diversity among them. Identifiable differences do not automatically instil dislike or hatred. These are learned emotions and attitudes. The more humans celebrate their diversity, the easier it becomes for each and every person to recognize and value the wellbeing and happiness of all humans, as one's own.

A close review of the ongoing major conflicts of identity politics shows that such conflicts arise from greed for power, hatred towards others based on their identities, or delusion on the part of the concerned politicians. There could also be a combination of these factors in a conflict of this type. Greedy politicians resort to identity politics as a means to gain power by enticing the majority community with promises of preferential treatment. Such politicians may not necessarily dislike or hate the affected minority groups. Unfortunately, this happens even in countries of established democratic practices. The primary goal of such politicians is to get power. They see identity politics as an easy means to accomplish their mission. On the other hand, some politicians engage in identity politics because of their strong dislike or hatred towards a specified group. Such politicians, as well as those motivated by greed for power, indulge in identity politics with a will.

Then, there are others indulging in identity politics under the auspices of democracy. At election time, they capitalize on the recognizable differences among the people, to their political advantage. They promise preferential treatment for some. After elections, they keep those promises, creating conflicts between those who have been favoured and the rest. However, these leaders think that ruling as representatives of the majority, solely for the benefit of the majority, is democracy. It is a false notion. They are deluded. The true meaning of democracy, in its simplest form, is the "rule of the people, by the people, for the people," as explained by Abraham Lincoln. In a democracy, all the people, not limited to a majority of any sort, should be taking part in making decisions that matter to them. In addition, governments must respect and safeguard the rights of minorities and apply justice that is equal and fair for everyone.

In the above situation, the solution to conflicts of this type lies in everyone's preparedness to *treat the wellbeing and happiness of all humans just as one's own*. Such an appreciation at societal level would help prevent those politicians who attempt to thrive on identity politics from coming to power. In their place, people would elect politicians who promote peace and cooperation instead of hatred, fear, suspicion and conflict.

A NEW BEGINNING FOR HUMANKIND

It is clear from the above that the key to lasting peace on Earth lies in four noble human virtues: caring and sharing; forgiving and forgetting; acting responsibly in a trustworthy and reliable manner; and appreciating the wellbeing and happiness of all humans, just as one's own. These are four distinct facets of universal loving kindness and compassion. Lasting peace can be guaranteed, however, only if all the four noble human virtues exist simultaneously. They also need to exist at all levels of humanity: personal, communal, societal, and global. This, in fact, calls for nothing short of an altogether *New Beginning for Humankind*.

Such a New Beginning may appear to some as a mere daydream. This is understandable. Many people around the globe thought the same way when it was first proposed to end slavery, fascism, Nazism, and other forms of authoritative rule. However, history has repeatedly proved that all such doubting Toms were wrong. Right now, we should not ignore our ability to make the world what we want. The destiny of humanity, and the world, is, indeed, in our own hands. The question we should be asking is not whether such a *New Beginning for Humankind* could ever be possible, but how we could make that New Beginning a reality.

However, this is not something we can accomplish in a hurry. It may take a considerable number of years or even decades. In any event, for anything of this magnitude and significance, first we need a steadfast process. In this particular case, it should be a process leading to an altogether new generation of humans endowed with all the four noble virtues. The time that it may take to realize the New Beginning should not scare anyone away from the process. The earlier we start such a process, the earlier we should be able to realize such a New Beginning. If we do not start such a process, we will never realize the desired New Beginning.

If we choose not to start such a process, the world will continue to remain in a fragile state of tension, subject to dangerous power struggles. And history would repeat itself with worldwide catastrophes similar to WWI or WWII. It is also important to understand that every time such a global catastrophe occurs, the destruction to life and property is greater than ever before. A comparison of the losses experienced during WWI and WWII clearly demonstrates this. For example, as indicated in chapter 1, the total number of human lives lost in WWI was 15 million and in WWII, 65 million. The estimates of civilian deaths were as high as 750,000 (5 percent) and 40 million (65 percent), respectively. These undeniable and frightening facts do call for our total commitment to a meaningful process designed to bring about lasting peace on the planet.

A convenient starting point for such a process could be a few minutes of daily contemplation of the four noble human virtues by every able living person. Such contemplation could take the form of some simple thoughts of determination to live up to the four noble virtues. There is no one particular set of words to verbalize such thoughts. Any set of words would be acceptable, as long as it explicitly refers to the four noble virtues in question. A specific set of words suitable for adults, however, may not be equally suitable for children. Children should have an especially composed set of words in a child's diction. At the same time, there is no need for anyone to learn a new language to start contemplating on these virtues. It can be done in any language, anytime, anywhere. A simply worded daily contemplation for young people in English could be as follows:

- *I shall care for the needs of others and share what is available in an equitable manner.*
- *I shall forgive and forget any harm done by others.*
- *I shall always act responsibly in a trustworthy and reliable manner.*
- *I shall appreciate the wellbeing and happiness of all humans, just as my own - regardless of race, ethnicity, tribe, religion, language, culture, and ideology.*

Such loving kindness and compassionate thoughts and words of contemplation are consistent with the teachings of all major religions. For example, the Bible (Christianity) tells us, "Let all bitterness and wrath and anger and clamouring and blasphemy be put away from you, together with all malice; and be kind one to another and tender-hearted, forgiving one another, even as God has forgiven us through Christ" (Ephesians 4:31 & 4:32). The Quran (Islam) tells us, "O mankind! We created you from a single [pair] of a male and a female, and made you into nations and tribes, that ye may know each other [not that you may despise each other]. Verily the most honoured of you in the sight of Allah is the most righteous of you" (Al-Hujurāt 49:13). Basavanna of Hinduism says, "You need to show compassion to all living beings. Compassion is the root of all religious faith" (Vachana 247). Sutta Pitaka of Buddhism says, "As a mother would risk her life to protect her child, her only child, even so should one cultivate a limitless heart with regard to all beings" (Karanīya Metta Sutta, Verse 7). The Oral Torah of Judaism says, "The world stands upon three things: upon the Law, upon worship, and upon showing kindness" (Mishnah, Abot 1.2). The scriptures of other religions also support such viewpoints. There is also no reason to believe that those who do not claim any religious identity will find such human virtues to be offensive or unacceptable.

It may be appropriate to reiterate that the Quran devotes itself to the ethics of loving kindness and compassion, like the main scriptures of other major religions. This reiteration is necessary as at times the Quran has been labelled as an instrument of violence and extremism. The critics of such labeling, however, say that the Quran speaks against aggression and calls for fights in the name of God only against those who have transgressed. In related comments on the Quran, Karen Armstrong says, "It's (the Quran is) not concerned with doctrine. It's about living justly and looking after the poor and vulnerable in your community" (Todd 2009, para. 28). Karen Armstrong is a renowned author of many books about Jesus, Buddhism, Jerusalem, Judaism, theology, and mysticism. According to the Islamic collection Hadith, Prophet Mohammed himself has said, "Not one of you can be a believer (of Islam) unless he desires for his neighbour what he desires for himself" ("Does the Koran say", n.d., para. 1). Many, in fact, believe that loving kindness and compassion are at the core of all religions.

Any person, whether belonging to a religion or not, could easily contemplate the four noble human virtues, like a mantra, on a daily basis. The best time for this could be either just before starting daily work in the morning or just before going to bed at night. Daily reflections of such words and thoughts have the power to change the mindset of humans at all levels. Another possibility is that all living humans could engage in this contemplation together, at a pre-determined time, perhaps once or twice a year. At the chosen time, all participants could reflect together on the four noble human virtues. Thus, all Christians,

Muslims, Hindus, Buddhists, Jews, and those of other religions or who have no religion, could reflect on the same thoughts and words at the same time. Together, they would represent all the world's racial, ethnic, tribal, linguistic, cultural, and ideological groups. Among them, there would be parents, teachers, and students, as well as farmers, anglers, tradespersons, factory and office workers, miners, marketers, shoppers, sailors, and road/water/air travellers. In such an event, the vibration of the simultaneous contemplation of positive thoughts and words by this great number around the globe would be phenomenal, and would bring phenomenal results.

Schools, in particular, could conduct special contemplation sessions for their students, say once a day. Such a session could be part of the agenda for the school general assembly, normally held in the morning before any classroom work begins. Another convenient time for such a session could be at the end of the last classroom session. As an alternative, schools could incorporate such contemplation sessions into their moral instruction classes. While conducting contemplation sessions, schools can also guide their students to put into practice the noble virtues they contemplate, in their day-to-day life. In so doing, students could be encouraged to maintain a journal where they could record on a regular basis all their acts of kindness and compassion towards their fellow beings. At the beginning, these acts could be as simple as helping a fellow student or a family member at home. Developing interest in such acts of kindness could also help eliminate the bullying problems generally associated with school settings.

With the help of these contemplation sessions and properly planned programmes for follow-up practice of kindness and compassion by students, schools could take the lead in building the desired new society. It would be a society where people would care and share, forgive and forget, act responsibly in a trustworthy and reliable manner, and treat the wellbeing and happiness of all humans just as one's own. Their care and compassion for their fellow beings would extend worldwide, beyond all identifiable differences based on race, ethnicity, tribe, religion, language, and other identities. This, in turn, would help the world find solutions to conflicts both within and among nations or states in a friendly, peaceful manner; such solutions will benefit all.

Research has shown that well-designed violence prevention and conflict resolution programmes in schools also can have significant positive impact on students. The Resolving Conflict Creativity Program in the United States is one such programme. The initiators of this programme, the US Educators for Social Responsibility (ESR), had extended it to four hundred schools by 2005. According to Joan Almon, the US coordinator of the Alliance for Childhood, an independent evaluation of this programme has found that it "successfully teaches young people the skills of negotiation, mediation, and peacemaking" (Benjamin & Evans 2005, 47). At the same time, Almon believes that in these schools, educators, in fact, were better prepared for the 9/11 event. In explaining this further, Linda Lantieri, the founding director of this particular school programme, said, "Children in our programmes have learned the healing power of love and respect and understanding. They see the connection between the way they treat one another and the way they will treat the world when they are in charge. (Benjamin & Evans 2005, 47)

Such school programmes even in other areas of human endeavour have produced similar, positive results. The success of an elementary-school programme aimed at improving pedestrian road manners in Zambia is a case in point. In my first visit to that country in the late seventies, I was pleasantly surprised by the extremely high standard of road manners of its pedestrians. The way they used their roads at the time was much superior to anything I had seen in any of the other countries I had visited by then, developed or developing. In my quest to understand how Zambian pedestrians had achieved such high standards, I realized that a 25-year old elementary-school programme had done the trick. This particular programme required every elementary-school community (students and teachers), especially in the cities, to spend a few minutes at their morning assembly to contemplate on road manners, on a weekly or daily basis. At the assembly, typically one student would come to the podium and lead the audience in chanting a few lines of instructions for proper road use. For example, the instructions for crossing a road at a marked crossing read "Look right; Look left; Look right again; if the road is clear cross over, but do not hurry." The repetition of these and other road manners by elementary school students on a regular basis had produced the generation of Zambians I encountered in the late seventies. As seen in these examples, such school programmes have the ability to bring about positive reinforcement in society by applying new behaviour patterns and creating new mind sets, in any area of human endeavour. If we implement such a school programme across the globe, its results would also be felt globally.

The implementation of such school programmes and pre-arranged group contemplation sessions worldwide requires the active support of many groups. These groups include religious and political leaders of all stripes, local governments, state governments, the UN, and all other national and international peace organizations. The UN, in particular, could consider facilitating such a school programme worldwide with the cooperation of all independent sovereign states. In addition, it could consider facilitating the annual or biannual global contemplation sessions at pre-arranged dates and times. It would be most appropriate to have such a global session on the International Day of Peace, September 21st, each year. The involvement of the UN in all these would help spread, to every nook and corner of the world, the message of the four noble human virtues that support lasting peace. At the same time, such UN involvement would also strengthen the worldwide public resolve to avoid wars and to resort to non-violent means in solving ongoing conflicts.

However, no one around the globe should wait until the UN and these other groups have initiated such measures. Instead, all peace-loving people around the world should start doing what they can in the pursuit of lasting global peace. They could begin the process with the daily practice of contemplation of the said noble human virtues. Then, they could spread this practice among their family, friends, workmates, and so on. At the same time, they could also form special peace contemplation forums, perhaps in the form of peace clubs and societies. They could do this at their places of study (colleges, universities, and training centres), work places, and community centres.

The entire process for the New Beginning for humankind should be open to voluntary participation at all levels, as individuals, local communities, nations, states, and as the global community. No individual, community, or organization has to stay away from participation in the process due to lack of resources, financial or otherwise. All that is required is the willingness to be a party to a message of loving kindness and compassion and to share it with others.

All the above individual, collective, and institutional measures together would help realize the desired New Beginning for humans. In this New Beginning, the mighty power of the four noble human virtues will triumph over the reasons that cause major conflicts in the world, ensuring lasting peace on Earth.

There is enough evidence to suggest that the process proposed for the realization of the New Beginning will meet with rapid success. The progress made so far by the modern environmental movement provides the most obvious of all such evidence. A highly recognizable signpost of the environmental movement began with just one man's idea to have a special teach-in day on the environment. In 1970, US Senator Gaylord Nelson of Wisconsin founded this day, which later became known as the Earth Day, to bring attention to the deteriorating environment. He planned to achieve this goal by having nationwide teach-in events on college campuses on this special day, every year. However, even the first Earth Day became much more eventful and influential than he contemplated. Now, millions of people around the world commemorate this day. A report prepared by World View, an international programme for educators of the University of North Carolina, explains, "Originally, Senator Nelson's plan was to start a nationwide 'teach-in' on the environment on college campuses, but soon others realized they shared common concerns and values. Grassroots organizations planned rallies, teach-ins, protests and more and soon the first Earth Day involved 20 million concerned citizens. By 2007, it is estimated that close to one billion people participated in events all over the world." ("Earth Day" 2010, para. 1)

The same World View report says that the 2010 Earth Day events spanned 192 countries and 19,000 organizations. The expected number of participants in these events was 1.5 billion worldwide. The 19,000 organizations include non-governmental organizations, quasi-governmental organizations, local governments, activist groups, and others. Together they focused on environmental education, public environmental campaigns, and environmental policies. In the process, they have summoned the public support, the energy, and the commitment to save the environment. All this has significantly changed the way we think and work as individuals, communities, and even governments. Many related activities around us speak for this. These activities include picking up trash, using blue boxes, and tree planting projects. Schools, special clubs, and societies dedicate their efforts to the environment and UN sponsored Earth Day events. Meanwhile, governments around the world have enacted numerous statutory acts to save the environment. These laws protect clean air, condemn environmental pollution, manage waste and water, and protect endangered species and habitat. All this shows how the Earth Day campaign, which was born out of one man's idea, has immensely contributed to the ongoing efforts to save the environment over the last four decades. The process for lasting peace on the planet with a New Beginning for Humankind could succeed in the same manner.

The process leading to the New Beginning would also achieve a higher level of global peace than anything that is possible through present, conventional peace efforts. However, this does not suggest in any manner that the ongoing conventional peace efforts are not important. The efforts made towards world peace by the UN, in particular, are commendable. All peace-loving people around the globe should be appreciating them. Among these efforts, the UN has established a list of fundamental common human values through a universal declaration, although it does need further improvement. In addition, the UN has also declared an International Day of Peace, and taken the lead in resolving international conflicts. These and other UN efforts have generated numerous peace activities around the world. These activities vary in nature. The ringing of the Peace Bell at the UN Headquarters, one or two minutes of silence observance, music and other entertainment shows, prayer vigils, and flag ceremonies for global peace are among them. Flying peace doves, school activities, writing competitions, special parades and festivals, and peace polls are also among them. These and other activities mostly take place on the International Day of Peace. Meanwhile, some groups of peace-loving individuals around the world have established peace organizations, such as the Peace in Our Life Time. Then, there are over three hundred special peace prizes given out every year to people who have dedicated their lives to promoting peace in the world. The most prestigious of them is the Noble Prize for Peace, which began in 1901. There have already been about 100 recipients.

All these conventional peace efforts need to continue and grow. Their primary focus, however, appears to be the need to end wars, rather than eradicating what causes wars. For example, the 2001 UN resolution on the International Day of Peace specifically declared, that it "shall henceforth be observed as a day of global ceasefire and non-violence, an invitation to all nations and people to honour a cessation of hostilities for the duration of the day" ("Resolution Adopted" 2001, para. 7). No doubt, it is a symbolic call. Still, the intent of the call does not go beyond the mere absence of war. This is not going to be good enough to ensure lasting peace on Earth. The New Beginning for Humankind described in this chapter takes the global peace mission to a much higher level, guaranteeing lasting peace for all our future generations.

Chapter 8:
Summary and Conclusion

THIS BOOK IS AN attempt to find out how to make the world we live in a safer and more peaceful place for our future generations. It started with a warning of a looming global nuclear catastrophe of unprecedented consequences. This warning came with two grisly reminders. One of them reminded us of the extensive and horrible destruction to life and property in Hiroshima and Nagasaki in 1945 caused by the first ever nuclear bomb attacks on the planet. The present looming nuclear catastrophe, if detonated, could repeat this history on a much, much larger scale. The other reminder warned us of the dire possibility that a violent conflict in any corner of the world, given the right conditions, could develop into a global fiasco; this, in fact, was what happened in WWI and WWII.

In any serious attempt to make our planet safer and more peaceful for our future generations, we must find answers to four critical questions. The book laid out these questions at the end of the introductory chapter, Chapter 1, hoping to answer them in the subsequent chapters. The first of these questions asked what the major violent conflicts in the world are today. The second asked whether there is any guarantee that none of the existing conflicts will deteriorate into a worldwide fiasco. Question three asked, in the event that there is no such guarantee, how we can prevent the outbreak of the looming global nuclear catastrophe. The fourth and last question asked whether there is anything more to be done to guarantee lasting peace on the planet.

Chapters 2 and 3, in particular, attempted to answer the first of these four critical questions. These chapters showed that there are many major violent conflicts in the world today. Some of them are among states, while others are within the boundaries of a single state. Then, there is also a special violent conflict with no borders, across the globe. Chapter 2 was fully devoted to inter-state and intrastate conflicts. It described in detail four inter-state and 17 ongoing intrastate conflicts. In addition, it gave a brief account of the recently concluded 11 inter-state and 30 intrastate conflicts. This helped the reader better understand the reasons behind such major conflicts. Chapter 3 separately discussed a special major conflict with no borders, showing its progress in what appears to be a never-ending series of bloody acts of terror. This chapter also explained how and why these terrorist attacks primarily target the citizens of the Western countries, and in particular the United States.

Some Islamic militant groups take responsibility for the terror attacks associated with this conflict. However, no one particular racial, ethnic, tribal, religious, linguistic, cultural, or ideological group appears to be behind the current world conflicts in general. Instead, one sees people of varied identities among the slaughterers as well as the slaughtered. The Islamic militant groups who take responsibility for the global terrorist attacks represent only a tiny fraction of the Muslim community. Irrespective of who should take the final responsibility for the existing major conflicts in the world, one thing is clear: all existing conflicts keep the world in a state of high tension. At the same time, there is also a real fear that any one of the major violent conflicts, given the right conditions, could soon detonate the looming global nuclear catastrophe.

The second question asked whether there is any guarantee that none of the ongoing conflicts could end up in a worldwide fiasco. To find the answer to this question, Chapter 4 first investigated in detail the ability of the existing global checks and balances to prevent such an eventuality. The global community is implementing these safeguards through the UN. This investigation focused on three aspects of these preventative measures: how they came about; their successes and failures; and the reasons for the failures. Next, Chapter 5 investigated the nature of the changing world dynamics, exploring their potential impact on ongoing conflicts. The findings of these two chapters provide only bad news: if the status quo remains, there is the dire possibility that one or more of the ongoing major conflicts could detonate the looming global nuclear fiasco. This answers the second question: there is no guarantee that none of the ongoing conflicts would end up in a worldwide catastrophe.

The third critical question specifically asked for what needs to be done in this grave situation. In answering this question, Chapter 6 showed that the prevention of such an eventuality is possible by taking immediate action in two main areas: reducing global tension and strengthening the global checks and balances now applied through the UN. For the reduction of global tension, this chapter proposed action in four main areas: ending global policing by powerful nations; ending the US-led WOT; destroying all WMD; and adopting non-violent means of conflict resolution. For further improvement of the present global checks and balances, this chapter proposed a complete overhaul or replacement of the UN. Of all the measures endorsed in this chapter, it is most important that unilateral global policing by major powers and the US-led WOT should end immediately. At the same time, the global community must find a way to destroy all stockpiles of weapons of mass destruction at the earliest opportunity. Further, all those engaged in violent conflicts must start afresh and seek to end them through non-violent means. Then, any exercise to overhaul or replace the UN needs to address effectively the reasons for its past and present failures.

All the above measures call for direct, positive action, specifically by state governments. The governments of the present and emerging global powers should take the lead in ensuring proper and timely implementation of these measures. The success or failure to end unilateral global policing, in particular, depends solely on how these particular nations themselves would act. Then, on its own accord, the United States, the number one global power, can implement the proposed actions to end the WOT. This should effectively end all US military missions still operating under the pretext of the WOT.

The destruction of all stockpiles of WMD requires positive action by the governments of the states that possess such weapons. This applies to all such states, irrespective of one's status as a global power or not. The other two measures, adopting non-violent means of conflict resolution and reforming or replacing the UN, call for cooperation and positive action by all governments around the globe. The stakes are too high for any state government to procrastinate or do nothing on any of these strategic measures. Time is ticking. All state governments should step up to the plate and attend to this critical need before it becomes too late.

These measures, no doubt, will have the ability to prevent the eruption of the threatening global nuclear catastrophe. However, the mere prevention of the outbreak of this impending catastrophe would not necessarily change the present human destiny of living under war threats every so often. Lasting peace on Earth is possible only if we also change this human destiny. The fourth and last critical question at the end of the introductory chapter specifically asked what more is required to meet this end.

Chapter 7 answered this question. First, it showed that it is, indeed, possible to change the existing dismal human destiny to one of lasting peace. However, the same chapter explained that this change will not result from any new treaties, pacts, or high-sounding speeches made by world leaders. Nor will it stem from any change in the power dynamics among the major global powers. Instead, lasting peace on Earth is possible only through a concerted effort by humans to subdue the enemies of peace within themselves.

The most significant of these internal enemies include greed, hatred, and delusion. In this context, greed refers to the excessive or uncontrolled desire for wealth or power. This kind of desire never ends. It simply grows and multiplies when more wealth or power is achieved. As discussed in Chapter 7, it is this insatiable desire that causes conflicts of economic exploitation. Such desire is also a main contributor to conflicts triggered by the misuse of state power.

Hatred refers to the emotions of strong dislike or resentment, rage, and envy towards a person or a group of persons. These emotions are the primary cause of conflicts of social and political vendetta discussed earlier in the book. Such emotions also contribute to conflicts of identity politics. Then, delusion refers to the wilful ignorance of reality. Chapter 7 discussed how delusion plays a key role in conflicts arising from the misuse of state power and identity politics.

The strategy suggested in Chapter 7 for subduing these internal enemies of peace is to create an altogether New Beginning for Humankind. It calls for a revitalized generation of humans endowed with four noble human virtues: caring and sharing; forgiving and forgetting; acting responsibly in a trustworthy and reliable manner; and appreciating the well being and happiness of all humans as one's own. These four noble human virtues have the power to subdue the enemies of peace that are primarily responsible for major conflicts among humans.

Chapter 7 also outlined a steadfast process for realizing the New Beginning for Humankind. It is a credible, achievable, and proven process. Similar processes in the past have produced desired results. The same chapter described three such processes. They include the process used in the Resolving Conflict Creativity Program in the United States and the one used by the modern environmental movement. The other is a process implemented in Zambia some decades back. All such processes, indeed, have delivered their intended results. This is not all. The process now proposed for realizing the New Beginning for Humankind also aims at a much higher level of global peace than what could ever be possible with conventional methods of peacemaking. The conventional means of peacemaking only aim at avoiding and containing wars. It does not automatically result in lasting peace. In contrast, the process for the New Beginning for Humankind aims at achieving lasting peace on Earth.

The implementation of the proposed process for the New Beginning also requires the blessings and active support of all levels of governments. In addition, it calls for direct and active support from a number of other parties. These parties include all peace-lovers and their organizations, educators, religious leaders, and politicians of all shades and beliefs from all the countries in the world. In fact, it is a process where every living human being, young or old, can play a very important role. The more individuals and organizations join the process, the shorter the time it will take to deliver the intended results.

All this clearly indicates that there are two main challenges to overcome in order to ensure lasting peace on Earth for our future generations. The first and most urgent challenge is to prevent the outbreak of a looming nuclear world war. The potential destruction to life and property it could bring about is beyond anybody's power of comprehension. In comparison, the destruction suffered during WWI and WWII would seem negligible. Consider the sophistication of weapons now available and the modern techniques of warfare. Many agree that the next world war would have the potential to turn the entire human species into ashes within seconds. The survivors of a third world war, if any, would have to start anew in a devastated world. Repeated here are the warning words of Albert Einstein (1879 – 1955), "I know not with what weapons World War III will be fought, but World War IV would be fought with sticks and stones" ("Albert Einstein" 1998, para. 15). This clearly shows the great urgency to implement the measures required to prevent the eruption of the global nuclear disaster that threatens us all. The second challenge is to ensure that the world would remain peaceful with no further threats of looming global catastrophes any time in the future. The onus is on the present occupants of the planet to do their very best to overcome these challenges, together and now.

This book has not only identified the clear and inescapable challenges to world peace, but has also proposed some specific measures to overcome them. Further, it has identified the parties that should be taking the lead in implementing them. Now, these parties have two options. One option is to ignore all this and do nothing, in spite of the potentially catastrophic dangers. If this is going to be their choice, they would be providing the perfect conditions to fight the next world war with nuclear weapons, and, of course, the one after that with sticks and stones. Their other option is to implement the measures needed to prevent the detonation of the looming global nuclear disaster and to bring to life the proposed New Beginning for Humankind. If this were the option chosen, the world would be a place with no more wars and people all around it would be endowed with the said noble human virtues. In that future world, people will celebrate their diversity, respect their common values, and resolve their inevitable conflicts without resorting to violence. The choice between the two options, in the best interests of our future generations, is clear as crystal.

Doing nothing in the face of these challenges is certainly not an option for anyone to consider. Pursuing that option only provides a silent setting where evil will flourish. In the past, a number of great philosophers reminded us of this reality in numerous ways. For instance, in the eighteenth century, Anglo-Irish philosopher Edmond Burke (1729-97) said, "The only thing necessary for evil to flourish is for good men to do nothing" ("Quotes to reflect on", n.d., para. 8). Two centuries later, Albert Einstein said, "The world is a dangerous place, not because of those who do evil, but because of those who look on and do nothing" ("Quotes on Speaking Out", n. d., para. 20). These reminders can give strength to everyone's resolve to do what is needed to prevent the unthinkable and to establish lasting peace on Earth for the sake of our future generations. There is no excuse for inaction - for anyone. Let us all start now. Together we will succeed.

- *May everyone care for the needs of others and share what is available in an equitable manner.*
- *May everyone forgive and forget any harm done by others.*
- *May everyone always act responsibly in a trustworthy and reliable manner.*
- *May everyone appreciate the wellbeing and happiness of all humans, just as one's own - irrespective of race, ethnicity, tribe, religion, language, culture, and ideology.*

About The Author

R.B. HERATH IS A writer, poet, dramatist, and a political reformist. In all these roles, he has always strived for peace in difficult situations. He did this first as a student leader in his high school and university days and later as the leader of a political party in his country of origin, Sri Lanka. One of the primary aims of his party was to prevent the outbreak of a looming separatist war in the country. For this, it provided a political platform designed to ensure the civil, human, and political rights of the entire citizenry. After the separatist war broke out regardless, he left the country in 1984. He is well traveled, and has lived in several countries in Asia, Europe, Africa, and North America. He has an excellent knowledge of the international scene.

His earlier writings include four books, two in English and two in Sinhalese. The first book in English, *Sri Lankan Ethnic Crisis: Towards a Resolution* (Trafford, 2002), proposes a new, democratic model of governance for Sri Lanka as a political solution to its ethnic crisis. Canadian Foreign Minister Bill Graham, who was among the many reviewers of the book, forwarded it to others concerned (www.rbherath. com). The second book in English, *Real Power to the People: A Novel Approach to Electoral Reform in British Columbia* (University Press of America, 2007), reviews a unique experiment in democracy. In this experiment, the government of British Columbia (BC) gave its people the power to take control over its electoral reform process and to make a final decision, bypassing the BC Legislature.

Sri Lanka Desapalanaya, Ayanna, Aayanna, Eyanna, Eeyanna (Lankanatha, 1979) and *Desappremayen Odavadiwa Darudariyanta Kavivalinma Liyu Lipiyak* (Lankanatha, 1979) are the titles of Herath's books in Sinhalese. The English translation of the former reads as 'A, B, C, D of Sri Lankan Politics.' It analyses the politics of Sri Lanka up to the time of its separatist war. The English translation of the latter reads as 'A Letter to Our Children in Poems Written through Patriotism.' It conveys a message of love, peace, and unity to the children of Sri Lanka in a child's diction. The government of Sri Lanka at the time distributed it among the schools and municipal libraries of the country.

In his role as a dramatist, Herath first wrote and directed a stage drama, *Angulimala*, in Zambia in 1989. Later he wrote and directed three other stage dramas: *Hoisting the British Flag, Keppetipola Heroism,* and *The Independence Struggle.* He presented them at the 50th Sri Lankan Independence anniversary celebrations held in BC on March 7, 1998.

After immigrating to Canada in 1990, Herath pursued a career with the BC government. At the same time, he served as a member of the Board of Directors of the South Asian Network for Secularism and Democracy in North America for several years. In addition, he also served as a member of the Citizens' Assembly on Electoral Reform in British Columbia. He is married, and has three adult daughters and one granddaughter. He now lives with his wife in Surrey, BC, Canada.

References

Adolf, Anthony. 2009. *Peace: A world history.* Cambridge, UK: Polity.

Ahmed, Asso. 2008. "Iraq: Turkey's fight with Kurdish separatists." *The Babylon & Beyond Blog,* October 10. http://latimesblogs.latimes. com/babylonbeyond/2008/10/iraq-turkeys-fi.html.

"Albert Einstein: Man of Imagination." 1998. Accessed September 21, 2011. http://www.wagingpeace.org/menu/action/urgent actions/ einstein/

Algar, Hamid. 1983. *The roots of Islamic revolution.* Toronto, Canada: Open Press.

Ali, Abdullah Y. 1997. *The Meanings of the illustrious Qur'an: English translation.* New York: Alminar Publications.

Aljazeera. 2010. "Yemen rebels renew ceasefire offer." Last modified January 30. http://www.aljazeera.com/news/ middleeast/2010/01/2010130162418278418.html

"Al Qaeda leader Mutafa Abu al-Yazid." 2009. Accessed June 28, 2012. http://articles.nydailynews.com/2009-06-22/news/17925714_1_ nuclear-weapons-al-jazeera-al-qaeda

"America's image slips." *2006*. Accessed January 20, 2011. http://pewglobal.org/2006/06/13/americas-image-slips-but-allies-share-us-concerns-over-iran-hamas/

"Arab public opinion, Al-Qaeda & the long war." 2008. Accessed December 7, 2010. http://insurgencyresearchgroup.wordpress.com/2008/04/19/arab-public-opinion-al-qaeda-the-long-war/

Armstrong, Karen. 1991. *Holy war*. London, UK: Papermac Macmillan.

Avineri, Shlomo. 1981. *The making of modern Zionism: The intellectual origins of the Jewish state*. New York, NY: Basic Books.

Baranyi, Stephen, ed. 2008. *The paradoxes of peacebuilding post-9/11*. Vancouver, Canada: UBC Press.

BBC NEWS. 2003. "Palestinians get Saddam funds." Accessed November 26, 2010. http://news.bbc.co.uk/2/hi/middle_east/2846365.stm

Beg, Mirza A. 2005. DEBATE: Nuclear proliferation – a taxonomy. *Daily Times*. Accessed December 7, 2010. http://www.dailytimes.com.pk/default.asp?page=story_6-3-2005_pg3_6

Beg, Mirza A. n.d. *Emerging Multi-Polar World Order*. Accessed November 26, 2010. http://www.friends.org.pk/Beg/emerging%20multi-polar.htm

Belasco, Amy. 2011. *The Cost of Iraq, Afghanistan, and Other Global War on Terror Operations since 9/11*. Accessed October 30, 2011. http://www.fas.org/sgp/crs/natsec/RL33110.pdf

Benjamin, Medea and Jodie Evans. Eds. 2005. *Stop the next war now: Effective responses to violence and terrorism*. Maul, HI: Inner Ocean Pub.

Bergen, Peter & Paul Cruickshank. 2007. "The Iraq effect: War has increased terrorism sevenfold worldwide." *The Muslim Observer*, February 27. http://muslimmedianetwork.com/mmn/?p=752

Blix, Hans. 2003. "Oral introduction of the 12th quarterly report of UNMOVIC." http://www.un.org/Depts/unmovic/SC7asdelivered.htm

Brand, Laurie. 1988. *The Palestinians in the Arab world*. New York, NY: Colombia University Press.

"Brazil's nuclear ambitions." *2008*. Accessed March 12, 2009. http://www.coha.org/brazils-nuclear-ambitions-worrisome

"Cairo declaration of human rights in Islam – Diverges from the universal declaration of human rights in key respects." 2007. Accessed December 7, 2010. http://europenews.dk/en/node/3847

Caldicott, Helen. 2002. *The new nuclear danger: George W. Bush's military-industrial complex*. New York, NY: The New Press.

Cambanis, Thanassis. 2009. "Rocket fire from Lebanon unsettles Israel, but fears of a Hezbollah attack suicide." *The New York Times*. January 8. http://www.nytimes.com/2009/01/09/world/middleeast/09lebanon.html

Carter, Jimmy. 2006. *Palestine peace not apartheid*. New York, NY: Simon & Schuster.

Chomsky, Noam. 2006. *Failed states: The abuse of power and the assault on democracy*. New York, NY: Henry Holt Company, LLC.

"Classified key judgments." 2006. Accessed December 7, 2010. http://www.dni.gov/press_releases/Declassified_NIE_Key_Judgments.pdf

"Cold War 1945-1960." n.d. Accessed November 26, 2010. http://www.funfront.net/hist/europe/coldwar.htm

"Does the Koran say love thy brother." n.d. Accessed June 23, 2012. http://wiki.answers.com/Q/Does_the_Koran_say_love_thy_brother_as_thy_self_as_the_holy_bible_does

Downie, Andrew, and Sao Paulo. 2009. "Brazil's President Lula says G7 nations no longer speak for the world." http://www.telegraph.

co.uk/finance/g20-summit/5000495/Brazils-President-Lula-says-G7-nations-no-longer-speak-for-the-world.html

"Earth day: A global celebration." 2010. Accessed February 16, 2011. http://www.unc.edu/world/Global_Updates_2010/March_April/April_10.htm

Elmore, Mike. 2009. "Burma's ethnic minorities endure decades of brutality." Irrawaddy. Accessed April 14, 2009. http://www.irrawaddy.org/article.php?art_id=8891

Engelhardt, Tom. 2011. *How to End the War on Terror*. Accessed October 30, 2011. http://original.antiwar.com/engelhardt/2011/06/19/how-to-end-the-war-on- terror.

European Centre for Conflict Prevention (the Netherlands). 1999. *People Building Peace: 35 inspiring stories from around the world*. Utrecht, The Netherlands: Author.

Fisher, Suzanne W. 2009. *Amish Peace: Simple wisdom for a complicated world. Grand Rapids*, MI: Revell, a division of Baker Publishing Group.

Fisk, Robert. 2005. *The great war of civilization*. London, UK: Harper Collins.

Foot, Richard. 2009. "Harper's Afghan comments spot-on, says Manley." *Calgary Herald*, March 2. http://www.calgaryherald.com/news/Harper+Afghan+comments+spot+Manley+says/1345819/story.html

Fromkin, David. 1989. *A peace to end all peace*. New York, NY: Avon.

Fulford, Robert. 2011. "Bin Laden's cult of hate will live on." *The National Post*. May 7. http://fullcomment.nationalpost.com/2011/05/07/robert-fulford-bin-ladens-cult-of-hate-will-live-on/

Geopolitical Monitor. *2009*. "Indian Maoists take train passengers hostage." Accessed December 29. http://www.geopoliticalmonitor.com/indian-maoists-take-train-passengers-hostage/

"George Bush: The Taliban must hand over the terrorists, or share in their fate." Accessed December 6, 2010. http://www.independent. co.uk/news/world/americas/george-bush-the-taliban-must-hand-over-the-terrorists-or-share-in-their-fate-670249.html

Gerner, Deborah J. 1994. *One land, two peoples: The conflict over Palestine.* Boulder, CO: Westview Press.

Gerstenzang, James. 2008. "Bush to Russia: 'Bullying and intimidation are not acceptable'."*The Los Angeles Times*, August 15. http:// latimesblogs.latimes.com/presidentbush/2008/08/georgia-russi-1. html

Glick, Caroline B. (2011). "The PLO's desperate defenders." *The Jerusalem Post. May 6.* http://www.jpost.com/Opinion/Columnists/Article. aspx?id=219433

Griffiths, Rudyard. 2006. *Dialogue on democracy: The Lafontaine-Baldwin lectures 2000-2005.* Toronto, ON: Penguin Group.

Guardia, Anton L. 2009. "Lebanon bleeds as the whole world fights out its bloody wars." *The Telegraph.* March 1. http://www.telegraph. co.uk/comment/personal-view/3626455/Lebanon

Hafezi, Parisa, and Firouz Sedarat. 2009. "Iranian president raises stakes against Israel."*The Thompson Reuters,* September 18. http:// in.reuters.com/article/idINIndia-42553620090918

Hain, Peter. 2007. Peacemaking in Northern Ireland: A model for conflict resolution. Paper presented at the Royal Institute of International Affairs meeting held in Chatham House, June 12, in London, United Kingdom.

Hall, Richard. 2000. *The Balkan wars.* London, UK: Routledge.

Hanh, Thich N. 1991. *Peace is every step: The path of mindfulness in everyday life.* New York, NY: Bantam Books.

Hanh, Thich N. 2003. *Creating true peace: Ending violence in yourself, your family, your community, and the world.* New York, NY: Free Press.

Heacock, Paul, Carol-Jane V. Cassidy, John K. Bollard, and Julie Plier, Eds. 2009. *Cambridge academic content dictionary (1ˢᵗ ed.).* New York: Cambridge University Press.

Heacock, Paul, ed. 2009. *Cambridge academic content dictionary.* New York: Cambridge University Press.

Heacock, Paul. Ed. 2009. *Cambridge academic content dictionary.* New York: Cambridge University Press.

Herath, Ranbanda B . (2002). *Sri Lankan ethnic crisis: Towards a resolution.* Victoria, Canada: Trafford Publishing.

Herath, Ranbanda B. 2007. *Real power to the people: A novel approach to electoral reform in British Columbia.* Lanham, MD: University Press of America, Inc.

Human Security Centre. 2005. "*Human Security Report 2005: War and Peace in the 21st Century.*" Accessed December 6, 2010. http://www. hsrgroup.org/human-security-reports/2005/text.aspx

Hunt, Scott A. 2004. *The future of peace: On the front lines with the world's great peacemakers.* San Francisco, CA: HarperSanFrancisco.

IMEU. n.d. "*How many Palestinian refugees are there?* In *FAQ on the Nakba: The Nakba and Palestinian refugees today.* Accessed December 14, 2010. http://imeu.net/news/article001237.shtml

"India says Sino-Pakistan ties a 'serious concern.'" 2011. *The Express Tribune,* may 21. http://tribune.com.pk/story/173209/india-says-sino-pakistan-ties-a-serious-concern/

"India, Pakistan dialogue makes sense: Obama." 2009. *Indo-Canadian Voice World,* April 4.

"Iraq War and U.S. Global War on Terror." n.d. Accessed June 24, 2012. http://en.wikipedia.org/wiki/Iraq_War_and_U.S._Global_War_on_Terror

"Iraq war illegal, says Annan." 2004. Accessed December 6, 2010. http://news.bbc.co.uk/2/hi/3661134.stm

"Iraqi public on the US presence and the future of Iraq: A WorldPublicOpinion.org poll." 2006. Accessed November 23, 2008. http://www.worldpublicopinion.org/pipa/pdf/sep06/Iraq_Sep06_rpt.pdf

"Israeli minister threatens Iran." 2008. Accessed November 30, 2010. http://news.bbc.co.uk/2/hi/7440472.stm

Karon, Tony. 2009. "Behind Hamas' own war on terror." *TIME*. Accessed November 26, 2010. http://www.time.com/time/printout/0,8816,1917809,00.html.

"Key quotes on threat posed by Pakistan turmoil." 2009. Accessed November 26, 2010. http://uk.reuters.com/article/idUKTRE54D1JL20090514

Khoury, Jack. 2011. "Netanyahu: Hamas-Fatah unity pact is a victory for terrorism." *The Haaretz*. May 4. http://www.haaretz.com/news/diplomacy-defense/netanyahu-hamas-fatah-unity-pact-is-a-victory-for-terrorism-1.359821

Kile, Shannon N., Vitaly Fedchenko, Bharath Gopalaswamy, and Hans M. Kristensen. 2011. *World nuclear forces*. SIPRI. Accessed June 27, 2012. http://www.sipri.org/yearbook/2011/files/SIPRIYB1107-07A.pdf

Kirshon, John. 2009a. *UN adopts universal declaration of human rights: Eleanor Roosevelt led commission on human rights*. Retrieved December 7, 2010, from http://www.suite101.com/content/un-adopts-universal-declaration-of-human-rights-a178701

Kirshon, John. 2009b. *Cold War ends at summit in Malta: Gorbachev hails new era of peace*. Accessed January 11, 2011. http://www.suite101.com/content/cold-war-ends-at-summit-in-malta-a176321

Lama, Dalai and H. C. Cutler. 2009. *The art of happiness in a troubled world*. New York, NY: Doubleday Religion.

Lama, Dalai. 1999. *Ethics for the new millennium*. New York, NY: The Berkley Publishing Group.

"League of Nations," *Wikipedia,* Accessed September 25, 2007, http://en.wikipedia.org/wiki/League_of_Nations.

Lewis, M. Paul. *Ed. 2009.* "Ethnologue Languages of the World: Statistical Summaries".Ethnologue. http://www.ethnologue.org/ethno_docs/distribution.asp?by=size

"List of wars." 2008. Accessed January 12, 2011. http://althistory.wikia.com/wiki/List_of_Wars_%28Myers_Way%29

MacAskill, Ewen., and Chris McGreal. 2005. "Israel should be wiped off map, says Iran's president." *The Guardian,* October 27. http://www.guardian.co.uk/world/2005/oct/27/israel.iran/

Maich, Steve. 2009. "Can I see your passport, Mr. President." Macleans. Accessed November 26, 2010. http://wWWII.macleans.ca/2009/05/29/can-i-see-your-passport-mr-president

"Major religions of the world by number of adherents." 2007. Accessed April 10, 2009. http://www.adherents.com/Religions_By_Adherents.html

Margolis, Eric S. 2007. *War at the top of the world (3rd Ed.).* Toronto, Canada: Key Porter Books.

Margolis, Eric S. 2008. *American Raj: Liberation or domination.* Toronto, Canada: Key Porter Books Limited.

McCain, Patrick. 2009. "Obama Cairo speech (video, text)." Accessed June 23, 2012. http://www.rightpundits.com/?p=4045

McCormack, John. 2009. "Petraeus outlines Afghanistan strategy." *The Weekly Standard,* February 9. http://www.weeklystandard.com/weblogs/TWSFP/2009/02/petraeus_outlines_afghanistan.asp

"Message to Iraqis." 2003. Accessed October 19, 2003. http://www.facebook.com/topic.php?uid=2405481472&topic=2692

Middle East Online. 2009. "ElBaradei: Iran deal could change Mideast." Accessed December 6, 2010. http://www.middle-east-online.com/english/?id=35509

"Most people want Iraq pull-out." 2007. Accessed January 20, 2011. http://news.bbc.co.uk/2/hi/middle_east/6981553.stm

Nahmad, Claire. 2003. *The book of peace: Meditations from around the world*. Boston, MA: Journey Editions.

Nasiri, Omar. 2006. *Inside jihad*. New York, NY: Basic Books.

"NAXAL/MAOISTS threats and movements." n.d. Accessed December 29, 2010. http://www.defence.pk/forums/india-defence/47405-naxal-maoists-threats-movements.html

New York Daily News. "Al Qaeda leader Mustafa Abu al-Yazid: We'd use nuclear weapons against the U.S. if we could." June 22, 2009.

North Atlantic Treaty Organization (NATO). 1949. "North Atlantic Treaty." NATO. Accessed June 22, 2012. http://www.nato.int/cps/en/natolive/official_texts_17120.htm

North Atlantic Treaty Organization (NATO). 2007. "NATO's positions regarding nuclear non-proliferation, arms control and disarmament and related issues." NATO. Accessed December 6, 2010. http://www.nato.int/issues/nuclear/position.html

Novak, Jane. 2008a. "Al-Qaeda Escape in Yemen: Facts, Rumors and Theories." Global Politician. http://www.globalpolitician.com/21614-yemen-arab

Novak, Jane. 2008b. "South Yemen Forms Liberation Council." Worldpress. http://www.worldpress.org/Mideast/3273.cfm

O'Neil, Dennis. 2006. *World diversity patters*. Accessed June 25, 2009. http://anthro.palomar.edu/ethnicity/ethnic_5.htm

Pease, Kelly-Kate S. 2003. *International organizations: Perspectives on governance in the twenty-first century (2nd Ed.)*. Upper Saddle River, NJ: Pearson Education, Inc.

Phillips, Adam. 2005. "Hiroshima survivor recalls day atomic bomb was dropped." Voice of America. http://www.voanews.com/English/archive/2005-08/2005-08-05-voa38.cfm

"Quotation Details." n.d. Accessed June 24, 2012. http://www.quotationspage.com/quote/329.html

"Quotes on Speaking Out, Taking Action and Indifference." n.d. Accessed July 7, 2011. http://no2torture.org/quotes/quotes_speaking.shtml

"Quotes to reflect on." n.d. Accessed July 7, 2011. http://www.sambarforpins.com/quotes.htm

RAND Corporation. 2005. "The UN's role in nation building: From the Congo to Iraq." Accessed December 30, 2008. http://www.rand.org/pubs/monographs/2005/RAND_MG304.sum.pdf

"Resolution adopted by the General Assembly: International Day of Peace." 2001. Accessed June 23, 2012. http://www.un.org/events/peaceday/2003/a55r282.pdf

Rosenberg, Marshall B. 2005. *Speak peace in a world of conflict: What you say next will change your world*. Encinitas, CA: Puddle Dancer Press.

Rourke, John. 2001. *International politics on the world stage* (8th Ed.). Guildford, CT: McGraw-Hill/Dushkin.

"Russell-Einstein Manifesto." 1955. Accessed June 24 2012. http://www.pugwash.org/about/manifesto.htm

"Sa'dah insurgency," *Wikipedia*, last modified March 24, 2009, http://en.wikipedia.org/wiki/Sa%27dah_conflict

Said, Edward W. 2000. *The end of the peace process: Oslo and After.* New York, NY: Pantheon Books.

Schell, Jonathan. 1982. *The fate of the Earth*. New York, NY: Avon

"Share the world's resources." n. d. Accessed January 20, 2011. http://www.stwr.org/global-conflicts-militarization/endless-war-the-global-war-on-terror-and-the-new-bush-administration.html

Shultz, George P., William J. Perry, Henry A. Kissinger, and Sam Nunn. 2008. "Toward a nuclear-free world."Accessed November 26, 2010. http://www.nuclearsecurityproject.org/atf/cf/%7B1FCE2821-

C31C-4560-BEC1-BB4BB58B54D9%7D/TOWARD_A_
NUCLEAR_FREE_WORLD _OPED_011508.PDF

Siddiqi, Shahid R. 2010. *Pakistan: Why West fears theft of our nuclear assets.* Accessed November 28, 2010. http://news.dawn.com/wps/wcm/connect/dawn-content-library/dawn/news/pakistan/04-west-nuclear-fears-qs-05.

Simmons, Bill. 2009. *Now I can die in peace: How the sports guy found salvation, thanks to the world champion.* New York, NY: ESPN Books.

Singh, Patwant. 2004. *The world according to Washington.* New Delhi, India: Rupa.

"Somalis `at war` with Ethiopia." 2006. Accessed December 6, 2010. http://news.bbc.co.uk/2/hi/africa/6199239.stm

Spillius, Alex. 2008. "George Bush says Iraq intelligence failure is his biggest regret." *The Telegraph.* December 1. http://www.telegraph.co.uk/news/worldnews/northamerica/usa/3540733/George-W-Bush-says-Iraq-intelligence-failure-is-his-biggest-regret.html

"Statement by the Hon. Syed Hamid Albar." 2005. Accessed December 1, 2010. http://www.un.org/events/npt2005/statements/npt02malaysia.pdf

Steinmetz, Sol. Ed. 1997. *Random House Webster's College Dictionary.* (2nd ed.). New York: Random House.

Stevenson, Angus. Ed. 2010. *Oxford Dictionary of English.* (3rd Ed.). Oxford: Oxford University Press.

Stroupe, Joseph. 2006. "Part 5: Russia, China 'cooking something up'." http://www.atimes.com/atimes/Central_Asia/HI29Ag01.html

Thapaliya, Bhuwan. 2007. "Rising Maoists insurgency in India." Global Politician. http://www.globalpolitician.com/22790-India

Todd, Douglas. 2009. "Karen Armstrong's compassion charter unveiled in Vancouver." *The Vancouver Sun,* September 25, 2009. http://

communities.canada.com/vancouversun/blogs/thesearch/pages/
karen-armstrong-s-compassion-charter-unveiled-in-vancouver.
aspx

Tolle, Eckhart. 2001. *The power of now: A guide to spiritual enlightenment.*
Novato, CA: New World Library.

"Turkey-Kurdistan Workers' Party Conflict," *Wikipedia,* last modified
April 4, 2009, http://en.wikipedia.org/wiki/Turkey-PKK_conflict

U.S. Department of Defence. American Forces Press Service. 2005.
ScanEagle Proves Worth in Fallujah Fight, by Jim Garamone. Accessed
December 6, 2010. http://www.defense.gov/news/newsarticle.
aspx?id=24397

"United Nations Security Council," *Wikipedia,* Accessed January 5, 2011,
http://en.wikipedia.org/wiki/United_Nations_Security_Council

"Universal declaration of human rights." n. d. Accessed February
11, 2011. http://healthcare.reachinformation.com/Universal%20
Declaration%20of%20Human%20Rights.aspx

"Universal Declaration of Human Rights." 2009. Accessed June 24,
2012. http://passiontounderstand.blogspot.ca/2009/07/bloggers-
unite-for-human-rights.html

"Universal Declaration of Human Rights." 2011. Accessed June 23,
2012. http://www.absoluteastronomy.com/topics/Universal_
Declaration_of_Human_Rights

"User: Grant bud," *Wikipedia, Accessed* December 31, 2010.
http://en.wikipedia.org/wiki/User:Grant_bud/War_in_
Afghanistan_%282006-Present%29

"War on Terrorism," *Wikipedia,* last modified September 21, 2008,
http://en.wikipedia.org/wiki/War_on_Terrorism

"War on words." 2009. Accessed December 6, 2010. http://www.
thedailybeast.com/newsweek/2009/02/03/war-on-words.html

"Warsaw Security Pact." 1955. Accessed June 22, 2012. http://avalon.law.
yale.edu/20th_century/warsaw.asp

Water, Jim V. de. 2005. "The United Nations' success story." *San
Diego Union-Tribune*. Accessed November 26, 2010. http://www.
signonsandiego.com/uniontrib/20050224/news_lz1e24water.html

"Who said: the fourth world war." n.d. Accessed November 30, 2011.
http://www.online-literature.com/forums/showthread.php?t=36

Wirsing, Robert G. 1998. *India, Pakistan and the Kashmir dispute*. New
York, NY: St. Martin's Press.

Woodward, Bob. 2010. *Obama's wars*. New York, NY: Simon &
Schuster.

"World view of US role goes bad to worse." 2007. Accessed May 23, 2007.
http://news.bbc.co.uk/1/shared/bsp/hi/pdfs/23_01_07_us_poll.
pdf

"World War II: Atom bomb and Hiroshima Part 5 eyewitness report."
n.d. Accessed March 30, 2009. http://www.trivia-library.com/a/
world-war-ii-atom-bomb-and-hiroshima

Your World Today. 2007. Washington: CNN International, May 25.
Television broadcast.

Zihala, Maryann. 2003. *Democracy: The greatest good for the greatest
number*. Lanham, MD: University Press of America, Inc.

Index

A

abuse of state power 61, 62, 177, 179-181
Afghanistan 23, 31, 37, 44, 46, 47, 65,
  69, 70, 72, 73-76, 79, 85, 86, 90, 94,
  96, 128, 132, 135, 138, 153, 155,
  156, 157, 160, 186
Ahmadinejad, President Mahmoud 19
Al-Aqsa Mosque 12
Algeria 33, 49-50, 94, 126, 135, 145, 147
al-Qaeda 23, 25, 35, 37, 38, 44, 46, 50,
  51, 70, 72, 73, 74, 75, 76, 79, 81, 82,
  84, 86, 87, 88, 89, 91, 94, 95, 154,
  155, 156, 157, 158, 159
American Peace Society 98
Amphictyonic League 98
Angolan Civil War 56
Antony, A. K. 24
arms race 5, 10, 21, 24, 114, 119, 122,
  125-127, 129, 138, 164, 166
Armstrong, Karen 192
Assyrians 11, 60

B

Babylonians 11
Balkan conflict 67
Baluchistan conflict 135
Bangladesh 32, 43
bin Laden, Osama 23, 37, 46, 47, 50,
  51, 70, 72, 73, 74, 76, 81, 84, 87, 94,
  95, 154, 155, 156, 158

BRIC countries 178
Buddhists 22, 49, 62, 193
Burundi Civil War 55
Bush Jr., President George 73, 77, 84,
  153, 154, 155, 160, 166
Bush Sr., President George 77, 117,
  130, 138, 165
Byzantines 11

C

Cambodia 31, 32, 59, 61, 62, 132, 181
Camp David Accord 13
Carter, President Jimmy 42
Chad Civil War 135
Chechnya 36, 81, 95, 146
chemical weapons 127
China 20, 22, 24, 26, 27, 31, 60, 88, 104,
  109, 114, 116, 126, 128, 129, 132,
  136, 137, 138, 139, 140, 142, 143,
  144, 145, 146, 147, 149, 153, 159,
  166, 172, 180, 186
China Arms Control and Disarmament
  Association 27
Christians 12, 38, 56, 62, 69, 90, 193
Church of Holy Sepulchre 12
Cold War 6, 31, 32, 116, 127, 133, 134,
  135, 138, 141, 144, 155
Columbia 34-35, 65, 170, 186
Congo 29, 53, 56, 116, 135, 177, 178
Crusades 70

D

da Silva, President Luiz Inacio Lula 140
detente 128-132
deterrence 127-128, 167
Dome of the Rock 12
drug trafficking 35, 49

E

Earth Day 196, 197
Ecuador 34, 141, 186
Educators for Social Responsibility 194
Egypt 13, 31, 39, 51, 68, 141, 164, 186
Einstein, Albert 5, 204
environmental movement 196, 203
Eritrean-Ethiopian War 29
Ethiopia 29, 51, 59, 104, 105, 132, 135, 186
Euskadi ta Askatasuna 35

F

Fatah 13, 14, 15, 39, 42, 43, 91, 92, 133
Ferdinand, Archduke Frank 4
Food and Agriculture Organization 113
France 19, 33, 35, 38, 66, 69, 77, 78, 98, 99, 102, 104, 105, 106, 107, 109, 114, 116, 122, 123, 126, 139, 141, 153, 159, 172, 177, 186
France-Algerian War 33

G

G4 countries 140
G7 countries 139, 140, 141
G20 countries 140
Gadhafi, President Moammar 39
Gaza Strip 10, 11, 14, 15, 89, 91, 92, 95, 133, 160
genocide 29, 57, 61, 148, 176, 180, 182
Georgia 83, 116, 123, 145, 153, 166
Germany 5, 20, 60, 66, 78, 98, 99, 102, 104, 105, 106, 107, 115, 122, 124, 125, 126, 127, 130, 131, 139, 140, 148, 159, 180

Grand Design 98
Greece 65, 97, 102, 103, 106, 115, 124, 127, 136, 186
Grey, Edward 99
Grotius, Hugo 98
Guatemala 56, 140, 186
Gulf War 30, 61, 76, 138, 166, 177

H

Hachiya, Dr. Michihiko 2
Hamas 10, 14, 15, 21, 41, 42, 43, 68, 91, 92, 95, 133
Hasmoneans 11
Hebrews 62, 116, 133
Hezbollah 21, 28, 40, 41, 92, 93
Hindus 21, 22, 62, 193
Hitler, Adolf 4, 60, 105, 106, 180
Holocaust 19
Hussein-McMahon Correspondence 12

I

Identity politics 181-190
India 10, 21-25, 43-44, 62, 65, 67, 70, 73, 94, 112, 114, 126, 133, 134, 135, 136, 137, 138, 139, 140, 142, 143, 144, 145, 146, 147, 148, 153, 163, 166, 182, 186
Indonesian Civil War 60
industrial revolution 122
International Atomic Energy Agency 19, 25, 164, 165
International Day of Peace 195, 197, 198
International Monetary Fund 113, 139
Intifada 14, 135
    First Intifada crisis 13
    Second Intifada crisis 135
Iran 9, 14, 18-21, 30, 37, 41, 42, 68, 69, 73, 81, 92, 93, 95, 114, 126, 132, 133, 135, 137, 138, 143, 145, 147, 148, 164, 165, 182, 186, 187
Iraq 5, 13, 30, 36, 38, 45, 65, 76-85, 89, 94, 103, 116, 135, 136, 137, 155,

158, 159, 160, 165, 186
Irish Republican Army 56, 160
Islamic Courts Union 50, 86
Islamic militant groups 7, 23, 65-96,
    119, 138, 158, 178, 200
Israel 9, 10-18, 18-21, 28, 30, 41, 42, 43,
    62, 67, 70, 72, 85, 89, 91, 92, 114,
    116, 126, 133, 134, 135, 138, 146,
    148, 163, 164, 165
Ivory Coast 53-54, 182

J

Japan 10, 25-28, 70, 83, 102, 104, 106,
    107, 122, 126, 136, 137, 138, 139,
    163, 166
Jerusalem 11, 12, 13, 17, 18, 69, 192
Jewish temple 11
Jews 11, 12, 16, 60, 62, 67, 193
jihad 23, 24, 37, 66, 74, 75, 80, 81, 89,
    96, 160
Jordon 68, 164
Justice and Equality Movement 51, 52

K

Kant, Immanuel 98
Karzai, President Hamid 75, 160
Kashmir 10, 22, 23, 25, 43, 67, 87, 134
Kenya 50, 65, 66
Kissinger, Henry 6
Kivu conflict 135, 178
Korean War 25, 33, 128
Kurdish Workers Party 36, 85
Kurdistan 36
Kuwait 30, 65, 77, 89
Kyrgyzstan 65

L

Lashkar-e-Tayyiba 23
Laurent Nkunda 29
League of Nations 13, 97, 99-107, 111,
    115, 118, 168, 171
Covenant 99
Lebanon War of 1982 13
Liberation Tigers of Tamil Eelam 55

Liberian Civil Wars 58
Limited Test Ban Treaty 163

M

Maghreb insurgency 135
major global powers 69, 119, 123, 136,
    139, 143, 171, 202
Mamluks 11
Manchuria 4, 106
Meshaal, Khaled 43
Middle East 9, 10, 17, 18, 20, 21, 30, 34,
    37, 38, 39, 42, 68, 69, 70, 85, 89-91,
    116, 122, 128, 134, 138, 148, 157,
    164
Morocco 39, 65, 68, 135, 164
Mountbatten, Lord Louis 6
Mozambique 58
Mughal Empire 70
Mujahedeen 31, 85, 95
Mumbai 10, 23, 24
Muslims 12, 21, 24, 47, 49, 50, 56, 57,
    61, 62, 65, 66, 67, 69, 70, 72, 94,
    133, 187, 193
Mussolini, Benito 105, 106
Myanmar 47-49, 134, 145, 181, 181,
    186

N

Nagaland 135
Naxalite communist insurgency 43
Nelson, Senator Gaylord 196
Nepalese Civil War 55
New York Peace Society 98
New York World Trade Centre 66, 71
Nicaragua 34, 58, 83, 132, 186
Nicholas II, Czar 98
Non-Aligned Movement 115, 129, 132,
    136, 164
North Atlantic Treaty 75, 78, 94, 96,
    115, 124, 125, 128, 131, 132, 136,
    138, 149, 156
North Korea 10, 20, 25-28, 33, 57,
    62, 114, 126, 129, 132, 133, 135,
    136, 137, 138, 139, 147, 148, 163,

166, 180
Nuclear Non-Proliferation Treaty 20, 25, 114, 115, 129, 163
Nuclear proliferation 135-138, 152
Nuclear weapons 126
Nunn, Sam 6

O

Obama, President Barack 17, 145, 154, 162, 184
Ogaden insurgency 135
Okello, President Tito 53
Oslo Peace Process 14
Ottoman Empire 11, 12, 70

P

Pakistan 10, 21-25, 31, 32, 37, 38, 44-47, 62, 65, 67, 73, 75, 76, 86-88, 94, 95, 96, 112, 114, 126, 133, 135, 136, 137, 138, 141, 145, 146, 148, 153, 157, 158, 159, 160, 163, 165, 186, 187
Palestine 9, 10-18, 42-43, 62, 67, 69, 85, 89, 91-92, 94, 133, 148, 164
Palestine Liberation Movement 13, 14, 15
Palestine National Authority 14, 15, 133
Palestinian Territory 42-43
Penn, William 98
Pentagon 66, 71, 72
Permanent Court of Arbitration 98
Perry, William 6
Peru 58, 65, 140, 186
Philippines 57, 81, 83, 86, 88, 95, 134, 141, 186
polarity
    bipolar system 123
    unipolar world system 133, 135, 139, 141, 142, 145

R

Roman Empire 11, 12
Russell, Bertrand 5

Russia 17, 19, 26, 36, 65, 73, 78, 81, 94, 98, 104, 106, 114, 116, 122, 123, 126, 127, 131, 132, 135, 136, 139, 141, 142, 143, 144, 145, 146, 147, 149, 152, 153, 161, 163, 166, 172, 180, 181

S

Saleh, President Ali Abdullah 37
Saudi Arabia 14, 31, 39, 65, 68, 69, 70, 72, 73, 81, 86, 89, 95, 138, 143, 164, 165, 186, 187
Schell, Jonathan 5
Second Chechen War 135
Second Congo War 29, 116
Security Council 15, 17, 74, 77, 78, 83, 109, 113, 114, 115, 116, 117, 118, 119, 124, 125, 129, 141, 142, 164, 165, 172, 173
Shultz, George 6
Sierra Leone 54, 56
Singh, Prime Minister Manmohan 24
Siniora, Prime Minister Fouad 40
Sino-Vietnamese War 31
Six-Day-War 13, 128
social and political vendetta 61, 93, 177, 202
Somalia 50-51, 86, 116, 134, 138, 143
South Korea 10, 25-28, 33, 83, 126, 136, 137, 138, 145, 163, 166
Soviet Union 60, 69, 74, 94, 105, 106, 112, 114, 123, 125, 126, 127, 129, 130, 131, 132, 134, 137, 138, 144, 147, 153, 163
Spain 35-36, 78, 83, 102, 105, 122, 134, 139, 159, 177
Spanish Civil War 105
Sri Lanka 10, 45, 55, 91, 145, 157, 182
Stalin, Josef 60, 180
Strategic Arms Limitation Talks 161
Strategic Arms Reduction Treaty 130, 162
Strategic Offensive Reduction Treaty 162
Sudan 51-53, 61, 86, 111, 181, 187

Suu Kyi, Aung San 48
Syria 13, 39, 41, 42, 81, 92, 95, 114, 137, 165, 186

T

Tajikistan 57, 138
Taliban 44, 46, 72, 73, 74, 75, 76, 87, 88, 94, 95, 156, 157, 159, 160
Tanzania 65, 66, 141
Thailand 47, 48, 49, 83, 94, 95, 135, 141, 181, 186
Treaty of Brussels 124
Treaty of Versailles 99
Tuareg Rebellion 135
Turkey 19, 36-37, 60, 85, 95, 103, 115, 124, 127, 134, 159, 181, 186

U

Uganda 53, 134
UN Human Rights Council 15
unilateral global policing 113, 152-154, 169, 172, 201
United Kingdom 21, 38, 65, 68, 72, 74, 77, 78, 79, 81, 83, 99, 102, 107, 109, 114, 122, 126, 139, 141, 169, 173, 186
United Nations 13, 15, 16, 17, 18, 19, 20, 28, 33, 36, 39, 40, 51, 52, 54, 74, 77, 78, 79, 83, 84, 86, 97, 107-119, 124, 125, 129, 132, 141, 142, 151, 152, 153, 164, 165, 168, 171-173, 175, 179, 181, 186, 187, 188, 195, 197, 198, 200, 201
UN Charter 107
United States 2, 5, 6, 14–21, 24, 26, 27, 30, 31, 32, 33, 35, 36, 38, 41, 42, 44, 45, 46, 47, 50, 56, 58, 65, 66, 67-70, 71-96, 99, 102, 106, 107-118, 122, 123, 124, 125, 126, 127, 128, 129, 130, 132, 133, 134, 135, 136, 137, 138, 139, 140, 141, 143, 144, 145, 146, 147, 149, 152, 153, 154, 155, 156, 157, 158, 159, 160, 161, 162, 163, 164, 165, 166, 168, 171-173,

182, 184, 186, 194, 196, 200, 201, 203
Universal Peace Union 98

V

Venezuela 34, 141, 186
Vietnam 31, 32, 79, 82, 127, 128, 132

W

War on Terror 44, 46, 72, 73, 75–77, 84, 85, 87–89, 91, 92, 94, 96, 135, 152, 154–161, 165, 168, 201
Warsaw Pact 125, 128, 131
Weapons of Mass Destruction 79, 84, 85, 126, 127, 130, 132, 136, 137, 158, 161–166, 173, 201
West Bank 10, 11, 14, 15, 16, 17, 18, 89, 91, 92, 133
Western European Union's Defence Organization 124
Wilson, President Woodrow 99
World War I 1, 2, 4, 6, 7, 63, 97, 99, 103, 106, 111, 118, 122, 127, 148, 176, 191, 199, 203
World War II 2, 4, 5, 6, 28, 29, 63, 97, 105, 107, 109, 111, 118, 121–123, 127, 135, 147, 148, 169, 171, 176, 191, 199, 203

Y

Yellow Sea Island 26
Yemen 37–39, 66, 94, 181, 209
Yeonpyeong 26
Yom Kipper War 13
Yom Kippur War 13, 128
Yugoslavian Wars 57

Z

Ze-Dong, Mao 60